Imperial Russia and the Struggle for Latin American Independence, 1808–1828

Russell H. Bartley

Institute of Latin American Studies
The University of Texas at Austin

International Standard Book Number 0-292-73811-0 (cloth)
0-292-73812-9 (paper)

Library of Congress Catalog Card Number 77-89770

The Latin American Monographs Series is distributed
for the Institute of Latin American Studies by:
  University of Texas Press
  P. O. Box 7819
  Austin, Texas 78712

In cherished memory of my father
and for Mary, who shares that memory

Contents

Illustrations

Tables

Preface

The present volume originated with an interest in Russian source materials for the study of Latin American history. It gradually evolved into an investigation of tsarist responses to the collapse of the Spanish and Portuguese colonial empires and finally broadened into a general study of Russo–Latin American relations. It is thus envisioned as the first volume of a more extensive work spanning the full course of these relations from their inception in the eighteenth century to the recent Soviet past.

The struggle for Latin American independence provides a natural focal point for this study in that it marks the beginning of a generalized process of change that at once shaped the future of Latin America and would determine its relations with the major industrial powers, including Russia. While overshadowed in the nineteenth century by England, France, and the United States, Russia nonetheless established and maintained a presence in Latin America that, with the emergence of the Union of Soviet Socialist Republics in the present century, acquired profound influence.

A study of Russo–Latin American relations addresses itself to but one limited dimension of Latin America's past. The significance of those relations in the present, however, points to the importance of investigating their antecedents. Not only does such a study broaden our knowledge of the external relations of Latin America, but it relates ultimately to the larger question of neo-colonial dependency in the age of decolonization and national liberation.

Inasmuch as this study embraces fields of historical specialization that are rarely combined, some passing explanations of a technical nature are in order.

The difficulty of citing Russian-language sources in their original Cyrillic form has made transliteration a standard practice of scholars writing in English. With minor modifications, the Library of Congress system for the natural and social sciences has been used in the present volume (see the transliteration table that follows this preface). Where it occurs, old Russian orthography has been transliterated in accord with the new revised orthography.

In general, personal names of Russian subjects have been transliterated following the Library of Congress system. Exceptions include tsars and non-Russians in the tsarist imperial service whose names are either Anglicized or given in their most common form. Non-Russian names of Russian subjects are transliterated in the text, but frequently appear in differing forms when cited in English- or other Western-language sources. Excepting Moscow and St. Petersburg, Russian place names have also been transliterated.

Dates, too, may be a source of confusion. In tsarist Russia, the days and months of the year were calculated according to the Julian calendar, which differed from the more widely used Gregorian calendar by eleven days in the eighteenth century and twelve days in the nineteenth century. Unless otherwise indicated, all dates have been converted to coincide with the Gregorian calendar, except in those few instances in which it was not possible to determine precisely the original dates.

A study of this nature rests necessarily on the advice and assistance of many people. For financial support that allowed me to pursue research in Europe and Latin America I am deeply indebted to the Foreign Area Fellowship Program, the International Research and Exchanges Board, the American Council of Learned Societies, the National Endowment for the Humanities, and the Graduate School and Center for Latin America of the University of Wisconsin-Milwaukee. For invaluable guidance and aid, I am grateful to the staffs of the University of Helsinki Library; the Lenin State Library (Moscow) and the Saltykov-Shchedrin State Public Library (Leningrad); the Archivo General de Indias (Seville), the Archivo Histórico Nacional (Madrid), the Biblioteca del Museo Naval (Madrid), and the Biblioteca Nacional (Madrid); the Arquivo Nacional Tôrre do Tombo (Lisbon); and the Arquivo Histórico do Itamaratí of the Brazilian Ministry of Foreign Relations (Rio de Janeiro). Research was also facilitated at several institutions in the United States, for which I am equally appreciative, among them the Bancroft Library (Berkeley); the New York Public Library; the Hoover Institution on War, Revolution, and Peace (Stanford); and the Stanford University Libraries.

Of the many colleagues abroad who aided in the research of this study, I wish to acknowledge with special gratitude the late Dr. Maria Windäs, until her death the director of the Slavic Department of the University of Helsinki Library; Dr. L. A. Shur, Institute of Ethnography of the USSR Academy of Sciences (Moscow); Dr. B. N. Komissarov, History Faculty, Leningrad State University; Drs. M. S. Al'perovich, N. N. Bolkhovitinov, and L. Yu. Slëzkin, Institute of Universal History of the USSR Academy of Sciences (Moscow); and Dr. Alberto Gil Novales, Department of History, Universidad Autónoma (Barcelona, Spain).

Colleagues at various American institutions likewise offered invaluable advice and assistance in the preparation of this volume. I owe a particular debt of gratitude to Professor Philip Shashko (University of Wisconsin-Milwaukee), who read and perceptively scrutinized the entire manuscript. I am also indebted to Professors Lewis Hanke (University of Massachusetts), John J. Johnson (Stanford University), and Ivo J. Lederer (Stanford University), all of whom read an earlier version of the manuscript and offered insightful suggestions for revision. Among my immediate colleagues at UWM, an expression of gratitude is due Professors Ronald J. Ross, Walter B. Weare, and Charles A. Ward, who at different stages of the manuscript gave me the benefit of their professional talents.

As in any scholarly work, competent technical assistance has been a great asset. I am especially fortunate to have had the collaboration of Ms. Brigitte Taylor, who with skill and constant good humor greatly facilitated final preparation of this exceptionally complicated manuscript.

Finally, I owe a very special debt of gratitude to Diana Bartley, who in innumerable ways helped to bring this work to completion.

TRANSLITERATION TABLE

A	a	A	a	P	р	R	r
Б	б	B	b	C	с	S	s
В	в	V	v	Т	т	T	t
Г	г	G	g	У	у	U	u
Д	д	D	d	Ф	ф	F	f
Е	е	E	e	Х	х	Kh	kh
Ё	ё	Ë	ë	Ц	ц	Ts	ts
Ж	ж	Zh	zh	Ч	ч	Ch	ch
З	з	Z	z	Ш	ш	Sh	sh
И	и	I	i	Щ	щ	Shch	shch
Й	й	I	i	_	ъ	_	"
К	к	K	k	_	ы	_	y
Л	л	L	l	_	ь	_	'
М	м	M	m	э	э	E	e
Н	н	N	n	Ю	ю	Yu	iu
О	о	O	o	Я	я	Ya	ia
П	п	P	p				

See J. Thomas Shaw, *The Transliteration of Modern Russian for English-Language Publications* (Madison, Milwaukee, and London: The University of Wisconsin Press, 1967).

Imperial Russia and the Struggle for
Latin American Independence, 1808–1828

1. Introduction

The role and significance of foreign involvement in the collapse of the Iberian colonial empires in America has long held historians' interest.[1] Primary attention has focused on England, France, and the United States,[2] although the policies of Austria, Germany, Sweden, and the Netherlands, too, have received some study.[3] Russia, on the other hand, has elicited only passing notice in the historical literature, despite the fact that at the time of the struggle for Latin American independence it was a leading world power with imperial interests extending to the Western Hemisphere. The present volume addresses itself to this important gap in the literature, examining the relationship between Russia's evolving New World interests and tsarist responses to the separatist movement of early nineteenth-century Latin America.

What follows is a study in international relations. As such, it seeks to move beyond strictly diplomatic history to probe the specific circumstances, domestic as well as foreign, in which the affairs of tsarist diplomacy acquired form and meaning. The historian, observes Italian scholar Federico Chabod, must take into account "passions and affections, ideas and ideologies, the situation of the country and its people, in a word, everything which makes of foreign policy nothing more than a moment, an aspect of a most broad and complex historical process embracing the entire life of a nation and which does not admit of closed compartments."[4] A nation's external relations are inextricably linked to its internal order. To attempt to evaluate foreign policy solely on the basis of diplomatic correspondence, concludes Chabod, is like trying "to illuminate today's great cities with a few oil lamps."[5]

In order to grasp fully the nature of Russian objectives in colonial Latin America, it is essential to examine the economic and geopolitical determinants of tsarist New World policy. Indeed, a frequent weakness of studies on this subject lies precisely in their narrowly diplomatic focus. Even such disciplined scholars as Dexter Perkins and William Spence Robertson can be cited as examples. In their well-known ar-

ticles on Russia and the emancipation of Spanish America, both authors draw on diplomatic correspondence to the almost total exclusion
of other sources.[6] Having thus enclosed themselves in one of Chabod's
sealed compartments, they fail to ask the questions that would permit
an explanation of tsarist New World policy in terms of Russian national interests.

There are, of course, numerous studies of a nondiplomatic character
that treat of related topics. By and large, however, these, too, suffer
from a lack of perspective, focusing on specific incidents of tsarist New
World colonialism without reference to the broader imperatives of
Russian imperial expansion. Several scholars, for example, have drawn
attention to various eighteenth-century projects for the establishment
of Russian colonies in South America and the Caribbean.[7] Others have
written on Russian penetration into California and on related efforts
to occupy the Hawaiian Islands.[8] Yet even here little is said about
tsarist expansion as part of a broader imperial process, and then only
in reference to the northern Pacific basin. Indeed, Russian colonial
projects in Latin America are treated more for their curiosity value
than as reflections of an evolving geopolitical program.

The question of tsarist New World ambitions, of course, is closely
related to the genesis and nature of the Monroe Doctrine, and in this
connection, too, has attracted the attention of historians.[9] One long-
standing argument holds that Monroe enunciated the doctrine in response to Russian designs on the Pacific Northwest; another attributes
it to fears of European intervention in the Western Hemisphere, of
which Russia was allegedly the prime mover. Although largely dis-
proved by the careful researches of Dexter Perkins and others,[10] these
erroneous views continue to enjoy some currency. The doctrine,
according to one recent author, was first set forth as a unilateral
pronouncement of policy to deal with "the incursion or threatened incursion of European powers into the Western Hemisphere."[11] It responded, adds another writer, to Russian claims of "control over an
extensive area on the northwest coast of North America," and to rumors that "the Holy Alliance was considering the restoration to Spain of
the colonies in America."[12] Yet these allusions to "the subjugation of
South America by the Holy Alliance," concluded Perkins many years
ago, "are based on no sound interpretation of events; the notion that
any such course was intended is myth, rather than history."[13]

Soviet historians, too, have written on this problem. First among
them is N. N. Bolkhovitinov, a specialist in United States and Latin
American history who has made numerous contributions to the literature on the Monroe Doctrine and Russo-American relations.[14] "If there

had in fact existed a threat to the Western Hemisphere," writes Bolkhovitinov, "then, as numerous American historians hold, the Monroe
Doctrine would have been defensive in nature and the United States of
America and its leaders would have acted as the protectors of the
fledgling Latin American republics."[15] This was not the case, however,
for in 1823 there was no real danger of an allied intervention in Latin
America. The Monroe Doctrine was in fact directed against an "imagi-
nary threat."[16]

More important, argues Bolkhovitinov, the U. S. government was
fully apprised of the international situation and well knew that the
continental allies could undertake no aggressive venture in the face of
British opposition. Indeed, he suggests, the governments of England
and the United States sought to further their own interests in the
hemisphere by propagating the myth of an external threat. By casting
themselves in the role of "defenders" of the newly emancipated republics, they endeavored to extend their influence over these countries.
The real threat to Latin American independence, concludes Bolkhovitinov, came not from Europe, "but from quite another quarter,
namely the United States of America."[17]

Several fundamental contributions to the historiography of tsarist
New World interests have appeared in recent decades. One of the first
important Soviet works on the subject was S. B. Okun's seminal study
of the Russian-American Company, published in 1939, which, together
with L. S. Berg's earlier volume on the Bering expeditions and two
subsequent works on Russian geographic exploration by A. I. Andreev
and A. V. Efimov, laid much of the groundwork for a broader approach
to the history of Russian overseas expansion.[18] These studies, in turn,
have been supplemented by a number of publications, including a
revised edition of Efimov's standard work on the history of Russian
geographical discoveries.[19] Worthy of special note are a detailed study
of Russian geographic exploration down to 1917, by D. M. Lebedev
and V. A. Esakov,[20] and a monograph on the Russian presence in
North America to 1867, by S. G. Fedorova.[21] This last work adds much
to the writings of Hubert Howe Bancroft[22] and is a natural companion
volume to the Okun book. It also complements P. Tikhmenev's standard history of Russian America.[23] All of these works, in turn, are richly
complemented by the recent researches and publications of N. N. Bolkhovitinov, most notably his two volumes on Russo-American relations
in the late eighteenth and early nineteenth centuries.[24]

To date, historians have produced two major works on Russian
approaches to Latin America in the period before 1850. One, by the
German scholar Ekkehard Völkl, traces Russian interest in Latin

America from the eighteenth to the mid-nineteenth century.[25] The second, by the Soviet historian L. Yu. Slëzkin, examines tsarist policy toward the independence movement in Spanish America.[26] Because of their relevance to the present study, these volumes warrant some discussion.

In his examination of the century between the Bering–Chirikov voyage to Alaska and final Russian withdrawal from California, Völkl is the first non-Soviet scholar to view the entire Western Hemisphere as an arena of tsarist imperial expansion from the broader perspective of Russian national imperatives. While California was to be the southern anchor of Russia's territorial possessions in North America, he argues, Latin America was to serve as an economic anchor of Russian dominion throughout the Pacific basin. Efforts were made to establish direct commercial ties with the Spanish and Portuguese colonies, and, in the years 1825–1827, serious thought was given to converting Haiti into a Russian trading enclave.[27] An overriding preoccupation with events in Europe, however, and a long-standing fear of foreign entanglements frustrated the realization of tsarist New World objectives. In the final analysis, Völkl concludes, Russia was a land power ill-fitted to challenge the maritime might of Great Britain.[28]

Tsarist policy toward the New World colonies of Spain and Portugal, Völkl writes, actually evolved through three discernible stages: (1) serious consideration of direct trade and diplomatic ties with the rebel colonies in the period 1808–1812; (2) official recognition of crown rights in the colonies and active diplomatic support of those rights from 1813 to 1817; and (3) open hostility toward the colonial insurgents after the year 1817, which, in Völkl's view, was a turning point in tsarist New World policy marked by the cession of Russian warships to Spain. That celebrated act, Völkl holds, was of political as well as military significance, for it signaled the beginning of concerted Russian efforts to secure collective intervention in the affairs of colonial Latin America. Even following independence, he adds, tsarist adherence to the principles of legitimacy prevented Russia from recognizing the newly emancipated republics.[29]

The Slëzkin study at once complements and moves beyond the Völkl volume, although chronologically it is the earlier of the two works. Based on a wealth of Russian archival materials, including the important holdings of the historical archives of the Soviet ministry of foreign affairs, the book focuses on tsarist responses to the threatened demise of crown rule in Spanish America. Interestingly, Slëzkin coincides with Völkl in the periodization of tsarist policy toward the Spanish American colonies, although the two scholars differ in their overall appraisal of Russian New World interests during the independence period. The years 1810–1812 constitute the initial phase, spanning the period from the outbreak of insurrection in Spanish America to Napoleon's invasion of Russia. "In these years," writes Slëzkin, "the Russian government, responding to the specific conditions of the continental blockade, sought to establish friendly ties with the insurgent Spanish colonies, which it viewed as potential trading clients." Russia was also motivated in this, the author adds, "by a desire to strengthen and expand the Russian possessions in North America, where Spain laid its own claims and hindered the growth of Russian trade with California."[30]

The second phase spanned the years 1812–1816, corresponding to the tumultuous period of struggle against Napoleon and the immediate postwar period. The court of St. Petersburg, Slëzkin holds, was too preoccupied with events in Europe at this time to pay much attention to the political upheavals of Spanish America. Formal alliance with Spain, however, placed Russia officially on the side of the Spanish crown.[31]

The third phase of tsarist New World policy, in Slëzkin's view, ran from 1817 to the close of the reign of Alexander I and was characterized by tsarist efforts to promote allied mediation in the colonial dispute. "Not once," Slëzkin argues, "did the Russian government reveal any aggressive intentions toward the [Spanish American] patriots, nor did it raise the question of armed intervention in Spanish America by the European powers, . . . although it did endeavor to assist Ferdinand VII to preserve, if only nominally, his rights in the insurgent colonies."[32] Throughout the independence period, Slëzkin holds, Russia adhered to a constant policy of neutrality toward the Spanish American insurgents. While this policy tended to favor the rebels before 1812 and to oppose them after 1817, it was, he contends, nonetheless a policy of neutrality.

Not all Soviet historians share Slëzkin's views.[33] L. A. Shur and B. N. Komissarov, for example, describe post-1815 tsarist policy toward the insurgent colonies of Spanish America as openly hostile. Russia, they argue, accorded Spain both moral and material assistance, while agitating actively for the collective intervention of the European powers in the New World. As evidence, they cite the cession of Russian warships to Spain in the summer of 1817.[34] Slëzkin holds that this transfer was a purely commercial transaction without ulterior political objectives.[35] To the contrary, respond Shur and Komissarov, the transfer was above all else political in nature, acquiring meaning only against the backdrop of sedition in Spain's New World possessions.[36] The matter warrants further study, concludes Komissarov, "for on its resolution rests a general evaluation of Russian policy toward the insurgents of Spanish America in the years 1817–1820."[37]

The present study shares the broad perspective of the Slëzkin and Völkl volumes, taking as its point of departure the view that tsarist responses to the disintegration of the Iberian colonial empires in America were firmly rooted in the ongoing process of Russian imperial expansion initiated at the turn of the seventeenth century. It differs with certain of their conclusions, however, and seeks to refine others, elaborating at the same time basic aspects of this topic only incompletely known and little discussed in the available literature. Of particular import here is the place of Brazil in the total picture of Russian New World interests, a subject this study examines in detail on the basis of new documentation uncovered in Brazilian and Portuguese archives.[38]

Drawing on the investigations of Völkl, Slëzkin, and numerous other scholars, as well as an extensive selection of printed and manuscript sources, the following chapters attempt to isolate Russian New World objectives during the first decades of the nineteenth century and to relate those objectives to the formulation of tsarist policy toward the insurgent Spanish and Portuguese colonies in America. The conceptual thread that runs throughout this study is the indivisibility of foreign policy and local domestic interests. This does not exclude influences of personality, ideology, and circumstance from the shaping of such policy, but rather denies them the constancy of other determinants inherent in the evolution of a national policy. Accordingly, much space is given to a discussion of Russian interests in Latin America prior to 1815. This has been done to provide a basis for reevaluating the post-1815 period, which students of this subject have traditionally, if perhaps erroneously, deemed more significant.

On this latter point, observes Slëzkin, one finds in the literature a traditional preconceived notion that Russian responses to colonial emancipation in Latin America derived solely from a tsarist commitment to the principles of the Holy Alliance.[39] For a long time, adds N. N. Bolkhovitinov, "the historical literature has been dominated by a view which identifies Russia's attitude toward the war of independence in Latin America with the most reactionary designs of the Holy Alliance."[40] This approach is erroneous, both authors insist, and has led its adherents to focus on the years 1815–1826, thereby ignoring important antecedents in the period before 1815. Russia's position on the colonial question was determined "not only by its adherence to the Holy Alliance, but by many other factors as well."[41] Moreover, documentary evidence demonstrates that prior to 1815 "the Russian government by no means concerned itself with utopian schemes to restore the rule of the 'rightful' monarch in the colonies, but rather studied very seriously the possibility of establishing direct trade ties with the new [Latin American] states."[42] Russia's attitude toward Latin American independence, these scholars suggest, can be properly understood only by taking into account the many decades of Russian New World experience prior to the emergence of Congress Europe.

Two constants in Russia's approach to America were the interrelated interests of commerce and imperial expansion. These interests, it will be argued, were given initial articulation during the reign of Peter the Great (1682–1725) and imparted a distinct direction to tsarist New World policies long before European statesmen began to concern themselves with the political implications of revolution in colonial Latin America. As already noted, one implication of this approach relates to periodization. Whereas previous studies of independence diplomacy have tended to focus on the post-Napoleonic period, an investigation of the economic and geopolitical determinants of tsarist objectives in the Western Hemisphere must begin considerably earlier.

It is significant, for example, that the mounting scarcity of prized colonial imports occasioned in Russia by the continental blockade coincided with the flight of the Portuguese court to Brazil and the resultant transferal of European legations accredited in Lisbon to Rio de Janeiro. The establishment of direct Russian contact with this potential New World supplier of sugar, coffee, and dyestuffs, in turn, occurred at a time when tsarist maritime perspectives were rapidly expanding to include voyages of supply and exploration throughout the Pacific basin. In the early 1800s, Rio de Janeiro became a frequent port of call for Russian vessels and a key link in the chain of communications between European Russia and Russian America.

The deepening concern of the privileged classes of Russia over waning colonial imports found reflection in the periodical press of the period and was early communicated to the Russian government, which by 1810 was taking steps to promote trade with Brazil and neighboring Spanish America. At the same time, the Russian-American Company was endeavoring to secure supplies for its settlements in the Pacific through trade with Spanish California and the west coast of South America. These efforts led to the founding of Fort Ross in the summer of 1812, an added factor in the subsequent formulation of Russian New World policies.

These seemingly unrelated developments acquire meaning when viewed against the backdrop of expanding geopolitical horizons that obtained in early nineteenth-century Russia. This was a period of far-reaching geographic explorations, particularly on the seas. Russian maritime prowess won increasing recognition, with frequent circumnavigations of the globe. The exploits of I. F. Kruzenshtern, V. M. Golovnin, O. E. Kotzebue, and other Russian mariners were often featured in the leading journals of Moscow and St. Petersburg, and by 1815 enlightened Russians were at least passively familiar with such exotic place names as Tenerife, Rio de Janeiro, Nuku Hiva, the Marianas, Port Jackson, and Simons Bay. In addition, literate Russians of the day had ready access to information on political developments both in the Iberian Peninsula and in the American territories of Spain and Portugal. Indeed, the relative abundance of news carried in the tsarist press about the political turmoils of Latin America itself bears witness to Russian public interest in the future of the Spanish and Portuguese colonial empires.

If the outbreak of hostilities between Russia and France in 1812 caused the tsarist government momentarily to focus its attention on events in Europe, the basic continuity of Russian New World objectives remained unbroken. Moreover, it was precisely at this time that Russia first achieved a visible presence in Latin America. In the years 1813–1815, ships of the Russian-American Company sailed for the first time to Peru and Chile. In 1812, company agents penetrated California, and that same year a tsarist legation was established in Rio de Janeiro.

The years immediately following the Congress of Vienna proved decisive in the evolution of tsarist thinking on Russian New World objectives and the related question of colonial emancipation. During this period, Ferdinand VII found a ready ally in the Russian autocrat, to the consternation of the Portuguese court in Rio de Janeiro, which for its part sought territorial aggrandizement at Spain's expense along the eastern bank of the Uruguay River. Russia employed every practical means at its disposal, including military assistance, to promote a restoration of crown authority in Spanish America. In this regard, the cession of Russian warships to Spain in 1817–1818 is indeed significant, for this was the one occasion when Russia actually essayed a policy of coercion in the Spanish colonies. The object of this transfer, euphemistically described by the two courts as a commercial transaction, was to facilitate a Spanish offensive in the River Plate, viewed at the time as the key to royalist victory in South America. Failure of this offensive to materialize, in turn, had a decisive effect on subsequent tsarist policy in the New World.

The impracticality of assisting Spain in a militarily significant manner stemmed from a combination of factors that Russia gradually came to appreciate in the years immediately following the Congress of Vienna. The enormous logistical problems inherent in such an undertaking were apparent from the very start. Added to this was the chaotic state of Spain's internal affairs, as well as Russia's inability to secure from the major European courts a commitment to the principle of collective force in dealing with the Spanish American insurgents. A military solution to the colonial question thus threatened to exceed in cost the remunerative value of the colonies themselves.[43]

Having failed to achieve palpable benefits through the one act of military assistance that promised fruitful results, and unable to rally the other European powers behind the banner of collective intervention, Alexander I finally dismissed the feasibility of any further military cooperation with Spain in the matter of colonial pacification. This decision appears to have been made in the autumn of 1818, following the Congress of Aix-la-Chapelle, and remained unchanged throughout the remainder of the tsar's reign.

With the outbreak of liberal revolution in the Iberian Peninsula, Piedmont, Naples, and Greece, Russian concern focused once again on Europe, leaving events in America to follow their own course. By the time Iberian domestic affairs were put back in a legitimist order acceptable to Russia and the other signatories of the Holy Alliance, it was too late to consider a similar housecleaning in the Spanish colonies. In the interim, the United States had recognized the de facto independence of Mexico, Colombia, Peru, Chile, and the River Plate, while the U. S. Congress had appropriated funds to defray the cost of diplomatic missions to the newly emancipated republics. Great Britain showed signs of following suit, while the royal fleet stood between America and any intervening force that might threaten British commercial interests. From this point on, therefore, Russia offered Spain little more than moral support in the dispute with its colonies. At the same time, the tsarist government continued to pursue its long-standing interests in the Western Hemisphere.

Insofar as tsarist Russia supported Spanish objectives in America, it did so for clearly self-seeking reasons. While the doctrine of legitimacy made Alexander I and Ferdinand VII natural bedfellows, the tsar and his agents considered this relationship little more than an ideological mantle with which to veil the pursuit of Russian imperial objectives. The sacrifice of principle to practical circumstance during the Greek uprising of 1821 lends added weight to this view.[44] Measured support of Spain in the struggle to retain its American possessions was viewed by the court of St. Petersburg as the most expeditious way to further Russian interests in the New World.

Thus it was envisioned that a continuation of Spanish colonial authority in the viceroyalty of New Spain would create conditions propitious for an expansion of Russian influence in California. Were Spanish North America to become independent, it was feared, Russian interests in the area would be severely jeopardized by British and Anglo-American ambitions. Spain, on the other hand, was beholden to Russia for tsarist support in the colonial question and thus could be expected to favor Russian interests in Spanish North America. Available evidence suggests that Russia may even have anticipated territorial compensation along the Pacific coast in return for the tsar's endorsement of Spanish New World pretensions.

Elsewhere in Latin America, tsarist officials sought economic advantages that would contribute to the growth of Russia's expanding empire in the Pacific. With increasing frequency Russian ships carried consignments to Rio de Janeiro, while similar transactions were effected on a trial basis at the west coast ports of Callao and Guayaquil. From Brazil Russian diplomats filed detailed reports on economic as well as political matters in South America, while after 1822 a scientific expedition under the direct sponsorship of Tsar Alexander I reconnoitered vast expanses of the Brazilian interior. Significantly, its leader, Georg Heinrich von Langsdorff, was also the Russian consul-general in Rio de Janeiro.[45]

Thus by 1820, Russian interest in the Iberian overseas empires extended from Madeira, the Azores, and Brazil to the west coast of South America, New Spain, and Alta California. Although the specific circumstances of Russian relations with these diverse territories varied widely, the tsarist court viewed the trans-Atlantic possessions of Spain and Portugal as a geopolitical whole strategically related to Russian imperial objectives in the Pacific basin. Failure to attach due weight to the totality of tsarist interests in the Western Hemisphere, i.e., to the geopolitical constants of those objectives, has led historians to draw tacit and perhaps misleading distinctions between Spanish and Portuguese America in the formulation of Russian New World policy.

This is especially evident as relates to Brazil, where a unique process of national emancipation produced problems of diplomatic recognition. Yet even here, the present study argues, the continuities of tsarist imperial objectives were ultimately of greater consequence than changing considerations of diplomacy. These continuities precluded an actual severance of ties with Brazil, despite the withdrawal of ambassadorial representation following the return of the Portuguese court to Europe in 1821, and in fact permitted an uninterrupted pursuit of Russian interests in that country pending the restoration of full diplomatic relations more than seven years later. They also promoted further contacts between Russia and Spanish America, and, in 1826–1827, prompted efforts to occupy Haiti as a Russian commercial enclave athwart envisioned trade routes connecting the Atlantic and Pacific oceans.

There are two basic approaches to the international aspects of Latin American independence—one from a colonial perspective, the other from the perspective of the interested foreign powers. The first seeks to evaluate insurgent perceptions of the international situation and to relate those perceptions to specific decisions affecting or intended to affect the direction of the independence struggle. The second focuses on an evaluation of foreign interests and intentions in colonial Latin America. Both approaches are necessary for a proper analysis of the subject, and, although historians have thus far favored the latter approach, much remains to be done in each of these areas. The primary object of the present volume, as stated at the outset, is to probe the major determinants of Russian responses to the emancipation of colonial Latin America and to evaluate, from a European perspective, the actual impact of tsarist policy on the course of those historic events.

2. The Awakening of Russian Interest in America

Russian approaches to early nineteenth-century America derived in part from accumulated past experience, in part from the exigencies of imperial growth and international circumstance alluded to in chapter 1. Knowledge of the New World among lettered Russians can be traced back to the 1520s, when Dmitrii Gerasimov, Muscovite envoy to the Vatican, first reported Magellan's circumnavigation of the globe to Tsar Basil III.[1] Some years later, a Greek monk resident in Moscow made brief mention of Spanish and Portuguese overseas discoveries, including "a most spacious land called Cuba whose limits are unknown even to those who live there."[2] These early references to the Western Hemisphere were followed by a series of Russian-language editions of foreign atlases and geographic treatises that provided the enlightened of Muscovy with added and increasingly accurate information about the New World.[3]

Occasional sixteenth- and seventeenth-century Russian translations of Western writings about the New World, however, relate only tangentially to the gestation of active Russian interest in the Western Hemisphere.[4] The limited circulation of these works, together with the cultural and geographic isolation of Muscovy itself, precluded any early articulation of such interest among the peoples of Europe's northeastern periphery. Indeed, Muscovy was not yet ready to look far abroad, for it still had to realize its own territorial imperatives. Although the capitulation of Novgorod in 1478 gave Moscow access to the White Sea, and although subjects of Muscovy reached the Pacific in 1639, neither event provided the growing empire with viable maritime outlets. Not until the eighteenth century, under the heavy hand of Peter the Great, did Russia secure access to the Baltic and Black seas. Only then did there emerge a basis for the extension of Russian interests to the remotest corners of the earth.

Eighteenth-Century Antecedents

It was in large measure Peter (1672–1725) who finally propelled Russia into the larger world of Enlightenment Europe and beyond. In a brief three decades he made great progress toward bridging the gap opened by the Mongol conquest of the thirteenth century between Muscovy and the principal formative processes of modern Europe. The first Russian ruler to look beyond the confines of the Muscovite realm, Peter personally ventured abroad in 1697. Moved by an insatiable fascination with cartography, mathematics, astronomy, navigation, and military technology, he spent a year and a half in Holland and England querying all who showed accomplishment in these areas. The young tsar even busied himself in the Amsterdam yards of the Dutch East India Company in an effort to master the craft of shipbuilding.

Peter returned to Russia bent on sweeping change, for he had seen "what wealth, trade, manufactures, and knowledge meant to a country in terms of power and prosperity."[5] Obsessed with the material superiority of Western Europe, reflected in "the forest of masts on the watersides of Amsterdam and London," Peter determined to place Russia in the fore of civilized nations, pointedly bypassing the tortuous evolutionary paths traversed over the years by England and Holland.[6] Large numbers of Russians were sent abroad to acquire the basically utilitarian skills required to achieve modernity. At the same time, foreigners trained in the useful arts were brought to Russia, where they contributed to the mounting disruption of traditional Muscovite ways. In anticipation of war with Sweden, Peter created an up-to-date army commanded by foreign officers, while at Voronezh, on the River Don, he charged the construction of a navy—Russia's first—to a varied assemblage of Italian, Dutch, English, and local shipbuilders. The newly formed fleet, including a sixty-gun vessel designed by the tsar himself, marked the extension of Russian power to the Black Sea. Shortly thereafter tsarist authority was carried to the Baltic, where in 1703 Russian forces seized the mouth of the Neva. So important was this latter outlet to the sea that Peter ordered a city built on that very spot for the Russian court. A symbol of Russia's commitment to maritime power and world involvement, St. Petersburg replaced Moscow as the imperial capital.

Peter the Great sought both to increase and to disseminate exact geographic knowledge about the empire and the world at large. Typically, he was responsible for the first printing of a Russian geography. Entitled, "A geography or short description of the globe," the work appeared "by order of his Tsarist Majesty" in March 1710.[7] Several pages of text were devoted to America and included brief descriptions of Florida, New Spain, Brazil, Chile, and Peru. Though not a significant advance beyond previous manuscript compilations, the early Russian geography did enjoy a far wider circulation than any of its predecessors, as evidenced by two additional printings of the work in 1716.[8] This initial geographic publication was followed in 1719 by a Russian translation of Johann Hübner's *Kurze Fragen aus der alten und neuen Geographie* (1693), a serious treatise largely devoid of the fantasy so characteristic of earlier geographic works. Translated "by the order of the great and sovereign czar and grand prince Peter the First," Hübner's work offered literate Russians the basic geographic and geopolitical facts of the New World, including numerous place names transliterated for the first time into Cyrillic.[9]

Peter's interest in geographic exploration had been heightened as a result of discussions with European scholars in 1697–1698 about what might lie beyond the Kamchatka Peninsula.[10] The tsar was especially eager to learn whether or not Asia and America were joined by land, for were the two continents separated, he reasoned, Russia might profitably exploit a northeast passage to China.[11] Following his return to Moscow in 1698, Peter instructed the governors of Kamchatka to gather all available information on Japan and the Pacific islands. Later, in 1719, he dispatched two geodesists to eastern Siberia to determine whether or not Asia and America indeed constituted contiguous land masses. Although the expedition failed in its primary endeavor, the tsar was encouraged to try again. Only weeks before his death in the winter of 1725, he drafted instructions for a larger expedition, which, under the command of Danish mariner Vitus Bering, was to pursue this same objective. When Bering and his second-in-command, Aleksei Chirikov, finally sailed into Alaskan waters in the summer of 1741, the way was at last opened to Russian expansion eastward across the Pacific.[12]

At the same time, there is evidence that Peter's interest in the Pacific basin extended to Spanish America. The very spirit of Petrine Russia was one of practicality aimed at a progressive strengthening of the Russian state.[13] Within the broader context of modernization then in progress, this meant a conscious expansion of foreign trade. That, in turn, raised the question of commercial ties with the New World, considered by many Europeans a source of untold riches.

Significantly, Russia now pursued direct ties with Spain. Informal discussions on trade were initiated following the War of the Spanish Succession, with the Russian side anxious to supply naval stores, hardware, and shipbuilding materials to Spanish yards in return for silver specie.[14] In 1719, the tsar sent a number of cadets to the royal naval academy at Cádiz to be trained as officers for Russia's nascent imperial fleet.[15] By the summer of 1721, P. I. Beklemishev, an experienced diplomat and commercial agent of the Russian court, had been dispatched to Spain to investigate first-hand the possibilities of direct Russo-Spanish trade.[16] A year later, the tsar appointed Russia's first ambassador to Spain, S. D. Golitsyn.[17]

Russian interest in trade with Spain, it is clear, extended beyond the Iberian Peninsula, focusing from the outset on the bullion and other produce of the overseas colonies. In his very first report to the tsar, written in October 1722, Beklemishev called attention to the profitable contraband trade carried on between Spanish America and the principal maritime powers of Europe, detailing the various ways in which this illicit traffic was effected.[18] The tsar quickly became convinced of the benefit to be derived from commercial intercourse with Spain and, in the fall of 1723, dispatched a counselor from the *kollegiia* of commerce, I. A. Shcherbatov, along with two subordinates to establish a Russian consulate in Cádiz.[19] Meanwhile, the negotiations on bilateral trade were formalized, culminating in the summer of 1725 with the arrival in Cádiz of three Russian merchant ships, the first vessels of such registry to enter Spanish waters.[20]

At about this same time, Peter was instructing Bering to gather precise intelligence on the location and disposition of European settlements in America.[21] The only such settlements the Danish mariner could have anticipated encountering, of course, belonged to the Spanish crown, most notably those of New Spain and the viceroyalty of Peru.[22] By the end of Peter's reign, therefore, it appears that Russia had in fact begun, however tentatively, to approach Middle and South America, groping its way at once across the Atlantic and the Pacific. This intention is reflected in the almost simultaneous dispatch of these two expeditions, one directly to Spain, the metropolis; the other toward Spain's colonies in the New World.[23]

In this light it is not surprising that a number of specific proposals were advanced in the first decades of the eighteenth century for Russian intervention in Latin America. As early as 1711, for example, an English merchant by the name of Rupert Beck approached the tsarist court with a plan for the seizure of Tobago as a base for Russian commercial activities in the Americas.[24] A second and more ambitious project was presented to the tsar toward the end of his reign by an unidentified Dutchman, who proposed that Russia occupy territories in South America lying beyond the effective control of the Spanish and Portuguese colonial authorities.[25] The areas envisioned by the project's author stretched from Patagonia (*Magellaniia*) through the

Brazilian interior to the Amazon basin and the Guiana Highlands. They were said to contain many valuable products, including sugar, cochineal, indigo, tobacco, copper, tin, gold, and silver, and "awaited only to be taken by his Russian Tsarist Majesty."[26] The conquest of these territories, according to the proposal, would require an expeditionary force of some twelve thousand foot soldiers, four thousand dragoons, ten warships, sixty large transports, and thirty smaller vessels capable of navigating rivers. Allowing two to three years to complete the operation, the tsar could then expect to receive perhaps as much as eighty million guilders annually from his new possessions. Clearly appealing to Peter's sense of national priorities, the author of the project asserted that "in a short time it would be possible to send between 80,000 and 100,000 soldiers from these lands to Europe or Asia to fight either the Turks or the Persians, thereby permitting the conquest of many lands and cities for his Russian Tsarist Majesty, the liberation of many thousands of Christians from slavery, and the liquidation of the enemies of Christianity."[27] Peter, however, remained unpersuaded.

Another proposal for the occupation of peripheral territories in South America was presented to the Russian court during the reign of Anna Ivanovna (1730–1740) by an enterprising Portuguese merchant, João da Costa.[28] Inspired by a brother who for several years had engaged in the slave trade between Angola and Brazil, da Costa initially proposed the establishment of a British colony in unoccupied territory extending from Santa Catarina south to the eastern bank of the River Plate. Failing to secure a firm British commitment, however, he turned to the Russian ambassador in London, A. D. Kantemir, who had himself contemplated the possibility of establishing a Russian colony in Brazil and now encouraged da Costa to approach the court of St. Petersburg.[29]

Da Costa tendered his proposal in the spring of 1735. A year later, the Russian court tentatively agreed to a modified version of the plan. Shortly thereafter, however, it annulled that decision and abandoned the project altogether. In light of Russia's recently launched campaign against the Ottoman Empire, da Costa was informed, the tsarina wished to avoid all possible entanglements in Western Europe and for that reason could not then challenge the interests of other colonial powers in South America.[30]

In 1736, yet another colonial project was presented to the Russian court. Its author, one Simon Abrogam, proposed the creation of a Russian colony in the Orinoco delta region of South America. This scheme, too, appears to have received initial approval of the tsarist government, only to be abandoned—as had da Costa's project—because of anticipated international repercussions.[31]

There appear to have been numerous projects for the founding of Russian colonies in South America during the first half of the eighteenth century.[32] As noted in the case of the tsarist ambassador to the court of St. James, interest in these projects was shared by Russian subjects as well as foreigners. To learn more about America, declared an official of the admiralty in 1735, it was necessary to reconnoiter the Spanish territories as far south as Mexico.[33] In order to promote the development of Kamchatka and the lands discovered by Bering, added a member of the governing senate, Russia ought to establish ties with California and Mexico. While Spain jealously protected the mines of its New World possessions, he observed, time and the patient pursuit of friendly relations would one day give Russia access to the precious metals of those distant countries.[34]

As the eighteenth century progressed, Latin America increasingly attracted the interest of enlightened Russians. By the 1750s New World themes had begun to inspire such literary lights as M. V. Lomonosov (1711–1765) and A. P. Sumarokov (1718–1777), both of whom decried in verse the abandon with which Spain had plundered the New World. At the same time, Lomonosov extolled those "Russian Columbuses" who, scorning fate and struggling through floes of ice, would someday extend Russian power to America.[35] In the latter part of the century, a great deal of information about the New World was circulated in the form of travel accounts and other descriptive works translated into Russian from French and German originals.[36] To these works were added the accounts of Fëdor Karzhavin and Vasilii Baranshchikov, two Russian travelers who visited the West Indies in the 1780s. Baranshchikov's work, first published in 1787, evoked considerable interest. Entitled *The unhappy adventures of Vasilii Baranshchikov . . . in three parts of the world: America, Asia and Europe*, it saw three editions in only four years.[37] The Russian periodical press, for its part, also began in this same period to publish a growing number of items pertaining to the New World.[38]

Baranshchikov and Karzhavin were only two of various Russians to visit the New World during the second half of the eighteenth century. The first appear to have been two naval officers, Nikifor Poluboiarinov and a Lieutenant Kozlianikov, who, in 1763, visited Brazil aboard a ship of the British East India Company.[39] They were followed in the 1790s and early 1800s by several talented mariners sent to England for advanced training who in the first decades of the nineteenth century played a decisive role in extending Russian sea power around the globe. Prominent among them were L. A. Hagemeister (1780–1834), I. F. Kruzenshtern (1770–1846), and M. P. Lazarev (1788–1851). All three officers made training voyages to the West Indies, while Kruzenshtern also visited South America.[40]

The extent to which Russia's cumulative knowledge and awareness of Latin America had begun to influence geopolitical thinking at the Russian court in the latter part of the eighteenth century is suggested by one incident in particular, namely Catherine II's patronage of Francisco de Miranda, outspoken partisan of Spanish American independence.[41] Following an audience with Miranda in Kiev, in February 1787, the tsarina saw fit to honor the Venezuelan revolutionary with her personal favor and protection. In St. Petersburg, she accorded Miranda privileges normally reserved for members of the diplomatic corps, to the evident annoyance of some foreign envoys.[42] When, after almost a year, Miranda indicated a desire to continue his journey, Catherine is said to have urged him to remain at the Russian court indefinitely. He declined the invitation, however, quitting the tsarina's domains in September 1787 to pursue the cause of Spanish American independence. Interestingly, for several years thereafter Miranda continued to enjoy the full protection of the Russian court in matters political as well as financial.[43]

Although little has been written about Catherine's reasons for receiving the dissident Venezuelan, circumstantial evidence suggests that "the protection extended Miranda by the Russian empress derived not from personal caprice, but rather was occasioned by considerations of an exceedingly practical nature, related above all to Russian penetration in America."[44] As already noted, the idea of Russian expansion into Spanish America first gained currency in the early eighteenth century. The founding of a Russian settlement on Kodiak Island in 1784 opened new perspectives for a Russian advance southward toward Spanish California and Mexico. Indeed, merchants and government functionaries in the Russian Far East had long contemplated just such a possibility. "The Russians," wrote a Polish visitor to Kamchatka in the early 1770s, "will someday take California. . . . Sooner or later," he added, "the Spanish colonies will fall prey to them."[45]

Catherine learned of the new Russian settlement on Kodiak toward the end of 1786. Already inspired by the movement of Siberian fur traders into the Aleutians and the Alaskan mainland, the tsarina decided to assert crown rights in those distant territories. Less than three months prior to meeting Miranda, she ordered the dispatch of four armed frigates and a transport to the Pacific Ocean "for the defense of our rights in the lands discovered by Russian mariners."[46] The following spring, she assigned three additional warships to the Far East in an effort to establish Russian naval supremacy in the Pacific.[47]

Tsarist ambitions in the eastern Pacific are reflected in early Spanish concern over possible Russian encroachments on the northern frontier of New Spain. Indeed, following the Bering-Chirikov voyage of 1741 the notion of an eventual Russian presence in California gained wide currency outside of Russia. As early as 1759 a Spanish Franciscan, Fr. José Torrubia, published a volume entitled *The Muscovites in California*,[48] and, not long after, a Jesuit confrere, Fr. Miguel Benavente, called attention to "potential Russian establishments in the Californias."[49] By 1760, Charles III had formulated plans to secure Alta California within the administrative jurisdiction of the *audiencia* of Guadalajara, and in 1761 he instructed his ambassador at the tsarist court to obtain precise information on Russian voyages to the Pacific Northwest.[50] Reports of a new expedition in 1764 "confirmed Russia's intention to establish itself in North America."[51] Informed three years later that this expedition had landed several hundred tsarist subjects on the North American mainland, the Spanish crown instructed the viceroy of New Spain to take precautions against possible Russian incursions into Baja California. Subsequently, steps were taken to assure an effective Spanish presence in Alta California, resulting in the settlement of San José, Los Angeles, Monterey, San Francisco, and over twenty mission communities extending from San Diego north to San Francisco Bay.[52]

In these circumstances, Catherine the Great appears to have looked upon Francisco de Miranda as a convenient agent for the furtherance of her imperial ends. Anticipating a future confrontation with Spain over territorial claims in North America, she apparently entertained the thought of fomenting revolt in the Spanish colonies so as to remove the threat of a future thrust against the settlements of Russian America. The evidence suggests that sometime in 1787 Catherine proposed to send Miranda to Kamchatka, whence, with the support of Russia's nascent Pacific fleet, he might strike at the west coast of Spanish America.[53]

Events closer to home, however, soon frustrated any such project. In August 1787 war again broke out between the Russian and Ottoman empires, while a few months later Russo-Swedish relations, too, degenerated into open hostilities. The situation precluded assigning any vessels of the Baltic fleet to the Far East, as the tsarina had originally ordered.[54] Like Peter and Anna Ivanovna before her, Catherine had to abandon plans to test Spanish power in America. Nevertheless, these plans were not lost on Russian statesmen of a later moment, who, in responding to the real disintegration of Spanish and Portuguese colonial rule, drew upon more than a century of articulated thinking about Russian New World interests.

Socioeconomic Roots

If one can in fact point to an evolving Russian interest in colonial Latin America, that interest derived in large part from the changing socioeconomic configuration of post-Petrine Russia. Basic economic motives are apparent from the outset, developing in an almost predictable manner with the attainment of Russian maritime power. At the same time, the economic sources of tsarist New World interest responded to decisive changes in Russian society resulting from the inexorable process of modernization set in motion by Peter the Great.

Expanding steadily throughout the second half of the eighteenth century, by 1800 Russian foreign trade rested on an active exchange of foodstuffs, raw materials, semifinished products, and a variety of manufactured goods. Bread, flour, lard, flax, hemp, canvas, pig iron, and forest products were exported, primarily to Great Britain and the maritime states of continental Europe, while silks, woolens, raw and processed cotton, dyes, sugar, tea, coffee, and utensils were imported to meet the growing demands of Russia's domestic market. Between 25 and 30 percent of overall annual imports could be classified as colonial goods, a major portion of which originated in Latin America.[55]

Tea, silk, and spices reached Russia from Persia, India, China, and the East Indies. Cotton, sugar, coffee, dyes, and tobacco came mainly from the New World, although limited quantities of these items, too, were imported from Central Asia and the Far East.[56] The single most valuable item appears to have been cotton. During the years 1802–1806, for example, raw and processed fibers were imported at an average of three million pounds per year; cotton articles of clothing imported over the same five-year period represented an average annual value of about four million rubles silver. Dyes, tea, silk, coffee, spices, and tobacco followed in descending order of commercial significance.[57]

Primary colonial imports from America were cotton, sugar, and dyestuffs. Together with varying quantities of coffee, cacao, tapioca, spirits, and medicinals, these goods were supplied to the Russian market directly, as well as indirectly through the great commercial marts of England and the Baltic.[58] Commodities received directly from the Western Hemisphere were shipped mainly from ports along the eastern seaboard of the United States and with few exceptions were carried in Anglo-American bottoms. An important part of these shipments, however, was actually procured in the West Indies and South America. Sugar, for example, came almost entirely from Brazil and the Caribbean, as did coffee, cacao, and dyestuffs. Substantial amounts of cotton, a prime export item of the southern United States, also originated in the Spanish and Portuguese colonies, although it would appear that most cotton shipments procured in Latin America were transported in British rather than U. S. bottoms.[59] The maintenance of free ports in the British Antilles provided an important outlet for colonial produce of the Spanish Main, including cotton, coffee, cacao, and indigo from the viceroyalty of New Granada.[60] At the same time, large quantities of Brazilian fiber were shipped via Portugal to the cotton mills of Manchester and Birmingham, the source of many cotton drygoods exported to Russia.[61]

By far the larger part of New World colonial goods was shipped initially to Great Britain, Portugal, and the principal non-Russian ports of continental Europe. The Atlantic crossing was made primarily in British and Portuguese vessels. Frequently the various articles of colonial produce underwent some form of industrial processing and were then re-exported to Russia in ships of diverse registry, although here, too, much of the carrying trade fell to the British.[62] The significance of New World colonial goods in Russian foreign trade at the beginning of the nineteenth century is reflected in table 1. These are, of course, generic classifications and as such permit only a partial view of Russian commercial links with the New World. In addition to the

TABLE 1.

BASIC COLONIAL PRODUCTS OF THE NEW WORLD
IMPORTED INTO RUSSIA DURING THE YEARS 1801–1808:
ANNUAL AVERAGES

Goods	Wt. in Lbs.	Value in Rbls. Sil.	% of Total Imports
Raw cotton	291,852	—	—
Spun & dyed cotton	2,674,764	2,056,000	5.0
Cotton drygoods	—	4,029,000	9.9
Raw sugar	2,584,980	385,000	0.9
Refined sugar	5,623,056	4,040,000	9.9
Dyestuffs	5,655,420	1,896,000	4.6
Coffee	2,286,468	807,000	2.0
Tobacco	—	179,000	0.4

Sources: V. I. Pokrovskii (ed.), *Sbornik svedenii po istorii i statistike vneshnei torgovli Rossii*, I, xxix; M. F. Zlotnikov, *Kontinental'naia blokada i Rossiia*, pp. 42–44.

different grades and varieties of colonial imports, there were many articles of relatively minor commercial significance that do not conform neatly to the preceding categories.

A varied selection of products reached the Russian market, for example, from Brazil, including cacao, tapioca, vanilla, cinnamon, clove, pepper, rum, and tropical woods (see table 2). Brazilian sugar was available to Russian consumers in white, refined, and brown powder, as well as in loaves. Cotton of varying qualities was imported from Pernambuco, Maranhão, Bahia, Pará, and Rio de Janeiro, together with coffee, indigo, and numerous other commodities.[63] As noted previously, many of these same products also reached Russia from Spanish America.

The growing importation of colonial produce into tsarist Russia in the late eighteenth and early nineteenth centuries at once testified to and resulted from important changes in the size, composition, and distribution of the Russian population. It related increasingly to socially identifiable patterns of consumption that not infrequently bore on matters of state policy. These, in turn, were directly related to population growth. Whereas the Russian Empire counted approximately nineteen million inhabitants in 1762, by the turn of the century this number had nearly doubled.[64] Even accounting for the annexation of new territories during the reign of Catherine II, the bulk of this growth must be attributed primarily to an accentuated natural increase within the limits of European Russia.[65] In this area alone the population grew from nineteen million in 1762 to some twenty-five million by the century's end.[66]

Cities reflected the general rise in population. In relative terms, the urban segment of Russian society remained insignificant well into the nineteenth century. In 1796, there were fewer than two million urban

TABLE 2.

IMPORTS FROM PORTUGAL AND THE PORTUGUESE
COLONIES AVAILABLE IN ST. PETERSBURG: PRICES FOR
THE YEARS 1806 AND 1809 (in rubles)

Goods	Unit of Measure	1806		1809	
		Cash	Credit	Cash	Credit
Almonds:					
sweet	per *pud**	18.0	20.0	26.0	32.0
bitter	per *pud*	16.0	17.0	24.0	26.0
unshelled	per *pud*	14.0	15.0	22.0	23.0

TABLE 2. (continued)

Goods	Unit of Measure	1806		1809	
		Cash	Credit	Cash	Credit
Cacao:					
from Maranhão	per *pud*	16.0	18.0	20.0	25.0
from Caracas	per *pud*	25.0	26.0	30.0	35.0
Chestnuts					
from Maranhão	per *pud*	7.0	8.0	14.0	—
Cinnamon	per *pud*	50.0	—	80.0	—
Citrus rinds:					
bitter lemon	per *pud* ⎫				
bitter orange	per *pud* ⎬	5.0	6.0	14.0	—
sweet orange	per *pud* ⎭				
Clove:					
from India	per *pud*	80.0	—	150.0	180.0
from Maranhão	per *pud*	18.0	—	60.0	—
Cochineal	per *pud*	280.0	300.0	1,400.0	1,550.0
Coffee:					
from Rio (superior grade)	per *pud*	22.0	23.0	64.0	—
from Pará (medium grade)	per *pud*	18.0	19.0	54.0	—
Cork:					
pressed	per *pud*	2.5	3.0	15.0	—
stoppers	per *pud*	3.5	4.0	20.0	—
Cotton:					
from Rio	per *pud*	—	—	15.0	16.0
from Bahia	per *pud*	—	—	19.0	20.0
from Pará	per *pud*	—	—	17.0	18.0
from Pernambuco	per *pud*	—	—	23.0	25.0
from Maranhão	per *pud*	—	—	21.0	22.0
Figs (dried)	per *pud*	3.5	—	5.0	6.0
Fruit:					
sweet lemons ⎫					
bitter lemons ⎪	per case				
sweet oranges ⎬	of	(according to quantity imported)			
bitter oranges ⎪	300–400				
sweet limes ⎭					
Ginger:					
white	per *pud*	14.0	15.0	30.0	—
brown/black	per *pud*	5.0	6.0	8.0	10.0
Gums:					
elastic	per *pud*	14.0	15.0	18.0	—
Arabic	per *pud*	10.0	11.0	25.0	45.0
Indigo:					
from Guatemala (superior grade)	per *pud*	210.0	230.0	600.0	650.0
from Brazil (medium grade)	per *pud*	110.0	120.0	380.0	—

TABLE 2. (continued)

Goods	Unit of Measure	1806 Cash	Credit	1809 Cash	Credit
from Brazil					
(inferior grade)	per *pud*	60.0	70.0	225.0	—
Ivory	per *pud*	60.0	—	150.0	—
Medicinals:					
sarsaparilla	per *pud*	45.0	50.0	100.0	—
ipecac	per *pud*	2.5	3.0	4.0	—
copaiba balsam	per *pud*	30.0	35.0	40.0	—
Olive oil:					
yellow	per *pud*	18.0	20.0	30.0	32.0
light green	per *pud*	16.0	17.0	28.0	—
Pepper:					
black	per *pud*	8.0	9.0	60.0	65.0
white	per *pud*	12.0	14.0	45.0	50.0
Raisins	per *pud*	3.5	—	8.5	—
Rice:					
white whole	per *pud*	4.0	4.5	13.0	—
white cracked	per *pud*	3.0	3.25	12.0	—
Rum	per keg	20.0	22.0	100.0	—
Sugar:					
white powder	per *pud*	10.5	11.0	20.0	22.0
refined powder	per *pud*	11.0	11.5	25.0	27.0
unrefined	per *pud*	7.5	8.0	15.0	—
refined loaves (superior grade)	per *pud*	18.0	19.0	62.0	64.0
refined loaves (medium grade)	per *pud*	16.0	17.0	53.0	55.0
refined loaves (inferior grade)	per *pud*	14.0	15.0	36.0	40.0
Tapioca	per *pud*	3.5	4.0	5.0	—
Tortoise shell	per *pud*	250.0	300.0	1,800.0	—
Vanilla	per *pud*	150.0	160.0	250.0	—
Wood:					
pau da rainha (superior grade)	per *pud*	60.0	70.0	75.0	—
(medium grade)	per *pud*	20.0	30.0	25.0	—
pau santo	per *pud*	6.0	—	8.0	—
brazilwood	per *pud*	4.0	—	5.0	—
ironwood	per *pud*	3.0	—	7.0	—
pau campeche	per *pud*	18.0	20.0	17.0	—

* 1 *pud* = 16.38 kilograms, or 36.113 English pounds.
Sources: "Preço Corrente das Producções de Portugal e suas Colônias em São
  Petersburgo aos 30 Nov. de 1806" and "Preço Corrente das Producções de
  Portugal e suas Colônias em São Petersburgo ao 1 de Jan.ro de 1809," AHI,
  Vol. 338/3/2.

dwellers out of a total population of approximately thirty-six million subjects.[67] By 1800, perhaps 4 or 5 percent of the population could be considered urban, as compared with 7 percent in France and over 20 percent in Great Britain.[68] In European Russia the absolute number reached an estimated 2.8 million by 1811,[69] of which perhaps just over a million could be described as townsfolk. While available data is so imprecise as to preclude hard statements, figures offered by A. G. Rashin indicate that better than 50 percent of these people resided in communities of less than four thousand inhabitants, which suggests the difficulty of differentiating many presumed urban dwellers from the dominant rural populace. Indeed, scores of cities, so-called, were in truth little more than country villages.[70]

Despite the decidedly agrarian complexion of Russian society, cities of consequence had come into existence by the early nineteenth century, and the pronounced growth within their bounds of an urban bourgeoisie was a fact of ever increasing historical significance. By 1811, there were thirty cities in European Russia that numbered more than ten thousand inhabitants each, accounting for almost 44 percent of the region's urban population. Seven cities had between twenty thousand and thirty thousand inhabitants, and two between thirty thousand and forty thousand. Overshadowing them all were Moscow and St. Petersburg, with 270,000 and 335,000 respectively.[71]

The urban populace was composed of several broadly distinguishable groups. Most numerous in the early years of the nineteenth century was a variegated agglomerate of more than a million persons, including low-level civil servants of common origin, foreigners, and a wide assortment of peasant types who labored in or were otherwise attached to the principal towns and cities of the empire. This group accounted for approximately 38 percent of the total urban populace. It was followed in numerical importance by the petty bourgeoisie or artisan-shopkeeper class (*meshchanstvo*), which numbered some 950,000 and accounted for another 35 percent of the urban total. State bureaucrats, clergy, and the military comprised just under 16 percent, while merchants amounted to slightly more than 7 percent of the total, numbering some 200,000 persons. Finally, there was the numerically small but socially and politically influential nobility.[72]

In St. Petersburg, seat of the imperial Russian government and leading city of the empire, these percentages varied from the general norm (see table 3). Due to the presence of the tsar and his court, the nobility was predictably more numerous than elsewhere, numbering just over thirteen thousand and accounting for 6.5 percent of the capital's inhabitants. During the first decade of the nineteenth century, the nobility of St. Petersburg saw its ranks augmented to more than twenty-three thousand persons, and then all but doubled again between 1811 and 1821; this latter increase is explained in part by the flight of noble families from Moscow following that city's burning in 1812.[73] The relatively high number of state bureaucrats residing in St. Petersburg, in turn, was due to the presence of the imperial government. In 1801 there were perhaps as many as thirty-five thousand civil servants (*raznochintsy*). By 1811 this number had risen to a high of more than sixty-five thousand, an increase partly explained by the ministerial reforms of 1802. Over the next two decades this number fluctuated on a generally downward course, dropping to about fifty-nine thousand toward 1821, then rising again to some sixty-three thousand by 1831.[74] Artisans, guildsmen, and shopkeepers accounted for approximately 12 percent of the capital's populace, rising from twenty-three thousand in 1801 to just over thirty-seven thousand by 1811. Merchants, on the other hand, halved their numbers in this same ten-year period, falling off from around fourteen thousand in 1801 to about seven thousand in 1811; this, in turn, can be explained by Russia's infelicitous adherence to the continental system and the resultant stagnation of the country's foreign trade. Domestic servants numbered just over twenty-six thousand at the beginning of the century, but more than trebled their numbers following the destruction of Moscow. Police, retired officers, palace guards, and special regiments in the immediate service of the tsar accounted for more than 16 percent of the inhabitants of St. Petersburg, while foreign residents comprised around 4 percent of the total. The clergy was relatively insignificant, numbering a scant five hundred members in 1801, as compared to the several thousand clerics resident in Moscow.[75]

At the bottom of the social scale was the peasantry, which accounted for 35 percent of the capital's population.

The general growth of Russia's population, and more particularly the rise of its urban populace, affected the economy of the empire in numerous ways.[76] The emergence of an urban bourgeoisie in key population centers gave rise to a life style markedly distinct from that which prevailed throughout the limitless countryside—a life style ever more attuned to the cultural, political, and socioeconomic pulsations of Western Europe. Augmented private wealth among the merchants and petty bourgeoisie, together with a pronounced Europeanization of the Russian nobility, gave rise to increasing demands for a variety of nonessential goods, which, in the main, proved to be of colonial origin.[77] So great was the value attached to luxury articles by the affluent and socially dominant that some actually came to be regarded as items of

TABLE 3.

SOCIAL DISTRIBUTION OF THE URBAN POPULATION
OF ST. PETERSBURG: 1801–1821

Social Groupings	1801	%	1811	%	1821	%
Nobility	13,200	6.5	23,100	7.7	40,300	9.5
Clergy	500	0.2	600	0.2	2,000	0.5
Merchants	14,300	7.1	7,200	2.4	10,000	2.4
Petty bourgeoisie and guildsmen	23,400	11.6	37,200	12.5	31,400	7.4
Raznochintsy	35,000	17.3	66,600	22.4	59,200	14.0
Domestic servants	26,100	12.9	28,300	9.5	91,800	21.7
Military*	39,100	19.4	48,100	16.2	66,900	15.8
Peasants	50,500	25.0	74,400	25.0	108,000	25.6
Foreigners†	—	—	12,300	4.1	13,300	3.1

* The military grouping does not include regular troops of the line, but rather police, palace and other official guards, and retired officers resident in the capital.
† Although Rashin omits foreigners from his figures for 1801, it is safe to suppose that they were relatively numerous in this the most cosmopolitan of Russian cities.
Source: A. G. Rashin, *Naselenie Rossii za 100 let*, pp. 119–124.

prime necessity. Such, for example, was the case with sugar. "With the general spread of its use," wrote a Russian contemporary, "this product became one of the principal articles of trade in all of the European states and for many of them acquired a fundamental importance with respect to their policies, finances, and diverse interests of trade, agriculture, and manufacturing."[78] Sugar, observed Count N. P. Rumiantsev in 1806, "has become for us an indispensable article of consumption." Cotton, too, was an essential commodity. These two products alone, Rumiantsev informed the tsar, drained some eight million rubles from the country annually, and this exclusive of the not inconsiderable cotton imports procured in Asia.[79]

During the turbulent years of the Napoleonic era, these and other socially rooted consumer demands influenced variously the shaping of Russian foreign, commercial, and fiscal policies. To the degree that this was so, these policies can be attributed in large measure to the growth of cities, and more especially to Moscow and St. Petersburg. This, in turn, was a primary source of Russian New World interest on the eve of and during the struggle for Latin American independence.

3. The Continental System and Russian Commercial Interests in the New World

The mounting economic confrontation between France and Great Britain during the final decades of the eighteenth century acquired at the outset of the nineteenth century such dimensions that it quickly engulfed the whole of Europe. Frustrated colonial ambitions in America, together with a steady deterioration of the French merchant marine and the manifest inability of French industrialists to compete successfully with their British counterparts, led Napoleonic France to seek the effective isolation of the British Isles from continental Europe. As France gradually extended its control over the continent, the political and economic fortunes of the Russian Empire, too, became increasingly tied to the policies of Napoleon.

Despite early efforts in concert with Great Britain, Sweden, and Austria to combat burgeoning French influence in the affairs of Europe, Tsar Alexander I was finally forced to shift alliances. On 7 July 1807, at Tilsit, he and Napoleon signed a treaty of peace.[1] At the same time, the two emperors affixed their signatures to a secret treaty of offensive and defensive alliance that could only draw Russia into an eventual confrontation with Great Britain. The British government was given until the end of the year to accede, through Russian mediation, to predictably unacceptable terms of peace. A negative response from Great Britain would obligate Russia, together with France and the courts of Copenhagen, Stockholm, and Lisbon, "to close its ports to the English, recall its ambassador from London, and declare war on England."[2]

Post-Tilsit Economic Dislocations

The implications of closing Russia's ports to British trade were clearly seen by the privileged elements of Russian society prior to the actual implementation of this measure in late October 1807. As early as the spring of 1806 the tsarist minister of commerce, Count N. P. Rumiantsev, was voicing concern over the impact on Russian foreign trade of renewed Anglo-French hostilities. The blockade placed on the mouths of the rivers Ems, Weser, Elbe, and Trave, he advised the tsar, had inevitably to prejudice Russian commercial interests. In a single year, basic Russian exports to the key Hanse Towns of Hamburg, Lübeck, and Bremen alone had slackened by more than four million rubles. Normally, Emden, too, received substantial shipments from Russia. Closure of these international marts could not be viewed with indifference.[3]

Russia also imported goods from northern Germany, including refined sugar, cotton fabrics, and spirits. Of these, sugar was perhaps the most severely affected by the blockade, as Great Britain was by and large the sole supplier. In Hamburg alone, noted Rumiantsev, there were as many as two hundred mills refining raw sugar for re-export to the principal markets of Europe, making this the single most important article of trade for that city's merchants. Although Hamburg's supply of raw cotton was not totally dependent upon the British, much of it originating in the Mediterranean basin rather than America, it nonetheless suffered notably as a result of the blockade. The same was true of wines and spirits, which came largely from Spain, Portugal, and France.[4]

In these circumstances Count Rumiantsev argued energetically, and one might suppose not disinterestedly,[5] for an end to Russian dependence upon foreign merchants and merchant marines. Sugar of the finest quality was produced in Russia, he observed, but in very limited quantities due to prejudicial policies of the imperial government. "If these obstacles are removed," he stated to the tsar, "then we can procure raw sugar directly from America; the money now extracted from us for the commissions and profits of the Hamburg merchants would remain in state coffers and [domestic] sugar mills would multiply."[6] Taking Hamburg as an example, Rumiantsev invited the tsar to reach the following conclusions about the Hanse Towns as a group: (1) that they were ancillary to the needs of Russian commerce; (2) that Russia would derive great benefit from the establishment of direct ties with the sources of goods traded in the principal marketplaces of the Baltic; and (3) that this could best be accomplished by augmenting the size of the Russian merchant marine.[7]

In early January 1807, Count Rumiantsev again called the tsar's attention to the precarious state of Russia's foreign trade. While the general pacification of the seas following the battle of Trafalgar had momentarily stimulated commercial intercourse, he observed, the increasingly complex political configuration of Europe, together with the debilitated commercial position of Spain, Holland, and France, now permitted Great Britain to monopolize the Russian market and, consequently, to determine the prices of Russian goods. This clearly detrimental state of affairs, he suggested, could be at least partially alleviated by promoting direct trade ties with the United States. The British hold on Russian foreign trade would be broken by the active competition of American merchants, while at the same time Russia would secure an alternate source of primary imports. Here, again, sugar and cotton were uppermost in Rumiantsev's mind.[8]

An unmistakable symptom of economic malaise in post-Tilsit Russia was rising speculation in foreign goods. Throughout 1807 prices on imported merchandise appear to have risen steadily, with a particularly marked increase occurring in the wake of the tsar's announced embargo on British trade. In November of that year, the governor-general of St. Petersburg directed a note to the city *duma* protesting the sudden rise in cost of all foreign products, "especially sugar, coffee and other highly sought items."[9] The governor-general of Moscow addressed a similar note of protest to Count Rumiantsev, who now held the combined portfolio of commerce and foreign affairs. Throughout the summer of 1807, Rumiantsev was informed, sugar of the finest quality had sold in Moscow for twenty-one and twenty-two rubles per *pud*. By autumn, he noted, it had risen to twenty-eight rubles, and following the news of Russia's break with Great Britain it had suddenly jumped to thirty-eight rubles per *pud*. The life style of Moscow's residents,[10] asserted the governor-general, had made sugar an essential article of consumption, second only to the most rudimentary necessities of life. Such a rapid and excessive rise in price, in turn, was popularly attributed to speculative intemperances on the part of the city's merchants.[11]

Effective measures to alleviate scarcities arising from the dependence of Russian foreign trade on outside middlemen were demanded with increasing insistence by those most directly affected, while solutions to the mounting crisis were sought both domestically and abroad. Thus in the summer of 1808, the influential Muscovite monthly, *Vestnik Evropy*, editorialized against the excesses of the Russian nobility. "If only we will renounce foreign delicacies and luxury goods supplied by the English and others," lamented the journal, "if the wealthy, who wish as before to drink coffee, will endeavor to bring it by caravan directly from the Levant," an important first step would be taken to counter an already deteriorated situation.[12] There were, the journal acknowledged, certain luxury items "without which no one in the world can live." Such, for example, was sugar, "demanded by all of the European peoples and second in importance only to bread."[13] These facts, the journal concluded, "should move us earnestly to seek substitutes for West Indian sugar, in order that we may liberate ourselves from dependence on foreign merchants and manufacturers, and further to free ourselves from the despotic whims of the British ministers."[14]

While Russians of means loudly decried the severe shortages and exorbitant prices of luxury goods, obtained in large measure from the trans-Atlantic possessions of Spain and Portugal, the general fiscal state of the empire so degenerated under the imposed stresses of the continental system that by 1810 decisive corrective steps were imperative. Indeed, the post-Tilsit crisis in Russian foreign trade had severely undermined the empire's economy, already badly strained by foreign wars and the maintenance of large armies abroad.[15]

As noted by M. F. Zlotnikov, the Russian imperial budget had never rested on a sound financial basis. State revenues came from the manufacture and sale of spirits and from a selective soul tax (*podushnaia podat'*) levied on the peasantry and petty bourgeoisie. Some additional monies accrued from customs duties, although receipts from this source dwindled notably with the imposition of the continental blockade. Total revenues failed to cover annual state expenditures, and even during periods of relative international tranquility the Russian government had to face serious budgetary deficits.[16] In these circumstances, the levying of a total embargo on British merchandise, as well as on all goods carried in British bottoms or otherwise handled by British middlemen, could only lead to an economic crisis. That this in fact occurred is apparent in table 4.

The deepening fiscal crisis of the Russian Empire was at once reflected in and bound to a rampant inflation of the ruble. In its desperate efforts to offset mounting budgetary deficits, the Russian government

TABLE 4.

FISCAL STATE OF THE IMPERIAL RUSSIAN GOVERNMENT
IN THE YEARS 1801 and 1807–1811 (in rubles)

Years	Expenditures	Revenues	Deficit
1801	93,310,714	81,081,671	12,229,043
1807	162,252,987	117,377,146	44,875,841
1808	244,250,880	118,449,918	125,800,962
1809	279,246,791	121,741,699	157,505,092
1810	241,487,455	170,576,060	70,911,395
1811	300,335,002	234,679,204	65,655,798

Source: M. F. Zlotnikov, *Kontinental'naia blokada i Rossiia*, p. 339.

turned to an unchecked issuance of paper notes. From some 319 million such notes in circulation in 1806, the number rose to 577 million by 1810.[17] The average value of a one-ruble note declined from 67.5 silver kopeks in 1807 to 44.7 in 1809 and 25.4 in 1811.[18] At the same time, the ruble's exchange value abroad fell sharply, as seen in table 5.

By the fall of 1810, Russia's economic crisis was rapidly coming to a head. On November 12 of that year, Minister of Finance D. A. Gur'ev took the matter before the council of state.[19] It was imperative, he told the council, to consider those aspects of the empire's foreign trade "which in its present state are principally responsible for the debilitation of our exchange capabilities, so precipitously weakened over the past two years." In order to bolster the government's faltering credit at home and abroad, Gur'ev proposed two broad measures: (1) a curtailment of foreign imports, and (2) an increase in Russian exports. He hastened to assure the council that he did not envision these measures as permanent, but merely as a necessary response to a transitory situation.[20]

The proposed curtailment of imports directly threatened trade in colonial commodities. The minister of finance recommended that the imperial government prohibit the further importation of most luxury and all nonessential goods, and that tariffs be raised on most authorized imports.[21] Gur'ev proposed that raw cotton and medicinals be granted duty-free entry and that duties on dyestuffs remain minimal. He felt, however, that those luxury items "which, through force of habit, had become essential and were used by the middle and wealthy classes" should be assessed from 10 to 50 percent of their marketable value. In this category Gur'ev included sugar, coffee, and cacao, prime products of Spanish and Portuguese America.[22]

Less than a month after Gur'ev's appearance before the council of

TABLE 5.

RUBLE EXCHANGE RATES FOR THE YEARS 1807–1812

Years	Amsterdam (in stivers)	London (in pence)	Hamburg (in shillings)	Paris (in centimes)
1807	22.83	25.25	21.08	217.33
1808	17.58	22.00	16.33	186.67
1809	15.33	——	13.67	159.25
1810	10.25	——	9.75	113.25
1811	8.58	——	8.00	94.50
1812	12.33	20.20	11.25	130.55

Source: M. F. Zlotnikov, *Kontinental'naia blokada i Rossiia*, p. 336.

state, the merchants of St. Petersburg advised the government of their views on the empire's economic difficulties. Speaking through an elected committee of nine, the capital's merchant community addressed itself to the council of state in much the same manner as had the minister of finance.[23] They, too, called for a restriction on imports and an increase in exports. The committee asked that a temporary ban be placed on the importation of all foreign manufactured goods and that such luxury items as coffee, rum, and champagne also be excluded from entry. Restriction, they added, should not be placed on the importation of raw materials, dyestuffs, and "the basic necessities of life."[24] At the same time, they suggested, an effort should be made to alter the consumer habits of those who clamored for nonessential foreign products. "The prohibition of all luxury articles from abroad," declared the committee, "might well be supported by sumptuary laws capable of restraining the excesses that have infected all classes of society. Let the nobility be obliged to meet their sacred obligations! Let their example, so decisively influential on all the other classes, move them to renounce extravagance, the effects of which are so detrimental."[25]

The Russian government responded with the publication of the Neutral Trade Act for the Year 1811. Largely the work of Michael Speranski, the influential and highly esteemed administrative advisor of Tsar Alexander I, this document introduced a new set of regulations governing the flow of exports and imports through the customshouses of the White, Baltic, Black, and Azov seas, as well as overland across Russia's European frontier.[26] The document was prefaced with an imperial manifesto stating that in view of existing circumstances, and upon the advice of the council of state, it was necessary further to regulate the empire's foreign trade. The immediate purpose of the new regulations was "to stem the spread of ostentatious luxury, to curtail foreign imports, and to stimulate insofar as possible the products of domestic labor and industry."[27]

One immediate effect of the new regulations was to reduce the number of authorized imports from 600 to 208 separate articles. Prohibited imports included woolen, cotton, and silk drygoods, metal utensils, spices, spirits, and a variety of foodstuffs.[28] Of particular significance for nascent Russo–Latin American trade relations was a total embargo on refined sugar, together with a major tariff hike on raw sugar imports. Whereas previously raw sugar had been subject to an import duty of 20 kopeks per *pud*,[29] the rate now rose to 7 rubles (1 ruble = 100 kopeks).[30] Similarly, import duties on cacao and coffee were increased from 2 rubles and 3 rubles 20 kopeks, respectively, to 20 rubles per *pud* for both articles. In the case of dyestuffs, the Neutral Trade

Act reflected only in part the recommendations of Gur'ev and the St. Petersburg merchants committee. Thus the tariff on indigo was raised from 2 rubles 50 kopeks to 13 rubles 75 kopeks, while the duty levied on imported cochineal was reduced from 10 rubles to 75 kopeks per *pud*. Raw cotton and medicinals, in turn, remained duty-free.[31]

While perhaps less stringent than the measures envisioned by Gur'ev and some of the empire's leading merchants, the Neutral Trade Act did place strictures on the influx of foreign goods into Russia. In so doing, it also created obstacles to an early expansion of direct Russian trade ties with Latin America.

Approaches to Portuguese America

By 1808 tsarist officials and private citizens alike were searching for palliatives for the mounting economic dislocations of the continental system. Both sectors expressed concern over dwindling colonial imports and increasingly came to contemplate the distant overseas territories of Spain and Portugal as possible sources of commercial relief. Already in January 1808 Moscow's erudite *Politicheskii, statisticheskii i geograficheskii zhurnal* called attention to the untapped wealth of Portuguese America. "Brazil's position for trade," the journal stated, "is so extraordinarily felicitous that it is as if nature had meant it to be a universal trading place."[32] Basic products of the region included rice, citrus fruits, cotton, tobacco, coffee, sugar, dyes, spices, and lumber, and all that kept it from achieving great commercial prominence were the excessively protective policies of the mother country. Brazil, the journal concluded, "is a land that awaits only human hands to yield up its precious gifts; for this delightful country, one of the most favored in the known world, lies devoid of industry and agriculture due to a lack of inhabitants. Here, there remain buried mines which in their wealth surpass all others, and everywhere on the banks of rivers is found gold dust promising rich profits."[33]

Other organs of the Russian periodical press also began to carry articles on Portuguese America,[34] while in early July 1808 the *Sanktpeterburgskie kommercheskie vedomosti* informed its readers of a significant change in Portuguese colonial trade. The prince-regent of Portugal, the paper reported, had decreed that henceforth all goods carried on vessels belonging to Portuguese subjects or to the subjects of friendly powers would be permitted to enter Brazilian ports for purposes of trade. They would be required to pay an import duty of 24 percent market value on any goods brought into the country and, upon payment of existing tariffs, could export Brazilian produce to Europe.[35]

What appears to have been the first serious Russian attempt to establish direct trade relations with Latin America was made in the spring of 1808 by Ivan Kremer, a leading merchant of St. Petersburg who had large amounts of capital invested in foreign trade.[36] On June 4 of that year, Kremer addressed a formal proposal to Count Rumiantsev detailing a project he had already discussed with the minister orally.[37] Appealing to sentiments that Rumiantsev had himself expressed personally to the tsar and that undoubtedly were well known to the St. Petersburg merchant community, Kremer argued that in the existing circumstances Great Britain was unable to continue its practice of supplying Spanish and Portuguese America with such basic items as iron, linen, cordage, canvas, and sailcloth, traditionally of Russian manufacture, and that consequently Russia was now in a position to derive benefit from an otherwise intolerable state of affairs. Moreover, he added, vessels engaging in such trade would return to Russia laden with the sorely needed colonial produce of the New World.[38]

Specifically, Kremer proposed to send two ships to South America, both during the year 1808, if possible; if not, one in 1808 and the other the following year. Each would carry a cargo of goods produced in Russia. Upon reaching their ports of destination, they would take on as much local produce as receipts from the sale of the original cargoes would permit. To offset hazards inherent in the venture, including the possible seizure of ships and confiscation of cargoes, Kremer asked that the first vessel to return safely to Russia be exempt from all import duties, while the second be required to pay only half the established tariffs. He further requested that these concessions, and indeed the entire enterprise, be guarded in complete secrecy lest it be discovered by the British and thereby compromised from the start.[39] Recalling certain outstanding debts for which the imperial government was beholden to him, Kremer expressed confidence that he would be honored by the approval of his august monarch, as well as by the personal patronage of Count Rumiantsev.[40]

The Russian government did in fact approve the project, and Kremer outfitted for the voyage two vessels he had purchased in Sweden: the *Prinzessin* and the *Ostergotland*. There were serious obstacles to the realization of this venture, however, and, in the absence of corroborating documentation, its final outcome remains obscure.[41] What is significant is that a project of this nature should have been proposed at this time and, further, that it was sanctioned by the highest councils of the Russian state. Kremer, like other influential Russians of his day, was willing to go to great lengths to surmount the hardships that the

continental system had imposed on Russian commerce. In those difficult circumstances, he viewed the promise of profit in distant Spanish
and especially Portuguese America with rising expectations.

Kremer was not alone in his estimations of the benefits to be derived
from the establishment of direct trade ties with the New World, nor
did the impetus for such trade come solely from the Russian side.
Barely three months after the Portuguese court arrived in Brazil and
João VI opened Brazilian ports to foreign shipping, the Portuguese
foreign minister, Rodrigo de Souza Coutinho (Conde de Linhares), instructed his chargé d'affaires in St. Petersburg, Rodrigo Navarro de
Andrade, to inform him in all possible detail on the feasibility of promoting trade relations between Brazil and the Russian empire.[42] On
18 January 1809, Andrade filed a lengthy dispatch to Rio de Janeiro
in which he anticipated much of the information requested by Linhares. The principal Russian ports on the Baltic where merchants of
the New World could expect to carry on a lucrative trade, he observed,
were St. Petersburg and Riga. In St. Petersburg, Portuguese merchants
based in Brazil or elsewhere in the overseas empire could consign ships
and cargoes to the reputable trading firm of Dionizio Pedro Lopes,
while in Riga they were commended to Wenceslao Theodoro Ghama,
a Portuguese merchant established in that city. Andrade also considered Archangel a viable outlet for the produce of Brazil. Passage
through the White Sea, he noted, was not hazardous, and, in the port
of Archangel itself, shipments could be consigned to a Mr. Van Brien,
who served as the Portuguese consul.[43]

At the same time, Andrade noted, there were serious obstacles to the
promotion of Russo–Brazilian trade relations. Thus the great distance
separating the two countries required that ships engaging in direct
trade between them make at least one intermediary stop to lay in fresh
stores. The political situation in Europe, however, made it impossible
for vessels of Portuguese registry to call at British or continental ports.
It was both necessary and prudent, therefore, that these ships put in
to Madeira or one of the islands of the Azores before proceeding on to
northern Europe, for should the French occupy Zealand without warn-
ing, Brazilian cargoes consigned to Riga and St. Petersburg would not
get past Helsingör. Finally, observed Andrade, the foreign minister
should recognize the limitations of his intelligence on the state of
Baltic commerce, since events were moving too precipitously to state
anything with certainty.[44]

Like Ivan Kremer, the enterprising Dionizio Pedro Lopes, too, saw
an attractive source of profit in the establishment of direct trade relations between Russia and Brazil. In early January 1809, he drafted a

memorandum on the subject, which the Portuguese chargé d'affaires immediately forwarded to Count Linhares with the recommendation that it be publicized among the merchants of Brazil.[45] "The memorable events which have occurred in Europe facilitate and make of the greatest importance and interest direct trade between the States of Brazil and the Russian Empire," wrote Lopes. "Almost all the products of Brazil have a ready outlet in Russia," he asserted, "and many goods produced and manufactured in this Empire can be exported to Brazil very advantageously."[46]

Lopes noted in his memorandum that, while St. Petersburg had close financial ties with Hamburg, Amsterdam, Paris, and London, the British capital offered Portuguese merchants the greatest advantages. As relations between Russia and Great Britain were at the time severed, however, he announced his readiness to provide merchants located in Brazil with the necessary credit "to initiate and promote their commercial speculations" in St. Petersburg. For those consigning shipments of Brazilian commodities directly to him, credit would be established on the basis of proceeds received from the sale of such shipments. To those wishing to purchase Russian goods for sale on the Brazilian market, he would advance credit at an annual rate of 6 percent. "As my firm is the only Portuguese establishment in this capital," Lopes declared, "I am confident that my compatriots will place their commissions and orders with me, it being well known in all the centers of Europe, and above all in those of Portugal, that I have always executed the very important commissions entrusted to me with honor, zeal and dispatch."[47]

Indeed, the import-export house of Dionizio Lopes figured among the first ten commercial establishments of the Russian capital, realizing in the year 1807 alone a total turnover of more than 1.3 million rubles.[48] Now, in the general crisis of Napoleonic Europe, Lopes sought to conserve and insofar as possible expand his financial gains. To this end, he undertook a fourteen-month journey to Brazil for the specific purpose of promoting trade between Russia and Portuguese America. Returning to St. Petersburg in the winter of 1812, he carried his promotional efforts to the pages of the widely read Portuguese-language monthly, *Correio Braziliense*, published in London. A frequent contributor, he reported exchange quotations, market conditions, changing trade regulations, and the movement of commercial shipping through Russia's Baltic ports.[49]

If by 1809 private entrepreneurs had begun actively to seek the establishment of direct trade ties between Russia and Portuguese America, the Russian and Portuguese governments, too, began to show interest in the promotion of such trade. At the beginning of January 1808, scarcely two months after the Portuguese court had sailed for South America, Count Rumiantsev assured Andrade that the transfer of the prince-regent to Brazil, far from weakening Russo–Portuguese ties, would, "given the advantages of direct trade between the two countries," in fact strengthen those ties.[50] At a subsequent meeting in February, Rumiantsev informed the Portuguese chargé that the Russo–Portuguese trade agreement of 1798[51] would remain unaltered and that Portuguese vessels sailing from the islands and ports of the overseas dominions could continue to call at Russian ports despite recent events in Europe.[52] As yet unaware of the *carta régia* published in Rio de Janeiro two or three weeks before, Rumiantsev also expressed the hope that in the event "any ship of the Russian-American Company should call at a Brazilian port prior to the issuance of new regulations governing foreign shipping," it would, in reciprocity, "be well received and permitted to take on a cargo of colonial goods."[53]

Rumiantsev did not make this remark unwittingly, for he almost certainly had in mind the three-hundred-ton sloop *Diana*, which, under the command of Lieutenant V. M. Golovnin, had departed Kronshtadt the previous month of July for Russian America.[54] The *Diana*, in turn, had been preceded by the Russian-American Company ship *Neva*, which, under the command of Lieutenant L. A. Hagemeister, called at the Brazilian port of Salvador early in 1807.[55] As Rumiantsev no doubt anticipated, the *Diana* put in to the island of Santa Caterina, where, in addition to taking on fresh provisions and a cargo of unrefined sugar, Lieutenant Golovnin gathered detailed intelligence on the island's potential for trade.[56]

Evidently unaware of the *Diana*'s proposed itinerary, Andrade limited himself to reporting without comment Count Rumiantsev's passing reference to ships of the Russian-American Company. Favorably impressed, moreover, by Rumiantsev's cordiality, the Portuguese chargé inquired of his home government if he might not profitably initiate formal conversations with the Russian minister of commerce and foreign affairs on the expansion of trade between the two countries. A reduction of duties on Brazilian coffee and raw cotton imported into Russia, he suggested, might be met with a reciprocal lowering of duties on Russian linens, oakum, and cordage imported into Brazil. Article nine of the Russo-Portuguese trade agreement, he added, provided for such alteration of the original treaty.[57]

In the spring of 1809, Andrade again spoke with Count Rumiantsev on the outstanding political and commercial matters of the moment. The Russian minister of commerce and foreign affairs had explicitly advised him, he reported to Count Linhares, that, while ships of neutral or Portuguese registry sailing from ports of the Portuguese overseas empire could continue to frequent Russian ports, vessels sailing directly from Portugal would no longer be permitted to do so.[58] Andrade vigorously protested the now official Russian stand on Portuguese shipping, roundly decrying its inequity and the prejudicial effects it would have on the interests of Portuguese merchants previously authorized to consign cargoes to Russia from Portugal proper. Rumiantsev, he informed Linhares, had nonetheless remained firm, explaining that in the existing circumstances the Russian government was obliged to adopt trade policies that in normal times would seem unjust.[59]

In December 1809, Count Rumiantsev broached the question of direct Russian ties with Latin America with the tsar. He drew Alexander's attention to a recent statement that had appeared in the press, according to which Russian subjects engaging in trade with Brazil would receive preferential treatment from Portuguese authorities. This was, he felt, a matter that merited further investigation. Apparently speaking to the tsar's heightened sense of idealism, Rumiantsev suggested that rather than simply seeking to profit from the misfortunes of Europe, the tsar should establish direct trade relations with Brazil and thus perform a lofty act of statesmanship worthy of his imperial person.[60]

The tsar, in turn, was himself cognizant of changing conditions in colonial Latin America, and, even before the outbreak of open and sustained hostilities against royal authority in the Spanish and Portuguese possessions, he expressed a personal interest in the pursuit of commercial advantage there. In the first days of 1810, Alexander advised his envoy to the United States, Count F. P. Pahlen, of his interest in future developments in the New World. Should fighting continue in Spain, wrote the tsar, he could foresee the formation of one or more independent states from the vast and rich territories which that nation possessed in America. "It is difficult to calculate just what changes such an event would produce in the political and commercial relations of Europe," he observed to Pahlen, "but it is easy to foresee that they will be of great importance."[61]

Alexander's desire to expand the empire's ties with Portuguese America was reflected at this same time in Count Rumiantsev's reply to a second petition tendered by Andrade for the admittance to Russian ports of Portuguese vessels sailing directly from Portugal.[62] Russia's adherence to the continental system, Rumiantsev informed the Portuguese chargé, made it impossible for the Russian court to consider Portugal a neutral nation. As long as that country was occupied by British forces, he declared, one could only suppose that it would serve as an entrepôt for British goods. Consequently, the imperial Russian government could permit neither the entry into Russian waters of ships sailing from mainland Portugal nor the entry into Portuguese ports of Russian vessels. The same, he hastened to add, would not hold for Brazil. As the place of residence of the prince-regent and the seat of his royal government, the tsar considered Brazil to be a case distinct from that of Portugal.[63] Reiterating what he had stated to Andrade previously, Rumiantsev again declared that Portuguese ships sailing from Brazil or any other of the Portuguese overseas dominions would be welcome in Russian ports and accorded all the rights and privileges stipulated in existing Russo-Portuguese treaties.[64] Having offered these assurances, Rumiantsev then requested a formal declaration from the Portuguese side guaranteeing reciprocal treatment for any Russian vessels that, sailing "from ports in the Empire or from its possessions in the northwest of America," might put in to Brazilian ports or elsewhere in the Portuguese colonies. The tsar sought these arrangements, asserted Rumiantsev, as a testimony of his consideration for the prince-regent.[65]

Both sides, however, were interested in more than pro forma expressions of mutual esteem and respect. The Portuguese chargé had understood that, for the time being, Russia could not alter its position with respect to Portugal. Protest though he might, it was impractical to pursue the matter further. Moreover, the Russian government had indicated a serious desire to maintain its long-standing ties with the Portuguese court and to promote trade relations with the overseas dominions. Andrade had kept his home government informed of these developments and had received an initially positive, if cautious, response from Count Linhares. Communications between Rio and St. Petersburg, however, were painfully slow, and distance now became a complicating factor.

By the spring of 1809, the Russian side had begun to make specific proposals for an expansion of trade between the two empires and to press the Portuguese chargé with growing insistence for a positive response on his part. Awaiting appropriate instructions from Rio de Janeiro, Andrade delayed until the end of 1809. Unable to wait any longer, he advised the Russian court on his own authority that a formal agreement governing such trade would have to provide for a reduction in tariffs on certain Brazilian goods imported into Russia. Count Rumiantsev responded favorably and asked Andrade to stipulate those goods. In the hope that his unauthorized action would meet with the approval of the prince-regent, he requested that duties be lowered on sugar, coffee, cacao, cotton, and rum (*aguardente de cana*).[66]

There followed a verbal exchange of views between the Russian chancery and the Portuguese chargé. In January 1810, Count Rumiantsev took the matter before the council of state, where he explained the need to alter the existing Russo-Portuguese accord and outlined the proposed revisions.[67] A gentlemen's agreement between himself and Andrade, he informed the council, would permit a continuation of such trade during the forthcoming season. However, he added, it was imperative that the government take a clear stand on the matter so as to allow a normalization of trade relations between the two empires.[68]

Tacitly recognizing the inevitable limitations of such trade in the circumstances of the moment, Rumiantsev drew the council's attention to the future. With the restoration of peace, he suggested, an expansion of commercial ties with Brazil would at once undermine British interests in the area and stimulate the growth of Russian trade and navigation. But, he argued, trade advantages of this import had to be secured immediately, and this could best be accomplished by "altering the treaty with the court of Rio de Janeiro in such a manner as to assure our products imported into Brazil those same advantages which we have enjoyed in Portugal."[69] The granting of similar advantages to Portuguese goods would give Russia access to a wide variety of valuable Brazilian products, including raw and refined sugar, coffee, cacao, vanilla, ginger, and dyewood. In addition, declared Rumiantsev, Russia would be able to obtain "diamonds and gold, as well as large quantities of silver, secretly exported by the Portuguese from Peru and Buenos Aires."[70]

Rumiantsev concluded his presentation to the council of state by stressing some relatively short-term benefits to be derived from the establishment of direct trade ties with Portuguese America. A mutual reduction of import duties, he declared, would prove exceedingly beneficial to Russian manufacturing interests, while at the same time access to this important new source of raw materials would stimulate the growth of the empire's light processing industries. Finally, he informed the council, the Portuguese chargé had intimated that limited quantities of gold and silver bars might be exported to Russia duty-free for the purpose of minting sorely needed specie.[71] The council was persuaded by Rumiantsev's arguments and approved his proposal.[72]

In early March 1810, Count Rumiantsev addressed a written note to Andrade detailing a provisional trade agreement approved by the tsar.[73] As compensation for those Portuguese goods to which circumstances had closed the Russian market, declared Rumiantsev, the tsar would allow a reduction of import duties on sugar, coffee, cacao, dyewood, rice, and medicinal drugs produced in Brazil or any other of the Portuguese overseas dominions. These goods would, however, have to be carried in vessels of Russian or Portuguese registry. Russian customs authorities, moreover, would require that their place of origin be duly established by the proper documentation. Indigo, tobacco, and wines from Madeira and the Azores would continue to be imported under existing treaty provisions.[74]

In return, Rumiantsev asked Andrade to commit himself, in the name of his court, to a formal declaration stating that all products of Russian origin enumerated in Articles seven and eight of the Russo-Portuguese trade agreement of 1798 would be admitted to Brazil and the other Portuguese colonies upon payment of half the established tariffs.[75] To these items, Rumiantsev proposed the addition of Russian cordage and fine linens. This, he asserted, was to compensate for the inclusion of medicinals in the list of Portuguese products admissible to the Russian Empire. Rum, he further observed, could not be included in any formal trade agreement given existing contractual relationships between the Russian government and local Russian distillers.[76]

Andrade replied to Rumiantsev's note within the week. The inclusion of cordage and fine linens in the list of proposed Russian exports to Brazil and the other overseas dominions, he advised the count, would not be acceptable to the Portuguese side. Unless these articles were dropped, he could not sign the proposed accord.[77]

The Russian response was almost immediate. Count Rumiantsev advised Andrade that the tsar had seen fit, for the present, to drop the matter of Russian cordage and fine linens. Moreover, he agreed in principle to the terms proposed thus far by his chancellor and the Portuguese chargé d'affaires. He desisted from further discussion about the exportation of cordage and linens, stated Rumiantsev, only to allow the necessary exchange of communications between the Portuguese chargé and his home government. Convinced that the prince-regent would concur in the legitimacy of his request, the tsar expected these two items to be formally included in the pending accord within a year of its final approval.[78]

Agreement appears to have been reached sometime within the next two months. On 19 May 1810, the *Sanktpeterburgskie kommercheskie vedomosti* carried on its front page an official edict from Tsar Alexander I advising the Russian merchant community of the new Russo-Portuguese trade agreement.[79] In view of the political events that had interrupted trade relations with Portugal and had led to the opening of Brazilian ports to ships of friendly powers, declared the tsar, and upon the advice of Count Rumiantsev, chancellor of the empire, and with the concurrence of the council of state, he had seen fit to incorporate a number of changes in the Russo-Portuguese treaty of 1798, namely: (1) to prohibit until further notice both imports from and exports to Portugal; (2) to annul tariff reductions established by the existing treaty on Portuguese wines, olive oil, and salt; (3) to allow tariff reductions stipulated by the existing treaty on Brazilian indigo and tobacco, and on wines from Madeira and the Azores when imported directly from the islands; (4) to reduce by one-half existing import duties on refined and unrefined sugar, coffee, cacao, dyewood, rice, and medicinals, when imported directly from Brazil and its colonies [sic][80] in Russian or Portuguese bottoms contracted by subjects of the Russian or Portuguese empires; (5) to make tariff reductions on Russian goods stipulated in Articles seven and eight and originally earmarked for export to Portugal, effective in the ports of Brazil and elsewhere throughout the Portuguese overseas empire; (6) to require documentary proof of itinerary from all vessels entering or departing Russian ports with shipments allegedly from or consigned to the Portuguese overseas empire; and (7) to limit provisions four and five of this agreement to a ten-month period ending on 15 March 1811. The edict appeared over the names of Alexander I and the chancellor of the empire, Count Rumiantsev.

The official sanctioning by the Russian government of direct trade ties with the Portuguese overseas dominions was in part a gesture made, as Rumiantsev had urged, with a view to securing future commercial advantage in the New World. As already noted, however, the practical implementation of such ties soon faltered in the face of rising economic difficulties and the resultant imposition of corrective measures embodied in the Neutral Trade Act of 1811. While the new trade restrictions did not totally preclude an expansion of Russian commerce with Latin America, they did pose serious problems. Recognizing this and seeking to preserve Russia's New World bridgeheads, however tenuous, Count Rumiantsev again took the matter of Russo-Portuguese trade before the council of state. On 3 March 1811, he advised the council that this trade could no longer be based on the informal understanding on which it had rested since the previous spring. The Portuguese chargé d'affaires in St. Petersburg, he added, had finally been empowered by the court at Rio de Janeiro to negotiate a new accord and had already agreed to tentative terms with the Russian chancellor. Rumiantsev submitted these terms in writing to the council for its consideration and approval.[81]

The embargo placed on refined sugar by the Neutral Trade Act, declared Rumiantsev, required that the Russian government allow alternative tariff concessions to the Portuguese. Brazilian cochineal, pepper, and cinnamon, he suggested, merited particular attention, for the first was an exceedingly valuable product, while the latter were of little commercial significance. Cochineal, he implied, would serve the needs of local industry; pepper and cinnamon, on the other hand, constituted relatively empty concessions by means of which the Russian side might attain substantial advantage in its negotiations with the Portuguese court.[82]

The statement of proposed terms that Rumiantsev submitted to the council of state envisioned a 50 percent tariff reduction on unrefined sugar, coffee, cacao, dyewood, rice, cochineal, pepper, cinnamon, and medicinals imported into Russia from Brazil. Wines from Madeira and the Azores, together with indigo and Brazilian tobacco, would continue to be imported under the terms of Articles six and eight of the Russo-Portuguese treaty of 1798. The Portuguese government, in turn, would allow tariff reductions on Russian products enumerated in Articles seven and eight of that treaty, plus a 50 percent reduction in duties on Russian cordage and linens imported into Brazil. Finally, the statement provided for a dispensation on Portuguese wines, salt, and vegetable oils at that time barred from entry into Russia.[83]

"Judging by the need that exists for our products in Brazil and all of the Portuguese colonies," declared Rumiantsev, "as well as by [Portuguese] trade ties with the Spanish possessions, where there is equal need of these products, one must conclude that this situation could be exceedingly advantageous for our trade."[84] Dwelling on a theme he had persistently advanced before, Count Rumiantsev again implied that Russia could realistically and profitably seek to replace Great Britain as the supplier of basic manufactured goods to Spanish and Portuguese America. Indeed, his proposed tariff reductions on Portuguese colonial imports reflected a greater concern with the promotion of Russo–Latin American trade than with an alleviation of the empire's pressing financial difficulties through strict compliance with the Neutral Trade Act of 1811.

Subsequent negotiations on the proposed trade agreement proved more difficult than Rumiantsev had anticipated in his February presentation to the council of state. Whereas the Russian chancellor had apparently reached some understanding with Andrade, the Portuguese chargé was soon replaced in these negotiations by a newly appointed minister plenipotentiary, João Paulo Bezerra.[85] Talks dragged on until mid-autumn 1811. Finally, after what Bezerra described as "long and extremely disagreeable discussions," the two sides reached a provisional accord that would regulate Russo-Portuguese trade until such time as a new and more equitable treaty could be drafted. Despite fundamental objections to the convention, Bezerra was at last moved to accept the document by the lateness of the season. It was necessary, he informed Linhares, to conclude a formal agreement before spring so as to avoid a total rupture of trade during the coming year.[86]

The convention consisted of fifteen articles detailing the terms of the accord, plus a secret article allowing for the reestablishment of trade between Russia and mainland Portugal "once Russia had made peace with England, or, in any event, whenever circumstances might permit."[87] It differed somewhat from the provisional statement of terms submitted to the council of state some eight months earlier. Rather than the 50 percent reductions envisioned by the previous document, import duties were now to be lowered by 37.5 percent. The new rates were to apply to raw sugar, coffee, cacao, dyestuffs, raw cotton, rice, spices, ivory, tobacco, precious metals and stones, salt, drugs, and medicinals imported into Russia from the Portuguese overseas empire;[88] and to hemp, hempseed, hempseed oil, linseed oil, iron of all sorts including staves, anchors and military ordnance, sailcloth, yard goods, fine linens, cordage, and all Russian manufactured articles exported from Russia to the Portuguese overseas empire on vessels of Russian or Portuguese registry.[89] Should the Russian embargo on refined sugar be lifted prior to the conclusion of a new commercial treaty, this commodity, too, would be subject to the 37.5 percent tariff reduction when obtained in the Portuguese overseas territories.[90]

Article fifteen of the convention provided that ratifications would be exchanged in St. Petersburg as soon as possible, and in no event later than nine months from the date of the accord's initial signing. The agreement was to become effective immediately upon signature by its chief negotiators, however, so as to permit Russian and Portuguese merchants to plan the coming year's sailings. On 8 November 1811, Bezerra sent a final version of the convention to Count Rumiantsev for official endorsement. The following day, he dispatched a report on his action to the court at Rio de Janeiro, together with a copy of the proposed accord for royal approval.[91]

Preoccupied with the progressive deterioration of Franco-Russian relations and with the anticipated outbreak of hostilities between France and Russia, the court of St. Petersburg delayed final approval of the convention. On December 11, Bezerra advised Count Linhares that he had not yet received word from the Russian chancellor on the status of the pending accord. This, he felt, resulted largely from pressures exerted by influential Francophiles closely tied to the Russian ministry of commerce. Despite these difficulties, however, Bezerra believed that the convention would be signed.[92]

In early February 1812, Bezerra informed Linhares that the Russian side still had not seen fit to sign the proposed convention. The matter had been complicated, he felt, by a reorganization of the ministry of commerce within the ministry of finance. Responsibility for the administration of Russian foreign trade had thus passed from Count Rumiantsev to D. A. Gur'ev, who, Bezerra believed, sympathized with the partisans of Napoleon and, consequently, was ill-disposed toward the pending Russo-Portuguese trade convention.[93]

Two months later, Gur'ev showed the Portuguese envoy to be correct. In a note to Count Rumiantsev, he expressed his profound displeasure with Article two of the proposed convention. This article, he argued, granted concessions to the Portuguese well beyond those contained in any previous accord between two powers. At the same time, it failed to provide adequate compensation for the Russian side. Moreover, he concluded, in the event of a rapprochement between Russia and England, the British would surely demand the same concessions for themselves, to the considerable detriment of the Russian government.[94] While the British might be useful allies in the struggle against Napoleon, Gur'ev suggested, Russia could ill afford a return to the economic dependency of the past. The granting to Great Britain of trade concessions like those extended to Portugal in the proposed Russo-Portuguese trade convention would constitute a major step in that direction.

Meanwhile, the Neutral Trade Act of 1811 had been extended for a second year.[95] The Portuguese envoy advised his home government that the revised tariff schedule differed only slightly from that of the previous year. Changes included additional import duties of three rubles per *pud* on unrefined sugar and one ruble per *arratel* (1 *arratel* = 1.012 pounds) on tea. The revised regulations also provided for the importation into Russia of hides from America, fixing the duty at sixty kopeks per hide.[96]

Despite Bezerra's repeated insistence that the convention be formally concluded, the Russian government continued to delay through the winter of 1812. Then, on 10 March of that year, Count Rumiantsev advised the Portuguese envoy that the impending outbreak of hostilities between Russia and France had moved the tsar to seek both a renovation of the old Russo-Portuguese trade treaty and the prompt conclusion of new and expanded commercial accords. The provisional convention then under consideration, Rumiantsev suggested, could now be set aside. Bezerra assented, but on the condition that formalities be concluded in the briefest time possible. The lateness of the season, he reminded the Russian side, required prompt action.[97]

After a further delay of some six weeks, Count Rumiantsev advised Bezerra that the tsar had authorized Gur'ev and A. N. Saltykov to negotiate an extension of the Russo-Portuguese treaty of 1798, as well as a new accord that would "set and consolidate in a permanent manner all commercial relations between the two powers." The new treaty, Rumiantsev added, would take into account "the changes effected in the commercial system of the Portuguese colonies."[98]

In an apparent effort to offset some of the losses occasioned by the failure to reach an accord prior to the opening of the year's sailing season, the Portuguese envoy had petitioned the Russian government for special concessions on the cargoes of two ships already en route to St. Petersburg. Both vessels had sailed under contract to Dionizio Lopes, who the year before had been named Portuguese consul-general in the Russian capital.[99] Insofar as this venture helped to establish direct trade ties with Brazil, wrote Rumiantsev, and wishing "to give the inhabitants of this interesting country proof of his personal interest," the tsar had seen fit to grant Bezerra's request. The two shipments consigned to the Portuguese consul general would be exempt from current import duties, having only to satisfy the tariff schedule in force prior to 1811. This concession, stipulated the Russian chancellor, would not be repeated again.[100]

The long and tedious trade negotiations between the Russian and Portuguese courts finally came to fruition in the spring of 1812, only three weeks before Napoleon's grand army marched against Russia. Unable to forestall any longer an open break with France, the Russian government agreed to permit trade with the entire Portuguese empire, including Portugal proper. On 10 June 1812, both sides signed a formal declaration extending the Russo-Portuguese treaty of 1798 for a three-year period ending 17 June 1815. The two sides further agreed to begin talks immediately on a new treaty which, as Rumiantsev had indicated previously, would "establish and consolidate on a permanent basis direct commercial ties between their respective subjects, possessions and states." The new accord would likewise reflect the interests of both powers, as well as "the changes occasioned in the commerce of the Portuguese colonies."[101]

Approaches to Spanish America

The politically more delicate question of establishing direct trade ties with the insurgent territories of Spanish America also received

Пис. Т Dav. 1828   Peint par G. Dawe, 1828
Графъ Николай Петровичъ   Le Comte Nicolas Petrowitch
Румянцевъ. 1754–1826   Roumiantzeff. 1754–1826

1. Count Nikolai Petrovich Rumiantsev, Russian Minister of Commerce (1802–1814) and Foreign Affairs (1808–1814), Chancellor of the Empire (1808–1814), architect of Russia's opening to the Americas

consideration by the Russian government. The leading proponent of such trade was again Count Rumiantsev. Moved by visions of maritime and imperial grandeur, the enterprising chancellor sought repeatedly to convince the tsar and his council of state that there were indeed very great advantages to be gained through a progressive expansion of Russian trade in that part of the world. His arguments were not without appeal in St. Petersburg, for the tsar himself had referred to possible Russian interests in Spain's New World possessions as early as December 1809.[102] The outbreak of widespread insurrection against Spanish colonial rule placed the actual pursuit of these interests in a changed light, moving Count Rumiantsev in the fall of 1811 to seek official authorization for the expanded trade.

The initial impetus to elaborate a policy on trade with Spanish America appears to have come from the insurgents of Venezuela, who, in the summer of 1811, approached the Russian government on the matter of direct commercial ties. In August of that year, the U. S. consul-general in St. Petersburg, Levett Harris, advised Count Rumiantsev that Cortland L. Parker, a fellow American and longtime resident of Caracas, had arrived in the Russian capital empowered by the new authorities in Caracas to represent the interests of Venezuela at the tsarist court. The provisional governments of northern South America, Harris reported, had opened their ports to all friendly shipping and, further, wished to establish direct trade relations with Russia.[103]

Rumiantsev received the special envoy from Caracas on two separate occasions.[104] At the initial meeting, Parker gave the Russian chancellor a detailed memorandum on the trade and produce of the insurgent colonies, including a price list for the period 1800–1810 on goods produced in Caracas.[105] He advised Rumiantsev that the provinces of Venezuela and Santa Fe (viceroyalty of New Granada) had broken completely away from Spain, that they had formed a government whose primary concern was to promote trade with all friendly nations, and that they were anxious to establish commercial ties with Russia. He had been authorized to negotiate an accord on behalf of the new government, Parker added, provided that ships sailing under its flag would be admitted to Russian ports on the same basis as neutral vessels of European registry.[106]

Rumiantsev reminded Parker that, despite the tsar's readiness to secure commercial advantages for his subjects, Russia's political commitments precluded the establishment of ties with Spanish America. Parker responded by suggesting that whatever the outcome of the war in Spain, the Spanish territories in America would not again submit to colonial rule. The newly constituted governments, he observed, continued to evoke the name of Ferdinand VII only to broaden public support. All official acts and dispositions, however, were issued in the name of the governments themselves.[107]

Rumiantsev replied that he did not wish to dispute the situation as described to him by the envoy from Caracas, but that the primary consideration for the court of St. Petersburg was its adherence to the continental system. The neutrality of a cargo, he declared, had to be established at its point of origin either by an authorized agent of the Russian government or by the government of the individuals to whom the cargo belonged. This, Rumiantsev felt, was not feasible in the case of Spain's rebel colonies. Parker countered that the necessary documentation for shipments originating in Spanish America could be issued by the Russian consuls accredited in various cities of the United States.[108]

Despite the objections that Count Rumiantsev raised to Parker's proposed establishment of trade relations between Russia and northern South America, it seems clear that he in fact favored the proposal. Immediately following his talks with Parker, Rumiantsev instructed N. Ya. Kozlov, newly appointed consul-general of Russia in the United States, to investigate the feasibility of establishing such ties. Kozlov was ordered to seek out Spanish American merchants who frequented Philadelphia and to advise them of the considerable advantages to be had in commercial dealings with the Russian Empire. He was, however, to speak only in generalities and to avoid all formal entanglements.[109] Rumiantsev further requested that Kozlov provide him with detailed commercial intelligence on "the provinces of Venezuela" and "the viceroyalty of Santa Fe," and that he keep closely abreast of all subsequent events in that region. Kozlov was also asked to report on the general state of affairs in New Spain and on the island of Santo Domingo.[110]

Count Rumiantsev next prepared a written statement on Russo–Spanish American trade ties, which, in September 1811, he presented to the council of state.[111] After first reviewing his talks with Parker, the chancellor vigorously argued for approval of the proposed ties. "There can be no doubt," he told the council, "about the extent to which our commerce would benefit from this new extension of direct relations to a region overflowing with all manner of products and even the most precious of metals, yet wanting for our surpluses." The only pertinent question one might conceivably pose, he declared, was whether or not the establishment of these ties would run counter to the empire's political obligations. This, however, had already been answered by Napoleon, who, Rumiantsev suggested, was the only person able to offer any objection. On 13 December 1809, the French emperor had stated that should Spain's colonies in America obtain their independence, France would not interfere so long as the new states did not enter into relations with England. Consequently, affirmed Rumiantsev, "I consider that not only can there be no difficulty in our opening trade relations with these colonies, but further that such trade should be allowed, with the sole condition that such authorization be based on the general principles of the continental system established for neutral powers."[112]

After prior consultation with the tsar, Count Rumiantsev had also drafted a proposed edict that would open Russian ports to ships of South American registry.[113] This document contained three provisions: (1) South American vessels would be admitted to Russian ports in accordance with the published regulations governing neutral shipping; (2) said vessels would be permitted to take on cargoes of Russian goods authorized for export; and (3) in addition to the normal documentation required by existing regulations, these ships would have to secure certificates of origin from the consuls-general of Russia resident in Brazil and the United States.[114] Rumiantsev submitted the draft edict to the council for its consideration and, he hoped, ultimate approval.

The council, however, failed to endorse the chancellor's proposal. On 21 October 1811, it met in general session to consider the matter of direct trade relations with Spanish America, and a majority of those present expressed opposition. While much of what transpired at that meeting remains obscure,[115] only four council members voted in favor of the proposal. Twenty-one others concluded that, "until such time as the government of the three provinces seeking to institute trade relations with us has been firmly established and formally recognized by us, it is neither proper nor convenient to honor the petition of the American, Parker."[116] Three weeks later, the council rendered its opinion in writing to the tsar, who in turn accepted the majority view.[117] For the time being, the matter was officially closed.

In January 1812, the provisional government of Caracas sought through its agent in London, Luis López Méndez, to reopen the question of direct ties with Russia by soliciting formal tsarist recognition of Venezuelan independence.[118] López Méndez enlisted the assistance of Levett Harris, who, as in the preceding year, again acted as intermediary between the South American insurgents and the court of St. Petersburg. Harris promptly presented the Venezuelan petition to Count Rumiantsev, together with his own personal endorsement of the separatist cause.[119] Tsar Alexander, in turn, restated his support in principle of colonial emancipation but declined to reverse the position taken by the council of state the previous fall. Given the general political situation in Europe, he advised Harris, Russia could not then extend recognition to the insurgent governments of Spanish America.[120]

Despite these official disavowals of direct and formal relations with the rebel territories of the New World, Russian interest in those territories did not subside.[121] Thus in the spring of 1812, N. Ya. Kozlov instructed Russian consular agents in Boston, Charleston, New Orleans, and Savannah to issue the necessary documentation to American shipmasters wishing to carry cargoes of colonial goods from Caracas, Veracruz, or any other neutral port to Russia. "Having carefully examined the matter," he advised the consuls, "I find absolutely nothing that could block their entry into Russia, regardless of their registry."[122]

In February 1813, Kozlov enlisted the services of a merchant by the name of Antonio Lynch to represent Russian commercial interests on the island of Cuba.[123] "Our goods are already known in the Spanish colonies," he observed to Count Rumiantsev. "They are furnished by the Americans, who even now continue to supply them through Havana in neutral ships." Our trade with Cuba, he added, "will consist of those same articles which we now sell to the Americans. Local prices for metal goods of all sorts, cables, rope, sailcloth, tallow, glassware and mirrors, are most advantageous; the greatest profits will be brought by our cloth and fine linens. In return, we shall receive sugar, coffee, indigo, cochineal, dyewoods, quinine, sarsaparilla, and all the other products of South America."[124] Lynch, Kozlov concluded, was the ideal person to promote this trade. A resident of Havana, he was intimately familiar with trade in the Caribbean and enjoyed the confidence of the Spanish authorities. Moreover, he spoke English, French, and Spanish.[125]

Kozlov's attempt to establish Russian commercial representation in Cuba, however, was of only limited success. In the fall of 1814, Lynch informed the Russian consul-general that, for personal reasons, he could no longer continue in his capacity as tsarist commercial agent in Havana. Kozlov, in turn, advised Rumiantsev that he would endeavor to find a responsible replacement.[126]

These actions by the Russian consul-general in Philadelphia reflected the spirit of Rumiantsev's instructions of 24 August 1811.[127] The naming of a commercial agent in Cuba, however, went beyond the specific provisions of those instructions and thus suggests additional directives from St. Petersburg authorizing such action. This is significant in light of the council of state's earlier rejection of the

Parker proposal for direct Russo-Venezuelan trade relations and the tsar's professed support of that decision. In actual fact, it would seem, Alexander endorsed Rumiantsev's New World priorities and here sought to circumvent the opposing council position by imperial fiat.

Events, however, soon overtook the gradual expansion of Russian ties with the New World. In the first days of summer 1812, Napoleon led his grand army of 600,000 men across the Niemen and into Russia. For the next three years, Tsar Alexander remained preoccupied almost solely with events in the Old World, and very few of those in his service could give even passing attention to the Americas. Europe was at war.

4. The Russian Presence in America

The imperial Russian government responded to the changing status of colonial Latin America in the pragmatic manner of a power with established New World interests. True, these interests were of recent articulation when contrasted with those of Spain, Portugal, and the other leading maritime powers of Western Europe. By 1808, however, they had come to occupy a significant place in the geopolitical thinking of the Russian court, influencing directly tsarist responses to the colonial upheavals of the New World.

As stressed in the preceding chapters, this growing attention to the affairs of Spanish and Portuguese America arose from the immediate economic dislocations of the Napoleonic period. It derived, too, from the centuries-long process of eastward expansion across Siberia and ultimately the Pacific. These convergent experiences, in turn, gave origin and force to an instrument of imperial expansion well proven in the West but as yet without firm roots in tsarist Russia—the chartered trading monopoly. Founded in the summer of 1799 as the Russian-American Company, this formally private enterprise at once stimulated and itself became an important vehicle of Russian state interests in the New World. As such, it is central to an understanding of Russia's presence in the Western Hemisphere during the early nineteenth century.

The Russian-American Company

"It has often struck me as a very extraordinary circumstance," wrote Georg Heinrich von Langsdorff in 1814, "that in a monarchical state a free trading company should exist independent as it were of the government, not confined within any definite regulations, but who can exercise their authority free and uncontrolled, nay even unpunished, over so vast an extent of country."[1] Appearances, however, were misleading, and Langsdorff failed to perceive the functional relationship that bound this supposedly private concern inextricably to the Russian state. Indeed, therein lay the utility of the chartered trading monopoly, for, while company interests coincided with those of the state, its contrived independence permitted tsarist officials to claim or disclaim at will responsibility for its acts.[2]

Effective government control over the Russian-American Company was implicit in the concern's founding charter, Article twelve of which obliged the company's governing board to inform the tsar of all administrative directives and related operations. To assure strict compliance, Tsar Paul I (1796–1801) created a special office under the direction of a personally appointed "correspondent," whose function it was to oversee company management. To this post the tsar named Nikolai Petrovich Rezanov (1764–1807), the principal architect of the Russian-American Company and himself a respected member of the St. Petersburg service nobility.[3] Thereafter, state controls on the company progressively increased. In 1800, Rezanov engineered the transferral of the company's main office from Irkutsk, central trade mart of Siberia, to St. Petersburg, seat of the imperial government. The accession of Alexander I to the throne a year later signalled a further assault on the company's operational independence.

Despite the fact that the controlling financial interest in the company lay with a small group of powerful merchants,[4] political control rested with the imperial government. As company resources grew and its activities broadened, the court moved ever more directly to regulate company affairs. In 1804, it replaced the office of correspondent with a provisional committee empowered to formulate company policy in matters affecting Russian foreign relations.[5] The provisional committee acted independently of the company's governing board and was not answerable to the stockholders. While two of the committee's three members were to be chosen by the company, the third was appointed by the tsar. In practice, moreover, all committee members usually came from the ranks of the service nobility and, consequently, represented crown rather than merchant interests.[6] The first committeemen selected, for example, were Admiral N. S. Mordvinov, minister of the imperial navy; I. A. Veidemeir, a senior official in the Russian ministry of foreign affairs; and Count P. A. Stroganov, vice-minister of the interior and personal adviser to the tsar.[7]

Although the terms establishing the provisional committee called for the rotation of one member each year, these individuals normally served for substantially longer periods of time, the committee's political complexion thus remaining constant.[8] Creation of this body, concludes S. B. Okun, "was the first step toward the transformation of a commercial organization into a direct agency of the crown."[9] This transformation advanced another important step in the fall of 1813, when the imperial government declared the provisional committee permanent. The process of restricting private control culminated five years later with the replacement of civilian by military authority in the company's New World settlements.[10]

Through the Russian-American Company, the tsarist government sought to transform the entire northern Pacific basin into an internal Russian sea. The northwest coast of America was to be occupied as far south as California, while existing Russian colonies in Alaska, the Aleutians, and Kamchatka were to be reinforced with strategically located settlements in Hawaii, on Sakhalin Island, and at the estuary of the Amur River. The immediate object of this grandiose scheme was to open the Chinese market to Russian trade, thereby laying·a viable basis for the economic development of the Russian Far East.[11]

While the northern Pacific basin clearly dominated the attention of those guiding Russia's eastward expansion, as subsequently it has dominated the attention of historians, tsarist geopolitical perspectives embraced more southerly latitudes as well. As already noted, Peter the Great appears to have envisioned direct trade ties with the Pacific coast ports of Spanish America. Later in the eighteenth century Grigorii Ivanovich Shelikhov (1747–1795), pioneer promoter of Russian settlement and founder of the North-Eastern American Company, a predecessor of the Russian-American Company, requested authorization of Catherine the Great to trade with the Spaniards in America.[12] Similarly, at the beginning of the nineteenth century, Count Rumiantsev proposed Russian trade ties with both the East and West Indies. "Given the opportunity to export lumber, fish and other natural products abroad," he advised the tsar in the winter of 1803, "the settlements of Russian America would attract a variety of people skilled in the sciences and the arts and would begin to develop factories and mills for the elaboration of metals, hides and other goods; in this way there would gradually evolve a society of artisans and craftsmen, and out of the settlements would emerge cities, forming a solid basis for trade with both the Indies."[13]

Rezanov, too, called for trade with the Spanish overseas dominions. While on an inspection tour of the Russian colonies in 1805–1806, he wrote the tsar that severe food shortages in the region could best be alleviated through trade with Chile and the Philippine Islands. Favorable exchange rates for the Spanish peso, he observed, would facilitate purchases of bread, rum, and sugar sorely needed in Kamchatka and Russian America.[14] It was necessary, he reiterated, to solicit authorization from the Spanish crown for the procurement of bread and other products in California, Chile, and the Philippines.[15] "The time has come," stated a company report in 1818, "to establish permanent intercourse with Canton, Chile, the Philippine Islands, Japan and other distant lands rich in natural resources."[16]

The active pursuit of these ambitious objectives required a fleet of deep-water vessels and experienced crews to sail them, a component of the Russian-American Company's assets conspicuous by its absence. Accordingly, a concerted effort was made to create a company fleet, with substantial sums earmarked early for the construction of ships.[17] Even more problematical than the acquisition of seaworthy vessels was the enlistment of experienced crews. In 1802, therefore, Alexander I authorized an unlimited number of officers and seamen of the imperial navy to serve on ships of the Russian-American Company, a measure that had the additional effect of restricting still further private control over company affairs.[18]

Thus began Russia's growth as a world maritime power, for it was precisely this unique combination of factors that first carried Russian ships around the globe in the early years of the nineteenth century. The decisive impetus for such voyages came from Captain I. F. Kruzenshtern, an experienced mariner who, in the course of advanced training with the British navy during the 1790s, had traveled to both the West and East Indies, including an extended stay on the Chinese mainland.[19] By his own account, Kruzenshtern had long lamented Russia's lack of active foreign trade and had concluded that even European Russia could derive great benefit from direct ties with China and the East Indies.[20] Anticipating views insistently reiterated by Count Rumiantsev,[21] he felt that Russian trade suffered excessive losses at the hands of foreign middlemen. The creation of a Pacific fleet, he argued, would eliminate the need to pay exorbitant prices for Chinese and East Indian goods to Danish, English, and Swedish carriers. Moreover, lower overhead would allow Russia to become itself the principal supplier of Far Eastern luxury goods to the lucrative north German market. The Russian-American Company, Kruzenshtern believed, "could not fail of becoming in time of so much importance that the smaller East Indian Companies of Europe would not be able to stand in competition with it."[22]

During his return voyage from China, Kruzenshtern prepared a memorandum in which he proposed "that two ships should be sent from Cronstadt to the Aleutic islands and to America, with every kind of material necessary for the construction and outfit of vessels." The Russian-American Company, he argued, must be given the means to build seaworthy vessels in the colonies.[23] Admiral Mordvinov and

И. Ф. КРУЗЕНШТЕРН
(род. 6 ноября 1770 г., ум. 12 августа 1846 г.)

2. Ivan Fëdorovich Kruzenshtern, commander of Russia's first round-the-world voyage (1803–1806), captain of the *Nadezhda*, first Russian vessel to visit South America

Count Rumiantsev agreed, as did the tsar, who at once appointed Kruzenshtern to command the proposed expedition. Two ships were purchased in London—the *Nadezhda*, a 450-ton vessel paid for by the imperial government, and the 370-ton *Neva*, bought jointly by Count Rumiantsev and the Russian-American Company.[24] As his second-in-command, Kruzenshtern selected Yu. L. Lisianskii (1773–1839), a service comrade of many years' experience.

Organization of the Kruzenshtern expedition reflected clearly tsarist geopolitical objectives in the Pacific basin as they had evolved since the reign of Peter the Great. The expedition was, moreover, to set the pattern of Russian involvement in that vast area for the next two decades, serving as a model for subsequent voyages to the New World. The *Nadezhda*, it was also decided, would carry a high-level embassy to Japan to seek trade ties with that bastion of the western Pacific. The tsar appointed Rezanov as his personal envoy to the Japanese emperor, bestowing upon him for the occasion the title of Grand Chamberlain, the highest rank at the Russian court outside the imperial family itself.[25]

Upon completion of this mission, Rezanov would make an extended tour of Russian America, as a result of which tsarist attention was further to be focused on neighboring Latin America. Rezanov was accompanied on these travels by Georg Heinrich von Langsdorff, who would subsequently serve as Russian consul-general in Rio de Janeiro and himself lead a Russian scientific expedition to Brazil. Also sailing aboard the *Nadezhda* were Lieutenant F. F. Bellingshausen and Otto Efstaf'evich Kotzebue, a cadet from the St. Petersburg officers school. Uniquely trained under Kruzenshtern's personal tutelage, these two men later commanded ships of their own on voyages to the New World.[26] Thus, in a real sense, the Kruzenshtern expedition extended Russian influence for the first time directly to Spanish and Portuguese America.

The *Nadezhda* and *Neva* departed Kronshtadt on 7 August 1803, sailing first to Copenhagen, then on to Falmouth, England, and the Canary Islands, reaching Santa Cruz de Tenerife in mid-October. After a week's layover, Kruzenshtern and Lisianskii again put to sea, charting a course for the Brazilian island of Santa Catarina.[27] Brazil, recorded Langsdorff, "abounding in gold and diamonds, with its splendid towns and rich plantations, had long been the leading object of interest among us; it had been the subject of our daily conversation, of our anxious curiosity. . . . Many of our ship's company," he noted, "wished earnestly to visit the town of Rio Janeiro. Captain Kruzenshtern, however, . . . determined rather to bend his course to Santa Catarina, an island three degrees farther to the south, which had many superior recommendations as a place of refreshment. . . ."[28] On 21 December 1803, the *Nadezhda* and *Neva* dropped anchor off the shore of Santa Catarina, the first Russian ships in history to enter Brazilian waters.[29]

Damage to the *Neva*'s main and foremasts forced Kruzenshtern to prolong his stay at Santa Catarina by several weeks. While he and Lisianskii attended to the needed repairs, Rezanov and his entourage took up quarters at the governor's residence in Nossa Senhora do Desterro [present-day Florianópolis], the island's principal town. Langsdorff, for his part, set out to examine with the naturalist's eye every aspect of this, one of the earth's "finest and richest spots."[30] Intoxicated by the island's natural luxuriance, he was, in contrast, distressed by the spectacle of Brazilian slavery. "It gave me a wholly new and very revolting sensation," he wrote, "when I went for the first time to Nossa Senhora do Desterro, and saw a number of these wretched helpless beings lying almost naked about the streets for sale."[31] At the same time, Langsdorff was impressed by the island's economic potential. "Should this fine country become hereafter more populous, and be less neglected by the government," he suggested, "it might, from its superabundant natural riches, be made one of the most important marts of commerce in Brazil."[32]

Kruzenshtern and Lisianskii generally concurred with Langsdorff's appraisal of Santa Catarina.[33] "Though this part of the Brazils produces cotton, coffee, rice, timber, and many other valuable objects of commerce," Lisianskii observed, "it is, generally speaking, extremely poor, from the prohibition of foreign trade. If, instead of being obliged to carry their merchandise to Rio de Janeiro, a free commerce with Europe were permitted," he speculated, "the inhabitants would soon improve and enrich themselves; since with all the disadvantages of the above restrictions, many of them live in comfort. What then might not be expected from proper encouragement?"[34]

"Of the whole of Brazil," Kruzenshtern added, "the island of St. Catherine, with that part of the main land adjoining it, has perhaps the least attracted the attention of the Portuguese government, much as it deserves it, on account of its situation, its healthy climate, fruitful soil, and valuable productions. . . ."[35] Any nation that should undertake to get possession of this colony," Kruzenshtern noted, "might do it as easily as the Spaniards did in 1777,[36] without so large an armament." But, he quickly added, "the impossibility of establishing a durable colony here, without having at the same time possession of some part of the adjoining coast, will deter any one from attempting so useless a conquest."[37]

The *Nadezhda* and *Neva* departed Brazil in the first days of February 1804, setting a course for Cape Horn and the Pacific. After a brief stop at Nuku Hiva, in the Marquesas, the two ships continued on to Hawaii, whence each struck out on a separate course—the *Nadezhda* to Kamchatka, the *Neva* to Kodiak.[38] Over a year and a half was to pass before they would again come together.

On 14 July 1804, nearly one year after leaving Kronshtadt, the *Nadezhda* dropped anchor in Petropavlovsk harbor, on the southeastern shore of Kamchatka. Eight weeks later, the tsar's special embassy embarked for Japan, arriving at Nagasaki in the early days of October. There, Rezanov sought unsuccessfully to surmount Japanese resistance to foreign intercourse, finally withdrawing in the spring of 1805.[39] On his return to Petropavlovsk, Rezanov quit the expedition, having resolved to visit the Russian colonies in America. Accompanied by Langsdorff, who now served as his personal physician, he set out in late July 1805 aboard the 150-ton brig *Mariia Magdalina*, of the Russian-American Company. After a short layover at Kodiak, they continued on to Sitka, where they were received by A. A. Baranov, chief administrator of the colonies and governor-general of Russian America.[40]

Rezanov quickly came to appreciate the precarious state of affairs that prevailed in the colonies. Indeed, so severe was the paucity of stores and basic necessities in Sitka that he resolved in the winter of 1806 to dispatch a ship to California for fresh provisions. "The Sandwich [Hawaiian] Islands might have been preferred for the purpose in an economical point of view," observed Langsdorff, "but political reasons led to the choice of St. Francisco."[41] Rezanov seems to have hoped that an appeal to humanity would open the door of commerce with the Spanish colonies otherwise closed to foreigners.[42]

Behind the immediate concern with securing a ready source of foodstuffs lay a desire to extend effective control over that source. Even prior to Rezanov's arrival in the colonies, Baranov had taken steps to expand the boundaries of Russian America. As early as 1802, he had been instructed by the directors of the Russian-American Company to extend Russian claims beyond the fifty-fifth parallel, southernmost boundary of the company's New World possessions as established in the imperial charter of 1799.[43] Now, only days before sailing to San Francisco, Rezanov wrote the company's governing board in St. Petersburg of the need to place Russian settlements on the Columbia River and to establish control over the straits of Juan de Fuca. From there, he proposed, "we can gradually move farther south to the port of San Francisco. . . . The Spaniards," Rezanov added, "are exceedingly weak in this area, and had our company been sufficiently strong to act in 1798, when war was declared on the Spanish court, we could easily have occupied California from the thirty-fourth parallel to the Santa Barbara mission and held this strip permanently. . . ."[44]

The expedition departed Sitka on 8 March 1806 aboard the *Juno*, a 250-ton brig built in Rhode Island and purchased the previous fall from New England shipmaster John DeWolfe. One month later, its crew racked by scurvy, the *Juno* slipped under the guns of the San Francisco presidio and dropped anchor off this, Spain's northernmost outpost of its New World empire. Already under royal orders to render every assistance to the vessels and crews of the Kruzenshtern expedition should they touch at that distant port, local Spanish authorities now tendered those same civilities to Rezanov and the men of the *Juno* despite the unusual circumstances of their visit.[45]

After first attending to the needs of his crew, Rezanov turned to the delicate matter of trade. Carefully selected gifts distributed among the Franciscan missionaries aroused calculated interest in the *Juno*'s cargo and it was soon proposed that the Russian goods be exchanged for a cargo of foodstuffs.[46] Such a transaction, however, required the approval of José Joaquín de Arrillaga, governor of Alta California. For this purpose, Rezanov requested an audience with the governor at his residence in Monterey, to which Arrillaga replied that, wishing to spare Rezanov the discomfort of the overland trip, he would himself come to San Francisco to meet with the Russian envoy. In this reply, Rezanov later wrote, "I detected the suspiciousness of the Spanish government which everywhere blocks foreigners from familiarizing themselves with the interior regions and observing the weakness of [the Spaniards'] forces."[47]

Arrillaga soon arrived at the presidio, where he received Rezanov in the same affable manner as had his subordinates. Apprised of the Russian's wish to exchange the *Juno*'s cargo for another of foodstuffs, the governor informed his visitor that existing colonial legislation precluded such a transaction. The most he could allow was the purchase of the desired provisions for cash, hardly a satisfactory solution for the fully laden *Juno*. As for regular commercial intercourse between the Russian colonies and Alta California, Arrillaga observed, not even the viceroy of Mexico could issue the necessary authorization. The governor finally agreed, however, to submit Rezanov's proposal directly to the crown, in Madrid.[48]

His immediate plans thus threatened with failure, Rezanov adroitly sought advantage in a budding personal relationship between himself and the daughter of José Darío Argüello, commandant of the San Francisco presidio. Apparently disenchanted with the isolation of California, the young woman reciprocated the envoy's cautious advances until he was emboldened to ask her hand in marriage. Legend and romance aside, expediency played a decisive role in this affair.[49] Rezanov, noted Langsdorff, "conceived that a nuptial union with the daughter of the Commandant at St. Francisco would be a vast step gained towards promoting the political objects he had so much at heart."[50] Indeed, once family and church consented to the marriage, Rezanov's position in San Francisco was so enhanced that, in his own words, he "managed this port of His Catholic Majesty as [his] interests required."[51]

Argüello, the chamberlain's father-in-law to be, now prevailed upon his old friend the governor to allow the proposed exchange of goods, to which Arrillaga reluctantly acceded. The problematical transaction at last completed, Rezanov took leave of his betrothed and, on 22 May 1806, sailed for Sitka. Upon his return to St. Petersburg, he had assured Arrillaga, he would travel to Madrid as ambassador extraordinary of the imperial Russian court for the express purpose of obviating any misunderstandings between the two powers. He would then return to San Francisco via Mexico "to reclaim his bride, and settle all matters relative to the commerce he so much wished to promote."[52]

Rezanov's thinking, however, went beyond the modest exchange he had outlined to Governor Arrillaga. Extensive commercial intercourse with California, he assured the tsar, "will inject life into [Russian] America, Siberia and Kamchatka; it will promote domestic industry in Russia, open new perspectives of imperial glory, and everywhere create plenty."[53] Such trade, he estimated, "can bring in at least a million rubles annually."[54]

Rezanov left San Francisco firmly convinced of the need to establish a Russian foothold in California. "If the Government had reflected earlier on this part of the world," he observed, "if it had properly appraised its worth, if it had steadfastly pursued the vision of Peter the Great, who, with the meager means at his disposal, sagaciously organized the Bering expedition, New California would never have been a Spanish possession. . . ."[55] Today," he wrote, "there remains [in California] an unoccupied stretch of most valuable land for which we have the greatest need. What," he queried rhetorically, "will posterity say if we allow it, too, to slip away?"[56]

Two years later, a metallic seal bearing the inscription "land of

Russian possession" was buried in the ground near Cape Mendocino. Not long after, a second was interred at Bodega Bay, a short distance north of San Francisco.[57] Finally, in the summer of 1812, an expedition from Sitka established a fortified settlement several miles above Bodega, Russia's first open challenge to Spanish authority in the New World.[58]

Even before Rezanov's visit to Sitka in 1805–1806, Baranov had taken steps to reconnoiter the California coast with a view to future hunting, trade, and settlement. Already in the fall of 1803 he had contracted with Anglo-American shipmaster Joseph O'Cain to transport a Russian expedition to San Diego and San Quintín Bay in Baja California, there to hunt sea otter. So successful was the venture that Baranov sent numerous other parties to California in subsequent years. He made six such contracts between 1809 and 1812, obtaining in this manner over eight thousand sea otter pelts from territory nominally belonging to the Spanish crown.[59]

Following Rezanov's departure from Russian America, Baranov sent his second-in-command and future commandant of Fort Ross, I. A. Kuskov, to explore the coast of Alta California. Upon his return in the fall of 1809, Kuskov advised Baranov that "sea-otter and fish abounded on the whole coast, that he had found many places well adapted for agriculture and ship-building, and that the whole country north of San Francisco Bay was unoccupied by any European power."[60] Baranov determined forthwith to establish a permanent settlement on the California coast, in consequence of which he ordered Kuskov to return to the area to search out a suitable site. It was not until early 1811, however, that Kuskov finally anchored in Bodega Bay, which he renamed in honor of Count Rumiantsev, principal mentor of Russia's New World enterprise. The immediate environs of the bay were found unsuitable for the envisioned settlement and Kuskov selected a site some eighteen miles up the coast, where he purchased a tract of land from the local Indians. He then sailed for Sitka to advise Baranov of his actions and to prepare for the actual founding of the new colony.[61]

Kuskov returned to the chosen site in the spring of 1812, accompanied by ninety-five Russians and some eighty Aleuts. There, on a bluff overlooking the Pacific, they erected a stockade and, within its enclosure, a number of log shelters. Amid much celebration, the settlement was formally christened Ross on 10 September 1812, name day of Tsar Alexander I. Thus began the twenty-nine-year history of the most distant outpost of the Russian empire. Thus, too, began a decade of territorial dispute between the courts of Spain and Russia.[62]

Word of the Russian settlement in California first reached Madrid at the close of 1813 in a dispatch from Félix Calleja, viceroy of New Spain.[63] José Luyando, then interim secretary of state, immediately notified Eusebio de Bardaxí y Azara, in St. Petersburg, instructing the Spanish envoy to lodge a protest with the Russian government. Spain, Bardaxí was to emphasize, "cannot view with indifference and would sorely regret that in so remote a place there should be cause for discord between two Governments so united. . . ."[64] In the course of the next few months, however, tsarist officials managed to convince Bardaxí that the Russian-American Company "is entirely independent and operates by itself with no intervention from the Emperor either in its management or in the colonies."[65] What these officials neglected to tell the Spanish envoy was that as early as the fall of 1809 the tsar had himself authorized the founding of a colony in Alta California.[66]

In Sitka and St. Petersburg alike the moment was judged propitious to press Russian territorial ambitions along the eastern shores of the Pacific. "As the central Spanish government, preoccupied with events in the metropolis, was unable to respond actively to events in its colonies," writes S. B. Okun, "the Russian-American Company saw no reason to provide legal justifications for this seizure [of California land]."[67] "Acting with feigned independence," adds L. Yu. Slëzkin, "the Russian-American Company was moved by the debility of Spain's authority in California to promote trade with this area in defiance of existing laws, and, foreseeing the final collapse of Spanish rule in the colonies, to expand the bounds of Russian America by founding the Ross colony."[68]

Indeed, as late as 1817 the tsarist government continued to profess total ignorance of the events surrounding the new settlement. Replying to a further protest lodged by the Spanish minister, Francisco de Zea Bermúdez, Nesselrode's associate in the ministry of foreign affairs, Count Ionnes Antonios Capo d'Istria, declared that prior to receiving Zea's note he had no knowledge of a Russian settlement in California. The Russian government, Zea was assured, had had no part in the founding of Ross.[69] Moreover, Zea reported, the Russian ministry of foreign affairs had "asked the Russian-American Company for an explanation of its agents' strange conduct." Once the company had replied, the tsar would take "whatever action the case might warrant."[70] The imperial crown, Zea was given to believe, sought "to determine the reasons and above all the cause and true object which the Company or its agents have had in committing this outrage. . . ."[71]

The object, hindsight reveals, was imperial expansion at the expense of the Spanish crown. The primary instrumentality employed in the pursuit of that object was the *fait accompli* obscured by diplomatic deception, which in turn sought to blur the boundaries between state and private enterprise. Such, in large measure, were the operative principles of tsarist New World policy throughout the period under consideration.

Maritime Contacts and Probings

By the time Rezanov set out on the arduous return journey across Siberia to St. Petersburg in September 1806,[72] Lisianskii and Kruzenshtern had brought their ships safely back to the port of Kronshtadt. After leaving Nagasaki in April 1805, Kruzenshtern had employed several months in reconnoitering the Kurile Islands, Kamchatka, and Sakhalin.[73] Lisianskii, for his part, had proceeded to Kodiak and Sitka, where he had helped Baranov to subdue the Tlingit tribes of the Alexander Archipelago.[74] In December 1805, the *Nadezhda* and *Neva* had rendezvoused at Macao. After exchanging their cargoes of furs for tea, chinaware, and nankins at Canton, they set out in February 1806 on the long return voyage to Russia, where they arrived the following August.[75]

The cumulative experience of the Kruzenshtern expedition imparted new direction to Russian overseas expansion. Previous thoughts of outfitting yards in the colonies for the construction of a Pacific fleet were abandoned and attention was turned to further voyages such as the one just completed by the *Nadezhda* and *Neva*. There were differences of opinion, however, as to the most advantageous course to follow.

Rezanov, for example, had argued that the Russian government should concern itself above all else with the strengthening of Sitka as the apex of a triangular trade between America, China, and Siberia. All vessels sent out from the Baltic, he had felt, should carry cargoes of goods essential to the development of the colonies and ought themselves to remain as part of the Pacific fleet. Only at such time as the Russian settlements in Siberia and America had been placed on a solid economic footing and were producing surpluses in excess of immediate demands should any consideration be given to regular maritime ties between European Russia and the Pacific.[76]

Kruzenshtern, on the other hand, considered such ties "as the only means of bringing the trade of the Russian American Company into a thriving state." To accomplish this "would require an entirely new organization" of the Russian-American Company, by which he appears to have meant the militarization of the existing structure.[77] This, subsequent events make clear, was the policy pursued.

South America figured prominently in Kruzenshtern's plan for maritime communications between European Russia and the Pacific colonies. Brazil was envisioned as a key source of stores for ships sailing around Cape Horn, and in actual practice became a regular stopping place for Russian vessels en route to the Pacific.[78] Ships bound for Kamchatka via the Horn, Kruzenshtern recommended, should sail straight to the Society Islands, where they could without difficulty replenish provisions consumed in the three-month voyage from Brazil. Ships sailing directly to the northwest coast of America, on the other hand, could most advantageously put into one of the ports of Chile, where they would find not only an abundance of shipboard provisions but also the maize and wheat so sorely needed in the colonies. "The run from Chili [sic] to Kodiak," Kruzenshtern observed, "is not too great; those who deem it so, may touch at the Sandwich islands, which do not lie much out of the way."[79]

Finding the *Neva* in exceptionally good condition after three years at sea, authorities in St. Petersburg decided to ready the ship immediately for a return voyage to the colonies, where it would remain in the service of the Russian-American Company. At the same time, I. M. Vasil'ev, the tsar's envoy to Lisbon, was instructed to seek free access for Russian merchant ships to the ports of Brazil. "If the Portuguese government cannot unqualifiedly grant this request," read Vasil'ev's instructions, "then let it at least permit ships of the Russian-American Company sailing from Kamchatka or Russian America to enter Brazilian ports and there purchase or secure through barter the products of that country." No effort should be spared, Vasil'ev was advised, to obtain this important concession.[80]

The *Neva*, it was further decided, would be accompanied by the 300-ton sloop *Diana* for armed escort. Delays in outfitting the *Diana*, however, so prolonged its departure that in mid-autumn 1806 the *Neva* set out alone, reaching Kodiak one year later. The *Diana* followed in July 1807. Neither ship again returned to Russia, nor was another dispatched to the colonies until the fall of 1813.[81] For over six years events in Europe severely hindered development of these fragile ties with Russia's far-flung colonies in the Pacific. The objectives, however, had been defined and no sooner did the Napoleonic threat begin to abate than they were again pursued with renewed vigor.

During the reign of Alexander I, twenty-five ships commanded by officers of the imperial navy sailed from European Russia on missions to the far side of the globe. Thirteen were naval vessels and eight belonged to the Russian-American Company. Four sailed more than once, while three failed to complete their missions. All but two put into Brazilian ports, several on both outbound and return voyages. Thirteen also entered Spanish American waters.[82]

In addition to these government-sponsored voyages, other vessels of Russian registry also appear to have visited Latin American ports at this time. Available evidence, however, is scanty and little of a conclusive nature can be said about them.[83] Some seem to have been chartered by the Russian-American Company for voyages to the colonies.[84] Others, bearing such names as *Hercules, Volga, Schastlivii, Natalia Petrovna,* and *Velikii Kniaz' Aleksandr,* belonged to private merchants —associates, perhaps, of the enterprising Ivan Kremer—who sought commercial profit in the turmoil of colonial emancipation. These ships appear to have frequented primarily the ports of Buenos Aires, Montevideo, and Rio de Janeiro, although there is also evidence of direct traffic between Kronshtadt and Havana.[85]

On 21 October 1813, the Russian-American Company ship *Suvorov* departed Kronshtadt for Sitka under the command of Lieutenant M. P. Lazarev. With its sailing began a five-year period in which Russia systematically pursued the objectives outlined by Rezanov, Rumiantsev, and Kruzenshtern, including bases of commerce and supply in Latin America. An unmistakable element of finesse and calculation now entered tsarist dealings with the Spanish and Portuguese crowns.

Prior to the *Suvorov's* departure, the Russian ministry of foreign affairs petitioned Eusebio de Bardaxí y Azara, envoy extraordinary of the Spanish regency, for a certificate of safe conduct, which, in case of necessity, would permit that ship to enter any port of the Spanish Empire. The *Suvorov,* Bardaxí was advised, would sail to Sitka and Kodiak, with intermediate stops in England and Brazil. No mention, however, appears to have been made of anticipated calls at Spanish American ports.[86] Yet on its return voyage in 1815–1816, the *Suvorov* touched at several points in Latin America. None of the visits was occasioned by "necessity," as stipulated in the Spanish passport issued to Lieutenant Lazarev.

The Russian-American Company's governing board had authorized Lazarev to amplify his instructions in any way that promised to further company interests.[87] Accordingly, he resolved on the return passage to reconnoiter the west coast of Spanish America. After taking on fresh provisions at San Francisco in August 1815, he charted a course for the Revillagigedo Islands, off the west coast of Mexico, and Cocos Island, not quite midway between the isthmus of Central America and the Galápagos Islands. Finding little of interest beyond prickly pears, seashells, and sharks, Lazarev touched only briefly at these points and soon continued on to South America.[88] On 10 October 1815, he dropped anchor at the mouth of the Esmeraldas River, on the Ecuadorian coast.[89] Here, he wished to survey the surrounding area, which he expeditiously accomplished in the company of local Spanish officials. Before again weighing anchor, he took on additional stores, including swine, coconuts, and fresh fruit.[90]

Whether by accident or design, Lazarev had failed to dispose of a substantial part of the *Suvorov*'s original cargo, which consisted mainly of goods earmarked for trade in Kamchatka, Okhotsk, and Russian America. For reasons not apparent from available documentation, Lazarev had completely bypassed Kamchatka and Okhotsk, sailing directly to Sitka from Port Jackson, Australia.[91] Rather than leave the remaining cargo in the colonies, Baranov had authorized some of the goods to be taken to the new Russian settlement in California, with the remainder to be sold or traded in Peru.[92] In view of the well-known prohibition against such commercial transactions' in Spain's New World possessions, this, like the founding of Ross two years before, can only be viewed as a calculated challenge to Spanish colonial authority. The principal object of this visit to Peru, wrote Lazarev upon his return to Russia, "was to initiate trade with the richest country in the world, where to date not a single European nation other than Spain has traded."[93]

On 6 December 1815, the *Suvorov* anchored in the port of Callao, where it remained for the next two and a half months while Lazarev adroitly pursued the ends of his visit. No sooner had the ship entered Callao than it was boarded by the port captain, who promptly requested the ship's log and related papers. "As no one could read our Russian documents," observed Lieutenant S. Ya. Unkovskii with thinly veiled amusement, "they were quickly returned to us."[94] Lazarev then traveled to Lima for an audience with the viceroy, José Fernando de Abascal (Marqués de la Concordia), who granted the Russian visitors permission to remain at their anchorage indefinitely. At the same time, Abascal assigned two customs officials to the *Suvorov* as a precaution against any illicit movement of goods ashore.[95]

While in Lima, Lazarev was introduced to Pedro Abadía, chief factor of the Royal Philippine Company and ready host to the visiting Russians.[96] Allegedly one of the wealthiest individuals in Peru, whose personal fortune Lazarev estimated at perhaps four million pesos, Abadía promised to facilitate an exchange of Russian goods for local Peruvian produce. In addition, he proposed the establishment of commercial links between the Royal Philippine and Russian-American companies, offering himself to act as intermediary in future bilateral transactions.[97] A unique concept at the time, Abadía's proposal was aimed apparently at circumventing crown restrictions on the movement of Oriental goods eastward across the Pacific.[98] Exactly how Abadía intended to consummate such an arrangement is not clear from the available documentation. In any event, he entrusted a large consignment of quinine to Lazarev for sale in Russia, thus marking, he hoped, the start of trade ties between the two countries.[99]

At Abadía's request, the viceroy authorized the exchange of goods that had in fact brought the *Suvorov* to Peru. Such license, observed Unkovskii, "was at that time granted no foreigner in the Spanish colonies."[100] Lazarev, for his part, seems clearly to have misrepresented the true situation aboard the *Suvorov* in order to secure this unusual dispensation. The Russians, Abascal was led to believe, lacked sufficient cash "to purchase what they needed to continue their voyage to Europe," in consequence of which he "allowed them to sell the residue of their cargo" and even exempted them from payment of import duties "amounting to several thousand pesos."[101] The goods marked for sale by Baranov were transferred to the Callao customshouse, where local buyers "offered the most advantageous terms of exchange for Chilean copper, quinine, Peruvian balsam, gamboge, vicuña wool, and cotton, as well as for cash. . . ."[102] The Russians also acquired a variety of Incan artifacts, including several priceless objects offered by the viceroy as a personal gift to Alexander I. In addition, Lazarev took on board nine live llamas, an alpaca, and a vicuña, zoological rarities never before seen in Russia. The total value of the *Suvorov*'s Peruvian cargo was placed at two million rubles, by no means an inauspicious introduction to the commercial potentialities of Spanish America.[103]

The visit of the *Suvorov* to Callao also provided the first opportunity for Russian subjects to observe directly the unfolding struggle for independence in Spain's New World possessions. "At the time of our stay in Lima," wrote Lieutenant Unkovskii, "the power of the crown in the colony had already been severely shaken, and everywhere there had been formed societies of creoles and mulattoes[104] opposed to the royal government, especially in Chile." The movement was exceedingly widespread, he added, and although Lima as yet remained quiet, even there "discontent was most apparent."[105] Indeed, shortly after Unkovskii made this observation, the *Suvorov* was itself caught in a skirmish between a squadron of insurgent vessels and royalist shore batteries in the port of Callao.[106]

The results of Lazarev's visit to Peru appear to have encouraged the Russian government to pursue its probings for commercial and strategic advantage in Latin America. Shortly after the *Suvorov*'s return in late July 1816, the tsar announced his intention to confer the Order of St. Anne, first and second class respectively, upon Abascal and Abadía in recognition of the services rendered to Lazarev and his crew.[107] The subtlety of this gesture deceived few, least of all Ignacio Pérez de Lema, Spanish chargé d'affaires in St. Petersburg, who decried "the pretext of actually needing provisions" with which Lazarev had abused the viceroy of Peru.[108] While not doubting the tsar's sincere desire to acknowledge the assistance accorded the *Suvorov*, Pérez de Lema was nonetheless inclined to believe that the Russians "wish to curry the favor of [Spanish colonial] authorities for future ventures which ships of the Russian-American Company may undertake in Lima and elsewhere in the King's dominions."[109] ·

Only the year before, the Russian ministry of foreign affairs had solicited a certificate of safe conduct for the Russian-American Company ship *Riurik*, which, under the command of Lieutenant Otto von Kotzebue, was to carry out a new voyage to the Pacific. The object of that voyage, the ministry had advised the Spanish chargé, was "purely scientific."[110] Pérez de Lema, however, harbored serious doubts. Despite the expedition's alleged scientific ends, he reported to Madrid, one should not rule out the possibility "that the Rurick might touch in California to promote trade with Sitka and the other colonies."[111]

The *Riurik* had departed Kronshtadt on 18 July 1815, bound for Kamchatka and Alaska. On the outward passage Kotzebue retraced much of the course sailed by the *Nadezhda* twelve years earlier, stopping, as had Kruzenshtern, at Santa Catarina, in Brazil. "Ships which intend to sail round Cape Horn," he noted, "do well to touch at this island, and not at Rio Janeiro; provisions are here cheaper; you enjoy a far better climate; and, above all, have the advantage of being nearer to Cape Horn."[112]

From Santa Catarina the *Riurik* proceeded to Chile, entering Talcahuano Bay at about the same time as the *Suvorov* was departing Callao. Kotzebue found much to recommend southern Chile as a place of refreshment for navigators doubling the Horn. He saw little, however, of commercial interest. "It is only to be regretted," he wrote in his journal, "that the Spaniards do not apply more to the cultivation of the country; their absurd jealousy likewise prohibits all trade, except with their own colonies, though they might carry on a flourishing commerce."[113] Chile, added the expedition's naturalist, "languishes in fetters, without navigation, commerce, or industry."[114] Perhaps because of these negative observations, the Russian court tempered its interest in trade relations with that distant country. Indeed, available records indicate that eight years were to pass before another Russian vessel entered Chilean waters. Fittingly, it was Kotzebue himself who, in January 1824, again dropped anchor in Talcahuano Bay.[115]

In late May 1816, as the *Suvorov* approached England and the *Riurik* neared Kamchatka, Count Karl Robert Nesselrode, the tsar's newly appointed foreign minister, informed Pérez de Lema of yet another expedition to the New World. The Russian-American Company, Nesselrode advised the Spanish diplomat, intended to send a shipment of supplies to the colonies aboard the ship *Kutuzov*, which in the course of its voyage would also undertake "geographic, historical and physical investigations" of interest and utility to all nations. In view of these ends, the Russian ministry of foreign affairs requested a certificate of safe conduct that would permit the *Kutuzov* to enter any Spanish American port that necessity might require.[116] Pérez de Lema provided the desired document.[117]

Shortly thereafter, it was decided to refit the recently returned *Suvorov* for a second voyage to the colonies. Having deemed it desirable for this ship to accompany the *Kutuzov*, Nesselrode now informed Pérez de Lema, the Russian-American Company wished to secure a passport that would allow it to touch in Spain's New World possessions should repairs so require or "should an unforeseen accident separate the two vessels."[118] As before, Pérez de Lema complied with the ministry's request, avoiding, however, any mention of unforeseen separations.[119] He then advised the Spanish court of the impending expedition.[120] Although he had authorized entry into Callao solely in case of necessity, he reported, it was doubtful "that, given the good reception previously accorded the Souvarow, the visit would be repeated out of sheer gratitude."[121] Pérez de Lema also wrote to Abascal, in Lima, apprising the viceroy of the circumstances that would bring the two vessels to Callao. "While I have issued them a passport in order that they might receive all necessary assistance," he pointedly observed, "it is not my intention to allow them to trade."[122] Nesselrode, for his part, had neglected to inform the Spanish chargé that the *Kutuzov* and the *Suvorov* would carry goods "for trade in a number of South American ports."[123]

The two ships sailed in September 1816, the *Kutuzov* under the command of Lieutenant-Captain L. A. Hagemeister, the *Suvorov* in the charge of Captain Z. I. Ponafidin. After a three-week layover in Rio de Janeiro, they continued on to Peru via Cape Horn, entering the port of Callao in late March 1817.[124] Here, they tarried for nearly eight weeks, during which time the principal order of business appears once more to have been trade. The journal of Ponafidin's executive officer, S. I. Yanovskii, indicates that Joaquín de la Pezuela, who had replaced Abascal as viceroy of Peru, at first refused to allow another exchange of goods like the one his predecessor had permitted Lazarev over a year before.[125] As on the previous occasion, however, the influential Abadía prevailed upon the viceroy to permit the exchange and Hagemeister was able to sell a part of his cargo.[126] Strict crown prohibitions on foreign trade, observed Yanovskii, were impoverishing a country rich in natural productions. Faced with such restrictions, local merchants reverted to illicit trade, which in Peru was extensive. "They bribe customs officials and guards," he wrote, "who quite openly allow everything. The viceroy knows this and may even be in collusion, or at least his closest officials conceal the sales and thus do not combat smuggling."[127]

In these circumstances, the exchange of Russian goods was accomplished to the apparent satisfaction of both parties. On 12 May 1817, Hagemeister hosted Abadía and some of his colleagues at a farewell dinner aboard the *Kutuzov*. After toasting the health of their respective sovereigns, accompanied by an eighteen-gun salute, the group drank to the growth and prosperity of the Royal Philippine and Russian-American companies, sealing the toast with an additional salvo of seven guns.[128] The door to continuing Russian commercial ties with Peru was thus set temporarily ajar.

Seven days out of Callao, the two ships parted company. Ponafidin charted a direct course to Sitka, while Hagemeister diverted the *Kutuzov* toward Guayaquil, there to probe further opportunities for trade. In all, the *Kutuzov* spent two months in the Gulf of Guayaquil, during which time a portion of the ship's cargo was transferred directly to "Spanish ships" in exchange for a selection of local produce.[129] While available evidence sheds little light on the *Kutuzov*'s movements, even these sparse details suggest an illicit transaction in contravention of existing Spanish laws, and, in fact, the incident subsequently elicited a formal protest from the Spanish crown.[130] At the end of July 1817, the *Kutuzov* set sail for California and thence to Sitka, where Hagemeister was to relieve the venerable Baranov of his charge as governor-general.

The basis for Russian trade ties with the west coast of South America was most succinctly summarized by Captain V. M. Golovnin, who, in February 1818, brought the naval sloop *Kamchatka* into the port of Callao. "The Peruvian trade could be exceedingly important," wrote Golovnin, "if only it were open to Europeans, or if the Spaniards were themselves as energetic as the English. . . ."[131] There is a market in Peru," he observed, "for the most valuable of European goods, especially those from Russia, including all manner of naval stores, such as rigging, sailcloth, copper sheets, and tar; also coarse linens, work clothes, yard goods, and many other products. . . ." Firearms constituted at that time the single most lucrative article of trade. Indeed, only the year before, the Russian-American Company ships *Kutuzov* and *Suvorov* had supplied a modest quantity of arms to the viceroy for a very substantial sum.[132]

As for Peruvian exports, the single most important article was the peso, "for here," wrote Golovnin, "silver can itself be called a commodity." Other products of the country included quinine, sarsaparilla, cotton, and vicuña wool.[133] Prices, however, were exorbitant when one had to pay in cash. There was simply too much specie in circulation, declared Golovnin. If, on the other hand, one could exchange a cargo of European merchandise for another of local produce, he could command the most advantageous of terms. But, here again, one was faced with the stringent restrictions of the Spanish crown.[134] In light of all this, Golovnin concluded, ships rounding Cape Horn would do well to make port at Valparaíso or Concepción. In contrast to Callao, he held, the ports of Chile "are safe and offer the navigator every possible advantage, besides which they are much closer to his course."[135]

Only a year before the *Kamchatka*'s arrival in Callao, Chile had been liberated by the armies of San Martín. This event, noted Golovnin, "had caused extraordinary confusion in Peru."[136] As for the supposed security of Chilean ports, Kotzebue found a highly volatile situation there six years later, when, alerted by rumors of a plot to seize his ship, he was obliged to force an exit from Talcahuano Bay against two Chilean warships that sought to challenge the Russian vessel.[137]

Tsarist maritime contacts with the west coast ports of South America failed to develop as Rezanov, Kruzenshtern, Rumiantsev, and other architects of Russian imperial expansion had envisioned. The half dozen or so visits to those ports by ships of the Russian flag during the independence period were significant, however, precisely in light of the views these influential figures held. In essence, they were voyages to test the feasibility of a grand imperial design embracing the entire Pacific basin. If in the end they demonstrated the impracticality of implementing the design, this in no way lessens their historical significance as indicators of a passing commitment to that design and to the concomitant policy decisions that defined Russia's position on the colonial question in Spanish and Portuguese America.[138]

5. Initial Responses
to Political Change in the Spanish and Portuguese Empires

The outbreak of rebellion in Latin America, followed by Russia's realignment with Spain and Great Britain against Napoleonic France, moved the court of St. Petersburg to examine more closely its evolving interests in the New World. French occupation of the Iberian Peninsula effectively severed metropolitan ties with the colonies, thereby opening those countries to widened intercourse with other European powers, including tsarist Russia. At the same time, international tensions and the related issue of legitimacy constrained Alexander I in his pursuit of expanded Russian ties with the Spanish and Portuguese territories in America. The result was a compromise, whereby the tsar attempted to further Russian New World interests through alliance with and manipulation of the Iberian crowns.

Tsarist concerns about hostilities in colonial Latin America are clearly reflected in the Russian periodical press of the period. Efforts to appraise more precisely the nature and significance of those hostilities led to an upgrading of tsarist diplomatic representation in the New World and an attendant expansion of direct Russian contacts with the Iberian colonies. Simultaneously, Russo-Spanish relations became increasingly intimate and tsarist influence at the court of Madrid grew rapidly. Commentary on Latin American independence in the Russian periodical press and official steps by the tsarist government to keep abreast of events in the Hispanic world reveal much about the nature of tsarist responses to the collapse of Iberian colonialism in the Western Hemisphere.

The Periodical Press

The Russian periodical press manifested an interest in the political future of Latin America from a very early date. Already in January 1807, readers of the *Sanktpeterburgskie kommercheskie vedomosti* learned of Francisco de Miranda's ill-fated expedition to the South American mainland. Miranda, they were informed, had failed in an initial move against Spanish colonial authority, having subsequently withdrawn his forces to the island of Grenada. Miranda himself, it was reported, had repaired to Barbados, where it was rumored that he would receive assistance from Great Britain.[1]

British meddling in the River Plate likewise aroused Russian public interest. The successful uprising of the populace of Buenos Aires against the occupation forces of Major-General William Carr Beresford was reported in March 1807. Spanish authority had been reestablished, it was stated, under the leadership of Santiago de Liniers. Some 1,200 British soldiers were erroneously reported to have perished in the clash with local forces.[2] The subsequent defeat of a considerably augmented British force in July 1807 and the resultant abandonment of British designs upon the River Plate led *Vestnik Evropy* to declare these attacks against South America to have been as precariously conceived as those perpetrated against Naples, Constantinople, and Egypt. "Not just the present order of things," asserted the journal, "but even the most favorable of circumstances could not for long permit England to preserve its conquests in Spanish America: Buenos Aires, as everyone predicted, has been quickly lost."[3]

The flight of the Portuguese court to Brazil, in turn, was viewed by at least some Russian observers as an occurrence of potentially greater political significance than the infelicitous projects of Miranda in northern South America or the military ventures of the British in the River Plate. "One can only conclude," declared *Vestnik Evropy* in January 1808, "that South America will soon be the theater of important events." Forced to choose between dependency on France and dependency on England, the unfortunate "ex-regent" of Portugal had chosen the latter and now willingly permitted England to maintain military units on Brazilian soil. "We shall soon know," the journal concluded skeptically, "the outcome of this decisive act."[4]

The first news of open rebellion against royal authority in Spanish America appears to have reached the Russian reading public in the summer of 1810.[5] On August 1 of that year, the St. Petersburg weekly *Severnaia pochta* reported that insurrection had broken out in South America the preceding month of April. It had started, according to the paper, in Caracas and La Guaira.[6] This same news brief appeared two days later in the *Sanktpeterburgskie vedomosti* and again on August 15 in the *Moskovskie vedomosti*. It was accompanied in these latter two papers by a second article that stated that the province of Caracas had declared its independence. "Having assembled 34,000 men," the article reported, "the inhabitants of this province placed Spanish customs officials under guard and sent them to Cuba. . . . Then, forming a provisional government, they declared their commerce to be free and totally independent of all political circumstances."[7] From this point forth, the Russian periodical press showed growing and sustained interest in the independence movements of colonial Latin America, an interest dampened only briefly by the Napoleonic interlude of 1812–1813.

Despite frequent inaccuracies in reporting, literate Russians had ready access to information about the troubled Spanish and Portuguese colonies. News from the New World reached Russia mainly through London, Paris, Hamburg, and Madrid, many articles in Russian periodicals being simply translations of items first published abroad. The British press was the principal source of information about Latin America, and prior to 1815, at least, the most informed, if not always the most disinterested.[8] At the same time, original reports began to appear in the Russian press on the course of colonial independence. These became more frequent following the issuance of directives to Russian diplomats in the United States to gather all available intelligence on the Spanish colonies,[9] and after the establishment in 1811 of direct diplomatic ties with Brazil. One could only conclude from a reading of the Russian press over the period 1810–1812 "that the independence movement in Spanish America was widespread and had achieved numerous successes."[10]

Like other European observers of the period, so, too, enlightened Russians early perceived fundamental weaknesses threatening the continued existence of the New World colonial systems, weaknesses that were especially pronounced in the Spanish colonies. And, as elsewhere in Europe, so, too, in Russia the individual most responsible for drawing public attention to those weaknesses was the renowned German naturalist, Alexander von Humboldt, who, accompanied by French botanist Aimé Bonpland, had spent almost five years studying the peoples, flora, and fauna of Middle and northern South America. Their monumental *Voyage aux régions équinoxiales du Nouveau Continent*, which first began to appear in Paris in 1807, provided much significant material for political commentary on colonial Spanish America.[11]

Already in September 1809, *Vestnik Evropy* drew its readership's attention to the fascinating geographic and statistical notices supplied by Humboldt and Bonpland about New Spain—notices, the journal observed, that unavoidably turned one's attention back to Old Spain. Alluding to the political turmoil occasioned in the mother country by Napoleon's occupation of the Iberian Peninsula, *Vestnik Evropy* suggested that for Russia the New World now acquired an added interest. "The future of Spanish America," it prophetically noted, "has not yet been decided."[12]

Commenting on the social and political tensions obtaining in New Spain, *Vestnik Evropy* reviewed Humboldt's general observations on creoles and native-born Spaniards. "Creoles," the journal stated, "are supposed to enjoy the same rights as Spaniards; however, the most important posts are entrusted only to the latter; as a result, both groups live in a constant state of enmity."[13] The journal further observed, albeit erroneously, that New Spain differed from other areas of America in that only the interior regions of the country had been developed, whereas elsewhere settlement had been limited largely to the coastal areas.[14] This was the best of the Spanish possessions in America. By all indications, the journal asserted, New Spain "would soon surpass even the mother country."[15]

In the case of Mexico, observed a subsequent issue of this same journal, "it can be said without hesitation that in the capital city and in many provincial places the urge to develop the useful arts is more apparent than in Spain itself."[16] Mexico City possessed exceptionally good educational institutions, where many talented men were trained in the various sciences. Similarly, the Mexican nobility were said to be far better educated than the nobles of Spain, while the local clergy had a greater appreciation of the legitimate ends of authority than did their Spanish counterparts. "In these circumstances," *Vestnik Evropy* editorialized, "it should be pointed out that, even without a change in government in Spain, the latter's colonies would most likely separate from the mother country; moreover, several, albeit unsuccessful, attempts have signalled the approach of independence, a fact that cannot be concealed from the observant political eye. Spain, like many other European states, erred in creating a colonial system that has always been unjust and that ultimately has become ruinous. Neither despotism nor the restriction of trade and other relations suffices to maintain forever the dependency of a land so rich in its own sources of wealth."[17]

By 1811, the Russian periodical press was unequivocally conveying to its readership the image of a rapidly disintegrating colonial order in the New World. *Vestnik Evropy*, for example, reported in February of that year that rebellion was daily spreading in South America. "Various regions belonging to Spain have declared their independence," it reported. "In west Florida there occur the very same changes as in Chile and Quito: the entire area has been declared independent."[18] "One cannot but think," the journal observed a month later, "that all of Spanish America will break away from the realm."[19]

"South America," observed *Istoricheskii, statisticheskii i geografi-cheskii zhurnal* in April 1811, "offers a spectacle similar to that seen over thirty years ago in North America. The battle for independence arises from a clash between the native inhabitants and the Europeans, and, in many places, has been accompanied by such bloodshed as to be indistinguishable from a revolution."[20] A month later, this same journal reported "further successes" in the struggle for Spanish American independence. It was quite remarkable, commented one writer, that Spanish colonial rule should have survived so long. "Now, it seems, the time has come when the [Spanish] Americans, oppressed for three whole centuries, will restore their independence and their rights. . . .[21] The idea of restoring independence," the journal added, "has spread from the southern half of America to Spanish North America. Mounting insurrection has shaken the viceroyalty of Mexico. . . . Already West Florida, a narrow, oblong strip of extraordinarily fertile land on the Gulf of Mexico, has detached itself from Spain. . . . The banner of revolution has even been carried to Spanish Middle America and to the West Indian island of Cuba. . . . Spain thus finds herself in danger of losing her *silver fleet*, not one of which, perhaps, will again enter Cádiz, as well as Havana, staging point for royal shipping. America," the journal concluded, "shall yet contribute much material to the history of the nineteenth century."[22]

By late spring 1811, a growing body of information led the Russian periodical press to refine its views of the independence movement in Spanish America. Whereas previous commentary had stressed the steadily mounting wave of revolution, attention was now drawn to the chaos of civil war. The inhabitants of Spanish America, observed *Istoricheskii, statisticheskii i geograficheskii zhurnal*, "have by themselves and of their own passionate nature split into two warring camps, locked in battle with one another. The cities of Caracas, La Guaira, Puerto Cabello, Cumaná, Barcelona, and other places are defending their independence. Puerto Rico, Maracaibo, Santa Marta, Santo Domingo, and Coro, on the other hand, have declared their support of the Regency in Cádiz."[23] However, the journal editorialized, "time will tell which system these vast and strange lands of the Spanish sceptre will adopt once Cádiz opens its gates to the French soldiers and there is no longer any Regency or *junta* in Spain; such a time, it seems, is already at hand."[24]

"Without a doubt," declared another Russian observer in October

1811, "still much time will pass before there arise from the agitation and anarchy that reigns in Spanish America new forms on which to establish the security and civil welfare of the inhabitants of that part of the world."[25] Moreover, he noted, the course of events in the New World was further complicated by a number of external factors, of which England was perhaps the most important. "The English, into whose coffers the gold and silver of the New World now flow, do not wish even to hear of independence. They seek to prevent free nations, possessed of the best mines in the world, from throwing off the yoke of English monopoly and from permitting other European vessels to enter their harbors."[26]

By the beginning of 1812, the Russian periodical press was reflecting renewed optimism about the independence movement in Latin America. "In brief, yet bloody battles," declared *Istoricheskii, statisticheskii i geograficheskii zhurnal*, "the New World has gained its independence. . . ."

> From the frozen rivers of Canada to the cold land of fire [Tierra del Fuego], near the south pole, all America is free and the inhabitants of this greatest and most beautiful part of the world celebrate with joy the first day of 1812, that day on which only a year before they still groaned under the yoke of Spanish fanaticism and the British tyranny of imposed trade. Only the city of Montevideo and the Kingdom of Brazil do not yet enjoy the freedom of their fellow peoples; but soon the first of these places will open its gates to the brave and triumphant besiegers; soon Brazil will dissolve the weak fetters imposed on her by a senseless Queen and her son, already a long-time instrument of the cabinet of St. James; for even there have reached the sparks of New World revival and there they will ignite into a blazing flame.[27]

America, the journal continued, would apparently break into four large republics: the United States of North America, with its capital at Washington; Mexico, "a beautiful country rich in gold"; and two South American republics centered respectively on the cities of Buenos Aires and Caracas.[28] The latter city, it was observed, had set an example for all South America, just as Boston had done for the English colonies some thirty-eight years before; an example set under the leadership of Francisco de Miranda, who had played a role in northern South America equal to that of "the immortal Washington" in North America.[29] The present, the journal concluded,

> promises an illustrious and fascinating future to coming generations [of Latin Americans]. Indeed, the present generation has already reaped some of the fruits of its new freedom: the inquisition has been eliminated; the Indians have been freed; the burden of taxation has been removed; com-

plete freedom of commerce has been promised; and the slave trade has been entirely discontinued. All estates and all religions will enjoy the same rights; beneficent institutions will be established like those in North America, and European arts and science will be fostered. In this way, a firm and stable foundation will be laid for the coming *century of pacification*. A beautiful flower promises beautiful fruit.[30]

In point of fact, the metaphorical flower failed to bloom for a long time and the quality of its fruit remains the subject of heated debate. Moreover, the immediate future of Russia itself was far from bright, with the result that journalistic interest in Latin America began to wane by the spring of 1812. One of the last reports on events in the New World prior to the full impact on Russia of war with France appeared in *Moskovskie vedomosti* one week after Napoleon's grand army had crossed the Niemen. The Spanish American insurgents, read the article, "win a victory in one place, while in another they are dealt severe blows; their numbers, however, continue to grow and everywhere they have followers."[31]

The trauma of 1812 temporarily erased Latin America from the columns and pages of the Russian periodical press. Napoleon's rapid advance and Alexander's apparent inability to meet the enemy straight on, dramatized by the successive capitulations of Vilna, Smolensk, and Moscow, at once surprised and shocked much of the Russian populace. These events, observed the great nineteenth-century historian V. O. Kliuchevskii, "evoked exceptional political and moral agitation; [Russian] society, moved by the great events in which it was obliged to take so active a part, became incited as never before."[32] Enlightened Russians in both official and nonofficial positions were caught up in the plight of the empire, many of them focusing their attention on the imperial government's failure to put its own domestic affairs in order. Articles began to appear on political freedom and freedom of the press; some journals even went so far as to advocate a constitution and representative institutions. "External events," wrote Kliuchevskii, "had placed Russia in conflict with the legacy of the French revolution."[33] It was in this context that Latin America attracted renewed interest in the Russian periodical press.

One of the first periodicals to turn its attention again to Spanish and Portuguese America was *Le Conservateur Impartial*, semiofficial organ of the Russian ministry of foreign affairs.[34] Thus, for example, in late summer 1813 this paper noted the harsh contrast between abundant mineral wealth and social injustice in Brazil. "The number of diamonds extracted every year from Brazilian mines," it observed, "is very considerable . . . yet, one can see nothing so wretched as those who live around the mines; they benefit not in the least from the riches extracted from their soil."[35]

The restoration of Ferdinand VII in March 1814 momentarily eclipsed notice of Spanish America in the Russian press.[36] By summer, however, the independence movement had returned to the news. *Vestnik Evropy* reported the perpetration of "extraordinary carnage" in Mexico, where allegedly both sides were executing prisoners of war; "to the shame of the century and humanity," the journal lamented, "on a single occasion Spanish General Llanos executed seven hundred men by the sword."[37] Similarly, *Le Conservateur Impartial* reported that in Venezuela all insurgents captured by royalist forces "were run through with the sword."[38]

Throughout the summer of 1814, the Russian press indicated the tide of battle to be running in favor of the Spanish American insurgents.[39] In Venezuela, according to *Le Conservateur Impartial*, Spanish General Cagigal had "barely escaped from the enemy; his battle gear, artillery, and a large number of prisoners fell to the insurgents."[40] And, in the River Plate, it was reported, insurgent warships had defeated a royalist squadron operating out of Montevideo; five hundred prisoners had been taken, together with seventy-three cannon.[41] Shortly thereafter, Montevideo itself was said to have capitulated to the insurgents of Buenos Aires.[42]

By autumn 1814, the Russian periodical press was reflecting renewed doubts about the outcome of the independence struggle in Spanish America. Royalist victories were reported with rising frequency.[43] As early as September 4 *Le Conservateur Impartial* reported a truce between insurgent and royalist forces in Chile.[44] By the end of September, some organs of the Russian press prematurely reported Chile to have been secured by the royalists.[45] At the same time, royalist forces were correctly said to have retaken Caracas and La Guaira, in northern South America.[46]

The fall of Montevideo, on the other hand, was viewed as a major victory for the insurgents. Not only had it provided them with an immense store of arms and munitions, but, of greater importance, it had deprived the Spanish crown of its only bridgehead in the River Plate. "The republicans will soon march on Peru," predicted *Le Conservateur Impartial*; "their superior numbers and artillery will force the royalist troops to withdraw into their fortified positions."[47]

Despite the increasingly confused picture of events in Spanish America following the restoration of Ferdinand VII, it seems clear that a decisive segment of the Russian periodical press sympathized with the New World insurgents, and, in the period under consideration, openly supported the independence movement. As noted above, this attitude arose at least in part from the domestic consternation of 1812, and was further strengthened by the manifest intransigence of the Spanish monarch, whose unwillingness to grant concessions to creole rebels evoked editorial censure from a number of leading Russian periodicals.[48] Fittingly, perhaps, the response of enlightened Russian society to the demise of colonialism in Latin America found special articulation in the St. Petersburg weekly *Syn Otechestva*. A vehicle of the new currents generated in Russia by the crisis of 1812,[49] this journal addressed itself both directly and indirectly to the question of Latin American independence. In February 1815, for example, it reproduced the following declaration issued to the royalist governor of Quito by the insurgents of northern South America:

> America has firmly decided to be free. Nothing can sway her from this course. Our demands differ so greatly from those of the Spaniards that any rapprochement is impossible. Spain wants to keep America in perpetual submission, in perpetual tutelage, in perpetual slavery. America has declared its freedom, its majority, and its independence. There is no compromise! America would sooner perish than bear an alien yoke.[50]

Ferdinand VII, declared *Syn Otechestva* in a subsequent issue, "has, upon his return, not only failed to contribute to a peaceful reunification of America with the mother country, but by his various actions has caused a veritable split."[51] Despite the lack of reliable information from official Spanish papers, the journal continued, it was evident from the English and American press that royalist forces had suffered numerous defeats. "What," it asked, "can a corps of ten thousand disgruntled soldiers dispatched by Ferdinand do in that country, in that alien clime, against the unlimited resources of the republicans, who have sixty thousand men, hundreds of cannon, and their own flotillas, especially when discontent reigns in the Spanish West Indies?"[52] Although for the present Brazil flourished under the benevolent rule of the prince regent, the journal added, "the proximity of the Spanish insurgents occasioned there considerable anxiety."[53]

Diplomatic Representation

On 20 June 1808, Tsar Alexander I appointed A. Ya. Dashkov as Russia's first diplomatic envoy to the United States.[54] One month later A. G. Evstaf'ev was named Russian consul in Boston.[55] The result of talks initiated in London the previous year by James Madison, the establishment of diplomatic ties with the United States was viewed from the Russian side as more than simple formalization of relations with a new government. From the outset, Russian statesmen contemplated America in all of its vast extension. While the nascent North American republic might provide relief for an economically distraught Russia, it also posed a potential threat to Russian interests in the Pacific basin. At the same time, the presence of Russian diplomats in the United States promised more accurate intelligence on the state of affairs in Spanish and Portuguese America and the possible implementation of direct trade ties with these areas.

Dashkov received the joint appointment of consul-general and chargé d'affaires, with residence in Philadelphia. Significantly, he was employed at the time of his appointment as an assessor in the Russian ministry of commerce. Shortly thereafter, he was named correspondent of the Russian-American Company and charged with furthering the interests of that company in the American Northwest.[56] He was also instructed to keep abreast of events in Spanish America. "Independently of news relating specifically to the country of your assignment," read his initial instructions, "you are especially requested to report as regularly as possible on the status of the Windward and Leeward Islands, as well as on that of Mexico, Tierra Firme and Peru."[57]

Dashkov arrived in Philadelphia on 1 July 1809. His colleague, Evstaf'ev, reached Boston one month later.[58] In the meantime, the U. S. government had approved the appointment of John Quincy Adams as minister plenipotentiary to the court of St. Petersburg, for which post Adams departed the United States on 5 August 1809.[59] Informed of the United States's intention to make this appointment, the Russian government had, in its turn, named Count F. P. Pahlen envoy extraordinary and minister plenipotentiary to the United States. At the same time, the tsar named P. I. Poletica and F. Ivanov to serve respectively as counsellor and secretary of the newly created mission.[60]

For the next several years, Count Pahlen was to be the ranking Russian diplomat in the New World. Tarrying in Paris while en route to the United States, Pahlen drafted in the autumn of 1809 a penetrating, even prophetic memorandum on the state of affairs in America. According to a universal law of nature, he wrote, new states grow and prosper while others crumble and decay. "In our times," he declared, "it is Europe that enters the fatal period of decadence and America that commences an era of prosperity, emerging from its lethargy and rising up on our ruins."[61] Pahlen referred not only to the United States but to the whole of America. "The immense New World possessions of Spain," he continued, "never dreaming of separation from the mother country in times of tranquility, now feel the necessity and advantage of becoming independent states and of assuming their natural place among the powers of the earth. Once there is no longer any hope for the salvation of Spain and we see the aged mistress of the New World fall beneath the yoke of France, then the germ of liberty shall manifest itself more openly in the different provinces of Spanish America, and above all in Mexico."[62]

Echoing observations made in the Russian periodical press,[63] Pahlen asserted that in the viceroyalty of Mexico "the sciences and the arts have made greater advances than in the United States, where the spirit of commerce seems to have encroached on all the other useful occupations. . . . Peru, Chile, Buenos-Ayres, Santa Fee and Mexico," he added, "each with different interests arising from their respective locations, products and needs, will not remain under a single government once the mother country succumbs. . . . One shall see the formation of as many states as there are viceroyalties, and this new order of things will produce a noticeable revolution in European commerce, in its results not unlike that occasioned by the discovery of the Cape of Good Hope.[64] The only European power to derive great benefit from the emancipation of America," Pahlen observed, "is England; now excluded from all the ports of our continent, those of the New World offer an immense outlet for the products of her industry, as well as vast stores of raw materials . . . formerly supplied by northern Europe. By forming new branches of commerce," Pahlen predicted, "English industry will in time quite easily dispense with our products, and, when better times once again permit all the nations of Europe to be at peace, one shall see the great injury America will have inflicted upon us."[65]

In the first days of 1810, the tsar sent his personal instructions to Count Pahlen, who still remained in Paris. Expressing deep interest in the future of Spanish America and possible emancipation, Alexander instructed his envoy to report regularly on developments in that part of the world. Revealing both foresight and an intuitive pragmatism, the tsar informed Pahlen that he had been moved to recognize Joseph Bonaparte as king of Spain in the interests of peace and because Joseph was, in reality, the only sovereign to be found in Spain. "But," he cautioned, "you are to show no particular partiality in the matter of my political relations with Spain. I am always guided," the tsar declared, "solely by that which benefits my Empire and I have not yet decided whether or not it would be advantageous for South America to remain tied to the throne of Madrid."[66]

Count Pahlen sailed for the United States in the spring of 1810, reaching Philadelphia on June 10 that same year.[67] For the next two years, he remitted frequent reports to St. Petersburg on developments in Latin America.[68] Shortly after his arrival in the United States, he advised the Russian minister of foreign affairs that as the French achieved new successes in Spain, so the spirit of independence grew in Spanish America. As of the previous May, he noted, Caracas had ceased to recognize the central *junta* in Spain and had formed an independent government allegedly loyal to Ferdinand VII but in fact bent on independence. Something similar had occurred in Buenos Aires, he added, while the spirit of independence was equally widespread in Santa Fe (de Bogotá), Lima, and Peru.[69]

In October 1810, Pahlen informed Count Rumiantsev that news received from South America "spoke only of popular movements and a change of government."[70] Much violence had occurred in the province of Quito, with numerous atrocities said to have been perpetrated against the local populace by royalist forces. An insurgent army of volunteers from Cartagena, Popayán, and Pasto was reportedly preparing an action against the royalist occupiers of Quito. In Buenos Aires, the revolution had triumphed the previous month of June, and, Pahlen wrote, the insurgents of that region were now preparing campaigns against crown forces in Montevideo and Chile. The viceroy of Mexico had dispatched troops to combat the partisans of Quito, Santa Fe, and Cartagena, but, Pahlen concluded, "the independence movement is too widespread in all of South America to be quelled by a few thousand, poorly disciplined men."[71]

The following month, Pahlen advised Rumiantsev that gradually all the provinces of Spanish America were breaking away from the mother country. "Some form provisional governments," he wrote, "while others declare their independence."[72] The province of Paraguay had formed a *junta*, while in Buenos Aires the partisans had quelled royalist opposition in the interior settlement of Córdoba. Rumors also circulated to the effect that Chile and Peru would soon follow suit. "Never have colonies found themselves in such a situation," wrote Pahlen. "In every age," he observed, "provinces have broken away from Empires because of civil or religious oppression, but now for the first time history offers us the example of so many people being emancipated by the disappearance of a central government."[73]

The tsar and his minister of foreign affairs undoubtedly read Pahlen's dispatches with interest. Indeed, John Quincy Adams was struck by Rumiantsev's "peculiar interest" in South America.[74] On one occasion in February 1810, the two men discussed at some length the direction of events in the Spanish and Portuguese possessions. In the course of their conversation, Adams observed that among the articles imported into Caracas by North American shippers were Russian manufactured goods,[75] suggesting that here, as elsewhere in Latin

America, there were potentially important markets for both Russia and the United States. These remarks, wrote Adams, "touched upon a string to which the Count's feelings responded instantaneously."[76] Inquiring first about the facility with which U. S. merchant vessels entered Spanish American ports, Rumiantsev then turned to the political realities of colonial Latin America. He personally considered the restoration of Ferdinand VII unrealistic, and consequently felt it inconceivable that the overseas possessions should remain even nominally under his authority. Adams concurred, adding that Brazil, too, had attained independence by virtue of the royal presence in Rio de Janeiro. Rumiantsev, in turn, expressed "his most entire and perfect coincidence of opinion" with Adams's appraisal of these matters.[77]

There appears, in fact, to have been a growing coincidence of opinion among Russian statesmen with respect to the course of events in Latin America. Typically, Pahlen's colleague Dashkov reported in early 1811 that "by all signs the Spanish provinces of South America have decided to remain independent. The proclamations of the various *juntas* establishing new governments only until such time as these governments can again come under the authority of Ferdinand VII," he added, "are deceptive. . . . They make changes in order to be free, not to preserve their countries for the old government."[78] Count Rumiantsev, too, seemed convinced that independence was inevitable, and available evidence suggests that the tsar also shared this view.

As a result of Russia's expanding ties with America, and in response to the changing political status of the Spanish and Portuguese colonies, a decision was made in the early summer of 1811 to reorganize Russian diplomatic and consular representation in the New World. On 28 July 1811, the tsar appointed Count Pahlen Russian envoy to the Portuguese court at Rio de Janeiro,[79] naming Dashkov to replace him as minister plenipotentiary to the government of the United States.[80] Poletica and Ivanov were likewise reassigned to Brazil as counsellor and secretary, respectively, of the new Russian legation.[81] Thus, by 1811 Latin America had become of sufficient concern to the court of St. Petersburg to warrant the transferral of an entire, albeit small, embassy staff—its first with experience in the New World—from Philadelphia to Rio de Janeiro. Pahlen, observed Count Rumiantsev, seemed destined "to visit all the sovereigns of America." If still another state appeared in the Western Hemisphere, he added, the tsar might well charge Pahlen with the establishment of Russian representation there, too.[82] Pahlen himself, however, seems to have had serious misgivings about embarking on so exotic a venture. He finally accepted the post on the understanding that his tour of service would not exceed two years.[83] Poletica, on the other hand, declined the new assignment, fearing the possible effects of a "torrid climate" on his health.[84]

In September 1811, Alexander detailed the goals and objectives of Pahlen's mission in South America. With the removal of the Portuguese court to Brazil, the tsar wrote, a single object had held Russian interest in that distant country, namely trade, "the advantages of which seem unquestionable. The merchants all hold this view," he observed, "and the latest treaty signed in Rio de Janeiro with Great Britain further attests to its importance. In sharing this trade with the English, Russia will certainly acquire a good market, but Brazil, too, will discover great advantages. As a tributary of English trade, she has received not only the products of English industry, but also second-hand merchandise from northern Europe. In exchange, she can sell only a small part of the products of her soil, whereas Russia, supplying her own merchandise at a better price, has need of all the local products of the Portuguese colonies."[85]

It would appear, the tsar noted, that the Portuguese themselves appreciated the advantages of such trade, for despite his interdiction of commercial intercourse with Portugal proper, they had continued to cultivate Russian favor and had even sent a minister to St. Petersburg from Rio de Janeiro.[86] "In this state of affairs," the tsar advised Pahlen, "it is fitting that you cultivate the Portuguese minister's inclination to institute direct trade with Russia, assuring him of my complete concurrence in this matter. In keeping with this principle," he continued, "it is desirable that the court of Brazil not let the yoke which England has imposed on it through her treaties of alliance and commerce weigh too heavily. You will seek with as much circumspection as dexterity, if not to destroy [England's] political influence, at least to weaken her commercial influence by making clear that in both respects Russia offers fewer inconveniences and many more advantages."[87] Alexander further instructed his envoy to impress upon the Portuguese court the preferability of residence in Rio de Janeiro, as opposed to Lisbon. In Portugal, he observed, the crown's very existence was constantly exposed to the vicissitudes of power politics, whereas in Brazil, surrounded by the wealth of that vast territory, "it could at once guarantee its independence and attain a place among the great powers."[88]

The tsar also drew Pahlen's attention to the broader question of Latin American independence. "It is to be supposed," he wrote, "that the court of Rio de Janeiro follows very closely the affairs of Spanish America." On the one hand, he suggested, the emancipation of Spanish America might undermine the Portuguese monarchy, resulting eventually in the formation of several independent Brazilian states. On the other, the extinction of the male line in Spain might move the court of Rio de Janeiro, through the Spanish infanta, wife of the prince-regent, to lay claim to Spain's New World possessions. England, however, almost certainly would oppose any such aggrandizement of Portuguese dominion, in which case, the tsar speculated, Russia might effect a balance of power in the Western Hemisphere favorable to a furtherance of its own New World interests. Alexander thus instructed Pahlen to sound out Portuguese sentiments on these matters and to determine more precisely British thinking on the future of Brazil and the neighboring Spanish territories.[89]

Finally, the tsar ordered caution in responding to solicitations for support tendered by partisans of Spanish American independence. As such overtures had already been made directly to the court of St. Petersburg, he observed, Pahlen could expect more of the same during his residence in Rio de Janeiro. In that event, the count was "to refrain from making any commitments which might prove premature. Until such time as circumstances determine which side expediency would have us take," the tsar wrote, "it is best to ply [the insurgents'] ego with an adroitly qualified prospect of assistance should their new political existence one day be recognized." Insofar as possible, such implied offers of trade were to be couched in the rhetoric of already existing regulations permitting the entry of neutral vessels into Russian ports.[90]

Having decided to establish an embassy in Brazil, the tsar moved at the same time to create a consulate general, to which post he named M. I. Labenskii, a career diplomat who previously had served as Russian consul-general in Paris.[91] In lengthy instructions generally paralleling those issued to Pahlen, Alexander advised Labenskii that "the proximity of the Spanish possessions and their frequent and continual intercourse with Brazil" would allow him to gather "useful intelligence on the political status of these colonies, and, perhaps, to establish commercial relations with them." Whenever possible, Labenskii was to meet Spanish colonists present in Rio de Janeiro, and, through such acquaintances, to further Russian commercial interests in the neighboring Spanish territories. The home government, Alexander added, would render him whatever assistance propriety would permit in the pursuit of these ends.[92]

In addition to the embassy and consulate general in Rio de Janeiro, the tsarist government also opened a consulate in Funchal, on the island of Madeira, to which post it appointed the then director of the consular division of the ministry of foreign affairs, F. F. Borel.[93] The tsar was guided in his decision to establish this new consulate by a desire "to expand more and more the commercial relations of His Empire with the States under the dominion of His Highness the Prince Regent of Portugal." Included in Borel's jurisdiction were the Azores, the Cape Verde Islands, and the captaincy-general of Pernambuco.[94] Following his arrival in Funchal, Borel in turn named vice-consuls in Pernambuco and on the island of São Miguel, in the Azores, acting in both instances to promote what he viewed as the "incalculable advantages" of expanded Russian trade with the Portuguese overseas dominions.[95]

Count Pahlen departed the United States for Brazil in the spring of 1812.[96] One of his first official acts after arriving in Rio de Janeiro was to inform the Portuguese court of the tsar's desire to confer the Order of St. Anne (second class) on Navarro de Andrade in recognition of the latter's efforts "to promote trade relations between Russia and Brazil."[97] Permission to accept the Russian decoration was granted immediately, reflecting once again the mutual interest of both courts in expanding their commercial ties.[98]

In the meantime, difficulties arose in connection with Labenskii's appointment as Russian consul-general. The tsarist diplomat was known to sympathize with Napoleon and was even said to have received material favors from the French emperor.[99] In July 1811, the Portuguese envoy in St. Petersburg strongly urged that, upon his arrival in Brazil, Labenskii be placed under police surveillance.[100] Subsequently, his appointment was withdrawn at the request of the Portuguese court,[101] and he was replaced by Georg Heinrich von Langsdorff, who for the next sixteen years would devote uncommon energy to the promotion of Russian relations with South America and in particular with Brazil.[102]

Langsdorff was ideally suited for this post. "A scholar and traveller, a man of varied accomplishments who had mastered the Portuguese language, he was perfect," in the words of one historian, "for the dispatch of consular affairs in Rio de Janeiro."[103] Notwithstanding his total dedication to science, he never lost sight of the practical interests of trade and imperial expansion that had brought him to South America. In one of his first dispatches from the Brazilian capital, he emphasized the advantages of direct Russo-Brazilian trade. Our vast empire, he wrote, "offers a thousand interesting objects that our subjects could export to greater advantage than the other nations who purchase our products in order to sell them here at great profit."[104] In a subsequent dispatch, he specified those goods of Russian origin that could profitably- be exported to Brazil,[105] while during the first half of 1814 he explored the possibilities of expanded trade directly with interested

Brazilian merchants.[106] That same year, he reported with satisfaction the arrival in Brazil of the first Russian merchant vessels to enter South American waters.[107]

Count Pahlen, for his part, reported regularly on events in South America. Despite royalist victories, he remained convinced that independence was inevitable for all of Latin America. With clear insight, he wrote in October 1813 that Spain was "too weak and too preoccupied with her own self-preservation to be in any condition to force the recognition of her authority—from California to Cape Horn—by peoples aware of their own strength and who perceive the advantages of self-government."[108] He further observed that "the removal of the Portuguese government to Brazil has freed this country of colonial bonds forever; even if the court should return someday to Lisbon, it will be unable to restore the old restrictions; Brazil has occupied a place among the independent states."[109]

Pahlen's departure from Brazil in June 1814 closed, in a sense, the first period of Russian diplomatic endeavor in America.[110] Achievements were modest, but not without significance. In a few short years, Russia had learned much about the Western Hemisphere, and, its European preoccupations notwithstanding, had managed to establish a formal presence in both North and South America. From this point forth, Russian responses to developments in the New World would become increasingly complex.

Relations with Spain and Portugal

Much of the growing complexity of Russian responses to political change in Latin America derived from Russia's formal relations with the crowns of Spain and Portugal. Severely strained in the first years of the nineteenth century by the conflicting alliances of Spain and Portugal, on the one hand, and by the ambivalent posture in European affairs of the Russian court, on the other, these relations were still further tried by the conclusion of the Franco-Russian accord at Tilsit in 1807.

Prior to Tilsit, Alexander I had viewed the Iberian Peninsula as a key link in a chain of alliances designed to constrain French expansionism. Accordingly, in May 1805, the tsar instructed his newly appointed envoy to the Spanish court, G. A. Stroganov, "to prepare the way for the most prominent and durable of ties between Russia and Spain, and, insofar as possible, to turn the court of Madrid from its servitude to France."[111] It was equally important for the "common cause," he declared, to reestablish peaceful relations between Spain and Great Britain. Barring such a normalization of ties, the tsar prophetically observed, Spain might stand to lose her overseas possessions.[112] Of more immediate concern, however, was the establishment of a "federative alliance" between Russia, Spain, Portugal, and the sovereign states of Italy, for this, Alexander held, was "the most effective means of containing France within her just limits and of assuring the tranquility and independence of southern Europe."[113]

Tilsit, however, precluded any further pursuit of these objectives. On 27 November 1807, the Portuguese court hastily abandoned Lisbon to Marshal Junot, embarking for South America under the protection of a British fleet commanded by Sir Sidney Smith. Shortly thereafter, Napoleon dispatched two additional armies to the Peninsula for the purpose of securing Spain, as well. In the resultant confusion, the Spanish royal family was lured to Bayonne, where on 5 May 1808, Charles IV abdicated in favor of the French emperor. The crown prince, too, was obliged to renounce all pretentions to the throne of Spain. Napoleon then maneuvered the Council of Castile to select his elder brother, Joseph, as the new Spanish monarch.[114]

Meanwhile, Spanish opposition to the French intruders resulted in the spontaneous formation of provincial *juntas* throughout the country. After an initial period in which these *juntas* vied for individual primacy, there emerged a central *junta* charged with prosecuting a war of liberation against the French and with forming a provisional government to rule in the absence of the king. Redoubled efforts by Napoleon to secure his Iberian flank, however, soon forced the central *junta* to withdraw from Aranjuez to Seville, and, subsequently, from there to the Isle of León, near Cádiz. There, on 29 January 1810, it created a five-man regency council and provided for the convening of a representative assembly, or *cortes*. Definite shape was thus given to a government that, existing precariously on an island only barely beyond the reach of Napoleon's occupying armies, held itself up as the sole legitimate repository of royal authority in Spain for the duration of the Peninsular War.

By the beginning of 1810, therefore, the proponents of Russian expansionism in the New World faced mounting obstacles to the realization of their ends. Direct ties with the Portuguese crown had been seriously impaired by the removal of that crown to Brazil. As already noted, it was not until the summer of 1812 that the tsar managed to place a diplomatic representative in Rio de Janeiro, while in the interim the Portuguese chargé d'affaires in St. Petersburg sharply scored the Russian court for its tacit complicity in the fall of Portugal.[115] At the same time, two contending régimes had appeared in Spain, each demanding formal recognition by the European powers. The pragmatism of Tilsit moved Alexander to extend such recognition publicly to Napoleon's brother, Joseph, whose envoy the tsar received as the accredited representative of the Spanish crown.[116] In the summer of 1809, however, the central *junta* approached Alexander through an undercover agent,[117] who sought to persuade the tsar that Russian interests lay in the preservation of Spanish independence and the restoration to the Spanish throne of Ferdinand VII. The tsar responded through an intermediary that circumstances did not permit him openly to support the Spanish opposition. Things might change, he added, and, in the meantime, it would be well for the *junta*'s agent to maintain his channels of communication.[118]

The events of spring and summer 1808 caused much confusion among foreign diplomats accredited to the Spanish court. While many chose to abandon their posts, the Russian minister determined to remain in Madrid. The tsar approved Stroganov's decision, instructing him in May of that year to establish formal relations with Joseph Bonaparte, who would soon enter the Spanish capital.[119] By the time Stroganov received these instructions, however, Joseph had already entered and quit the Spanish capital, withdrawing hastily to the Ebro River following the defeat of French forces at Bailén, in Andalusia. In the circumstances, Stroganov judged his instructions inapplicable, for any attempt to carry them out, he reasoned, would constitute an act of treachery in the eyes of the populace and provisional authorities. His presence in Madrid, therefore, ceased to serve any immediate purpose, in consequence of which he repaired to Lisbon.[120]

In one of his last dispatches from Madrid, Stroganov gave tacit endorsement to the central *junta*, as opposed to 'the collaborationist Council of Castile. The *junta*, he wrote, "was convened during those recent events which have removed Ferdinand VII from the throne of Spain; since then it has offered the most inflexible resistance to all measures tending to place Spain under foreign domination. . . ."[121] The Council of Castile, on the other hand, had discredited itself "in the eyes of the entire nation," for it was guilty of "criminal condescension toward the French authorities," of issuing edicts "in the name of a power which it had no authority to recognize," and, by complicity, of "the elevation of Joseph to the Spanish throne."[122]

Circumstances, however, precluded Russian recognition of the central *junta*. Indeed, the tsar soon appointed Count N. G. Repnin to replace Stroganov in Madrid, taking care to remind his new envoy that Russian foreign policy continued to rest on "a close alliance with France." The main objective of this policy, he observed, was "to reestablish peace on the continent by restricting the ruinous despotism which Great Britain exercises on the seas and which she is unable to consolidate except by dividing the continental powers. . . ."[123] Even here, however, the tsar revealed the deep pragmatism that underlay his approach to foreign affairs. In the event that Joseph Bonaparte were to invite the Russian minister to accompany him at the head of his Peninsular forces, Repnin, himself a military officer, was to accept without hesitation. "In this way," the tsar advised his envoy, "you will be so much better able to appraise the true state of affairs [in Spain] . . . and to keep my ministry precisely informed." But, he hastened to add, "you shall employ only the most reliable of means and occasions to relay this sort of information, so as not to compromise yourself. . . . Show much devotion to the king," concluded Alexander, "but do not commit yourself on anything, above all in my name. . . ."[124]

Repnin, however, failed even to reach his place of assignment, for Napoleon closed the Iberian Peninsula to foreign diplomats. The French government, Repnin reported in the fall of 1810, "viewed with repugnance" the presence of foreign envoys in Madrid, although he himself had managed to secure entry for one of his subordinates, P. O. Morgenheim.[125] Convinced that authorization to enter Spain would continue to be withheld from ranking diplomats such as himself, Repnin returned to St. Petersburg in March 1811.[126] Official relations between Russia and occupied Spain thus remained anchored in Paris.

Meanwhile, the newly formed regency, fugitive on the Isle of León, had dispatched an undercover agent to St. Petersburg to seek Russian support of the loyalist cause. The regency had acted on the advice of Antonio Colombí y Payet, a Spanish merchant and long-time resident in the Russian capital, selecting for the mission Francisco de Zea Bermúdez, also a merchant and member of an important commercial house in Málaga that was closely affiliated with Colombí's St. Petersburg firm.[127] Proceeding first to Madrid, where, through the office of Antonio Ugarte,[128] he managed to secure a French passport, Zea Bermúdez reached the Russian capital in December 1810.[129] There, once Colombí had assured official acquaintances that his associate was indeed an authorized representative of the regency, Zea entered into preliminary talks with the Russian court.[130] By order of Alexander I, these talks remained in total secrecy. The tsar chose not even to apprise his minister of foreign affairs, Count Rumiantsev, about them, preferring to entrust the entire matter to his personal friend and confidant, R. A. Koshelev.[131] Initial discussions examined a possible alliance between Russia and the Spanish regency in the event of a Franco-Russian conflict. In February 1811, the tsar informed Colombí that he had become convinced that war with France was all but inevitable and that once hostilities had actually broken out, he would conclude formal treaties of alliance with England and the Spanish regency. Colombí, in turn, communicated the tsar's views to Zea Bermúdez, who immediately embarked for Cádiz.[132]

Zea reached the loyalist stronghold in May 1811, reporting directly to the regency on Alexander's gradual return to the foreign policy assumptions of 1805. On June 29 he again departed for St. Petersburg, now empowered to conclude a formal treaty with the Russian court.[133] In a manner reminiscent of more recent times, Old World statesmen endeavored with mounting frenzy to dissipate the strength of a continental colossus through calculated entanglements on the European periphery. Spanish and English diplomats, notes one scholar, "pursued a single, exceedingly simple end: to induce Alexander to concentrate maximum forces on Russia's western border so as to occupy there a maximum of French forces." Alexander, for his part, sought to divert Napoleon from Russia by heightening hostilities in southwestern Europe.[134] If war should break out in the north, declared the tsar, Spain could best serve the common interest by driving at the very heart of France. If at the same time England were to launch diversionary actions against Italy and the Hanseatic towns, an end to the misfortunes of Europe would be assured.[135]

When Zea Bermúdez returned to Russia in the summer of 1811, he found the tsar again reluctant to deal directly with the Spanish regency.[136] While in part the result of Alexander's wish not to provoke Napoleon prematurely into war, the tsar's attitude appears further to have been influenced by the overtures of Cortland L. Parker, who, in the name of the provisional government of Caracas, sought Russian recognition of Venezuelan independence. "Under the overt protection of the French Ambassador, . . . and the covert but very active influence of the American legation," Zea reported, "the matter had already taken such shape that when at last I discovered it, it was in fact on the docket and about to be discussed by the council of state, with much probability of success. . . ."[137]

Having learned of the Parker mission, Zea vigorously protested the hearing Alexander had accorded the insurgents of northern South America, labeling them as "seditionaries and disrupters of the social order." Zea further underscored the devious ways of Napoleon's agents, the inviability of the Franco-Russian alliance, and the very considerable benefit to be derived by Russia from a rapprochement with Spain and Great Britain. So successful was his argument, he informed the regency, that both the tsar and his council of state had been moved to reject Parker's proposals.[138] While Zea may have held an inflated view of his powers of persuasion, Russia did in fact remain firm in the decision not to endorse the new political order in Venezuela.

By the first months of 1812, Alexander I had lost hope of any further accommodation with Napoleon,[139] and therefore set a course toward rapprochement with Spain and Great Britain. In February of that year, the tsar authorized Koshelev to inform Zea Bermúdez that henceforth Russia would (1) maintain a show of military force along its frontiers for the purpose of intimidating Napoleon; (2) seek no further accommodation with France; (3) endeavor, short of military action, to divert Napoleon's attention from the Iberian Peninsula to northern Europe; and (4) facilitate the entry of British vessels into its ports, despite the prohibitions then in force. In return, Koshelev advised Zea, Russia would expect England and Spain to take the appropriate military actions in support of a Russian effort should Napoleon launch an eastern campaign.[140]

As an indication of his commitment to the regency, Alexander at last authorized Count Rumiantsev to deal directly with Zea Bermúdez. Then, in April 1812, the tsar offered to sign an accord with the regency in return for a gratification of six million *pesos fuertes* (1 *peso fuerte* = 8 silver *reales*). Aware of the regency's severe financial straits and resultant inability to provide such a sum, Zea determined to solicit British assistance in underwriting the desired treaty. He departed for London almost immediately and there received guarded expressions of encouragement from Lord Castlereagh, who said he would pursue the matter through the British envoy to Stockholm. Zea's return to St. Petersburg, however, coincided with the French invasion of Russia and events now precipitated the pending realignment of European powers.[141] In the first days of July, Russia concluded a treaty of peace and alliance with Great Britain. On the twentieth of that month, a similar accord was signed at Velikie Luki between Russia and the Spanish regency.[142]

A paradigm of brevity, the Russo-Spanish accord consisted of a short preamble and five concise articles. It formalized an alliance between the two powers, committed each to prosecute the war against "the common enemy," and provided for the promotion of mutually beneficial trade relations. Politically, Article three was the most significant part of the accord. "His Majesty the Emperor of all the Russias," it read, "recognizes as legitimate the general and extraordinary Cortes assembled at Cádiz, as well as the constitution which they have decreed and sanctioned."[143] Russia thus became the first European power to endorse the Spanish constitution of 1812, an act it was later to disavow. Not even England, extending de facto recognition to the regency from its inception, offered formal approval of this liberal document.[144]

Conclusion of the Treaty of Velikie Luki opened the way for an exchange of ambassadors between the two governments. Indeed, the regency, even before learning of the accord, had appointed its former secretary of state, Eusebio de Bardaxí y Azara, to head the Spanish legation in St. Petersburg.[145] Tsar Alexander, in turn, named D. P. Tatishchev, an experienced diplomat of consummate finesse, to serve as his minister plenipotentiary in Spain.[146]

Bardaxí reached his new post toward the end of 1812. Shortly after his arrival in the Russian capital, he filed a lengthy background report to the regency on his counterpart, Tatishchev. The Russian envoy, he wrote, "belonged to one of the oldest families in Russia and was associated with the finest houses of the empire." He was not a wealthy man, however, and lived mainly from his salary as a government servant. "He is talented and knowledgeable," Bardaxí added, "and has always expressed opposition to the French, although not everyone agrees as to the strength of his principles." Moreover, he was said to have a great thirst for honors and money, and, allegedly, had hastened his departure from St. Petersburg because of mounting personal debts.[147]

Tatishchev's immediate objective was to determine the actual authority wielded in Spain by the regency, especially its ability to conclude binding treaties with foreign powers. The Russian court, it is clear, still doubted the stability of the provisional Spanish government. "Whatever Tatishchev's evaluation," Bardaxí advised the regency, "he will manage to secure the greatest advantage possible for his Government and Homeland."[148]

The regency and *cortes*, however, were spared Tatishchev's anticipated scrutiny, for the Russian envoy delayed his arrival in Spain until after the restoration of Ferdinand VII. Tatishchev had left Russia in December 1812, but proceeded only as far as London, where he tarried for more than a year before continuing on to his assigned post. It was during this sojourn in England that he first articulated his views on the colonial question in the New World. At this time, for example, he made special note of the impact of Anglo-American independence on Spanish America. "The emancipation of the English colonies," he wrote, "was too seductive an example not to sow the seeds of rebellion in the Spanish possessions. . . . At present they can be recovered, but everything indicates that this will require a long time."[149]

In the spring of 1814, Tatishchev again addressed himself to the colonial question. "In large part," he wrote the tsar, "Spain's overseas possessions are the victims of all the horrors of civil war, brutally perpetrated by both sides. The spirit of independence is spreading with such rapidity that it is already doubtful whether Spain will ever restore her rule."[150] The following fall, Tatishchev arrived in Madrid, there to mix increasingly in the internal affairs of the Spanish state.

The stage was thus set for a period of direct Russian involvement in the turmoil of Spanish America. Spanning the years 1815–1818, this involvement derived from a policy of calculated pragmatism that sought to advance Russian imperial interests at the expense of a prostrate Spain. The bases of this policy had emerged already in 1812, when the court of St. Petersburg first advanced the concept of direct material compensation in return for Russian political recognition. Although events had moved Alexander I to conclude the Treaty of Velikie Luki in the absence of compensatory gratuities, the underlying objectives of that policy continued to guide Russian relations with the Spanish crown in the post-Napoleonic period. Russo-Portuguese relations, in turn, were of an analogous nature.

6. Colonial Pacification
and the Dilemma of Intervention

The fall of Napoleonic France and the subsequent reordering of continental affairs gave play to the grand pageantry of congress diplomacy that was to dominate European politics in the immediate postwar period. The great gatherings of monarchs and statesmen and the often heated discussions of the principles of legitimate rule, however, were from the outset conducted against the backdrop of impending revolutionary change. Enlightened despotism, the cornerstone of eighteenth-century political philosophy, showed signs of stress in the face of incipient industrialization. In the generalized crisis of the Napoleonic years, the issues of the French Revolution acquired new urgency among a greatly widened circle of committed social critics.

While these issues would come to a head only after 1820, events portended a mortal challenge to the old order long before. Proclamation of the Spanish Constitution of 1812 and its summary revocation following the restoration of Ferdinand VII in 1814 dramatically revealed the tenor of future political struggles—struggles that within a decade would sweep across Europe's southern periphery, threatening the very foundations of absolute monarchy. At the same time, America began to represent a threat to the established political order of the Old World. European statesmen of absolutist persuasion found the example of the United States disquieting and even more so the specter of additional republican régimes in the New World territories of Spain and Portugal. The matter of colonial pacification, therefore, became a major issue in the diplomacy and politics of post-Napoleonic Europe.

Tsarist Russia, for its part, had achieved the pinnacle of power and influence on the European continent. From the signing of the Act of Holy Alliance in September 1815 to the Congress of Aix-la-Chapelle three years later, writes one historian, "St. Petersburg became the diplomatic capital of Europe."[1] In sharp contrast to the preceding years of continental blockade, Russia now entered a period in which it was at no time faced with serious military threats from abroad.[2] During these years, Tsar Alexander concerned himself not only with the pressing matters of continental reconstruction but also with the pursuit of Russian New World interests and the related problem of revolution in colonial Latin America.

The tsar's obsession with imparting a new moral order to the conduct of international relations, itself the driving force behind the Holy Alliance, has been the source of much confusion about the real nature of tsarist objectives in the Western Hemisphere. "The most striking thing about the attitude of the Tsar in the colonial question," wrote Dexter Perkins in 1923, "is its moderation. Here as elsewhere, Alexander manifests an earnest desire to practice that concert of action which he preached, not to dictate a policy of his own."[3] "But the Holy Alliance stood as a symbol of Alexander's craving for a more inclusive and autocratic organization," counters William W. Kaufmann. Indeed, the tsar merely used the colonial question to further Russian interests in Europe.[4] "The uprising of the [Spanish American] colonists against their 'lawful ruler,' " adds V. M. Miroshevskii, "was by its very nature inimical to the counterrevolutionary policies of Alexander I."[5] Tsarist policy toward the revolted colonies of Spanish America, according to William Spence Robertson, derived from "the doctrine of legitimacy," "certain principles enunciated in the Treaty [sic] of the Holy Alliance," and "the idealistic spirit of Alexander I."[6] Lobanov-Rostovsky, in turn, has written that "Alexander I was determined to help reinstate the dominion of Spain over her colonies in an effort to stem the tide of revolution which he rightly feared would eventually reach Spain proper."[7] From 1817 to 1825, concludes L. Yu. Slëzkin, tsarist policy toward the independence struggle in Spanish America rested on the principles of legitimacy, and, consequently, "sought ways and means to restore the sovereignty of Spain over her rebellious colonies."[8]

The issue has further been clouded by an incomplete understanding of the mechanics of tsarist diplomacy in the post-Napoleonic era, several students of this period having imputed an independence of action to Russian diplomats inconsistent with the personality and style of their sovereign. Particularly conspicuous in the diplomacy of colonial pacification were Carlo Andrea Pozzo di Borgo, Alexander's ambassador in Paris, and D. P. Tatishchev, Russian minister plenipotentiary in Madrid. These champions of the Spanish cause, wrote C. K. Webster, "devised extensive schemes in which even the conquest of Portugal was involved, . . ." yet they "never received the support of the Tsar. . . ."[9] "That the Tsar's sympathies were with Spain need hardly be doubted," asserts Perkins, "but the first move to identify Russia with the solution of the American question came not from him, but from Pozzo, acting . . . on his own initiative."[10] Tatishchev's scheme for "giving Russian naval support to a Spanish expedition against South America, . . ." declares Kaufmann, "lacked the official sanction of the Tsar. . . ."[11]

Each of these assertions suggests a lack of continuity in Russian foreign policy, which, upon closer examination, proves erroneous. As rightly noted by Robert M. Slusser, "Alexander's assistants in the execution of foreign affairs included a number of men of marked ability, but neither they nor the Ministry of Foreign Affairs were granted a share in the actual formulation of policy. They might advise, but it was the Tsar who made the final decisions and who frequently initiated policies without consulting his advisers."[12] "Although it is true that after the winter of 1812 Alexander I began to think of himself in Messianic terms as the liberator of the European nations," adds Hajo Holborn, "he did not forget even then the stark interests of Russian power."[13] Indeed, herein lies the significance of Count Rumiantsev's exit from the foreign ministry in February 1814: the tsar having taken full direction of all state business, there was no longer any place for an independent-minded foreign minister. Accordingly, the functions of that office were entrusted to the diligent but subservient Count Nesselrode.[14]

The years 1815–1818 mark a transition in tsarist New World objectives from the pursuit of broad commercial and geopolitical advantage throughout the Western Hemisphere to the defense of a modest presence in California and Brazil. In the flush of victory over Napoleon, Alexander I pressed for imperial advantage on all fronts, although almost immediately he began to obfuscate the practical considerations of *Realpolitik* with a decidedly Messianic view of Russia's historical destiny. Yet if, as suggested by Lord Castlereagh, Alexander was so absorbed in the "sublime mysticism and nonsense" of the Holy Alliance as to impair his perception of Russian interests in Europe, such impairment of judgment did not immediately extend to America. Here, he continued to pursue the pragmatic ends proposed by Kruzenshtern, Rezanov, and Rumiantsev. Indeed, even after leaving the ministry of foreign affairs Count Rumiantsev actively promoted those New World policies that, as foreign minister, he had himself helped to shape. For a time, it seems, he continued to enjoy the tsar's confidence in matters pertaining to overseas expansion and almost certainly was the guiding force behind the voyages of the *Suvorov, Kutuzov,* and *Kamchatka* to the west coast of South America. Significantly, Rumiantsev personally organized and financed the voyage of the *Riurik,* which in 1816 first carried the Russian flag to Chile.[15] Even the calculated bestowal of the Order of St. Anne upon Peruvian viceroy José Fernando de Abascal and Pedro Abadía, chief factor of the Royal Philippine Company in Lima, suggested the subtle hand of the artful count.

The shift to a less ambitious policy in Latin America reflected a sober reevaluation of attainable objectives in the New World. On the one hand, the restoration of Ferdinand VII to the Spanish throne soon involved the major European powers in Iberian colonial affairs, thereby restricting Russia's options for independent action in the Western Hemisphere. On the other hand, the experiences of Captains Lazarev, Kotzebue, Hagemeister, Ponafidin, and Golovnin revealed the absence of real advantage in direct trade ties with the west coast ports of South America. Though Russian ships had on two occasions effected modestly profitable transactions in Peru, the singularity of those transactions only underscored the marginality of such ties to the overriding object of tsarist concern in the New World, namely Russian America. At the same time, the original impetus for the creation of an independent merchant marine capable of competing with the British all but disappeared with the lifting of the continental blockade. Despite earlier pleas for the liberation of Russian trade from control by foreign middlemen, Russian imports and exports once again moved largely in foreign bottoms.[16] Indeed, direct trade ties with the sources of prized colonial goods ceased by and large to be an issue.

In these circumstances, Tsar Alexander abandoned further thought of concerted commercial expansion in Latin America, turning his attention instead to the preservation of limited Russian interests in Brazil and Alta California. Both of these areas, in turn, were directly related to the preservation of Russian holdings in the Pacific Northwest—Brazil as a key link in the chain of maritime communications between European Russia and Russian America; California as a source of foodstuffs for the colonies. Viewed in this light, tsarist responses to the independence movement in Latin America reflect a logic generally overlooked by those who have written on the subject, a logic rooted in the confusing interplay between international power politics, the ideology of legitimacy, and Alexander's gradual rethinking of his imperial priorities.

Collective Mediation

At Vienna, the allied powers excluded the colonial question from their discussions, for neither Spain nor Portugal desired outside intervention in this matter, nor was Great Britain willing to allow such intervention.[17] Accordingly, the Treaty of Vienna made only a single reference to Latin America, this in Article 107, which provided for the restitution of French Guiana to France.[18] The courts of Europe were too preoccupied with the immediate business of normalizing continental affairs to accord more than passing attention to political turmoil in the overseas empires of Spain and Portugal. Events in South America, however, soon thrust the colonial question before the diplomatic councils of the Old World.

In the summer of 1816, João VI moved to occupy the long-disputed territory of Uruguay, entrusting the campaign to General Carlos Frederico Lecor and the Divisão de Voluntários Reais, recently arrived from Europe. Numbering some 4,800 men, the royal volunteers bested the *montoneras* of Uruguayan patriot José Gervasio Artigas in several armed encounters and in January 1817 occupied Montevideo. For the next five years, the eastern bank of the River Plate remained at least nominally in Portuguese hands.[19]

Upon learning that Lecor had secured the Uruguayan capital, João VI addressed a personal letter to Ferdinand VII, in which he sought to justify the invasion on the grounds that Spain was unable to control the insurgents of the River Plate and that as a result Rio Grande de São Pedro [Rio Grande do Sul] was in imminent danger of attack "by the considerable forces which the audacious Artigas had assembled for this purpose." Anticipating that Ferdinand would doubt the sincerity of his intentions, he sought to reassure the Spanish monarch that Lecor's troops did not intend to conquer the Banda Oriental, "but rather to occupy it as the only line of defense available to Brazil as long as her security is endangered by the revolutionary state of the neighboring Colonies." He was, he added, ready to reach an understanding with Ferdinand on this and all other matters of mutual interest to the two crowns, "without the interference of any other Power."[20] Ferdinand, however, had already taken Spain's case to the allied powers. The dispute thus became an object of European diplomacy.[21]

From the first the Spanish crown sought the support of the court of St. Petersburg, apprising the tsar of Portuguese designs on the Banda Oriental even before those designs had been carried out. On 16 December 1816, Zea Bermúdez advised the Russian court of the impending invasion and requested the tsar's support of the reclamations that Spain would make against the court of Rio de Janeiro.[22] Alexander expressed dismay over the state of affairs described by Zea and took immediate steps to strengthen the Spanish position. "His Imperial

Majesty, earnestly desiring to see removed the just apprehensions occasioned His Catholic Majesty by the threatening measures of the Court of Brazil," Count Nesselrode informed the Spanish envoy, "has ordered His Minister in Paris to prepare with his colleagues an appeal to Rio-Janeiro for a redress of the grievances of the Court of Spain." Moreover, Nesselrode added, the tsar had instructed Pozzo to propose to the allied ambassadors that the Portuguese court be pressured into a prompt rectification of its actions in the River Plate by a threat of collective intervention on behalf of Spain.[23]

In actual fact, Nesselrode had not yet prepared Pozzo's instructions. He did so, however, three days later and in essentially the same language as he had expressed to Zea. Given the urgency of the matter and in order to avoid possible misunderstandings occasioned by the slowness of communications between Europe and Brazil, the tsar wished the allied powers to inform the Portuguese court that failure to explain promptly its actions in the Banda Oriental and to make the desired rectifications would oblige the powers collectively to assist Spain in the recovery of its occupied possessions, to which end they would employ "all their influence and all their energies." Pozzo was instructed to prevail upon the allied ambassadors in Paris to adopt a common stance on the matter of Portuguese intervention in the River Plate, and, with a single voice, to address the court of Rio de Janeiro in terms analogous to those outlined by the tsar.[24]

In February 1817, the plenipotentiaries of Austria, England, France, Prussia, and Russia met in Paris to consider the Portuguese intervention in Uruguay. After a month of deliberations, the five powers rejected the explanations offered by the Portuguese, to wit that (1) the court of Rio de Janeiro could no longer tolerate the threat posed to its southern frontiers by the existence of revolutionary régimes in the River Plate and (2) possession of the disputed territory had been taken in the name of Portugal rather than Spain so as not to arouse all the rebel forces of Spanish America against Brazil.[25] In a joint declaration issued on 16 March 1817, the powers announced their intention to mediate in the dispute, as requested by Spain, and to prevent "by all means at their disposal" a military confrontation between Spain and Portugal, as such an encounter would have grave consequences not only for these two states but for the whole of Europe as well. The powers demanded that João VI clarify his intentions and that he take immediate and decisive steps to rectify the indefensible occupation of the Banda Oriental. Should the court of Rio de Janeiro fail to respond in an appropriate manner, the declaration concluded, then Spain, "whose prudent and moderate conduct has been applauded by all

Нас. Илабе — Peint par Isabey

Графъ Карлъ Андреевичъ   Le Comte Charles Andréewitch
Пошцо-ди-Борго,   Pozzo di Borgo,
1764 — 1842   1764 — 1842

3. Count Carlo Andrea Pozzo di Borgo, Russian Minister Plenipotentiary to
France (1814–1834), senior tsarist diplomat on the European Continent

Europe, would find in the rightness of her cause and in the assistance of her allies ample means to repair the injuries which she had suffered."[26]

While containing a veiled threat of concerted military action on behalf of Spain, the March declaration fell short of the firm stand proposed by the court of St. Petersburg. "It is to be feared," Pozzo had advised Nesselrode a short time before, "that [the declaration] will not be as strong or as complete as both the nature of the case and my instructions would have me wish." Although it would serve to embarrass the Portuguese, he added, it would not convince them that the European powers spoke in earnest.[27] Nonetheless, the declaration bore a distinctly tsarist stamp, for its very wording paralleled that contained in Pozzo's instructions of three months earlier.[28] Indeed, Pozzo appears to have been the prime mover behind the Paris talks and the one most responsible for bringing the powers to a united, albeit temporary, stand on the Uruguayan question.[29] By this early date, the tsar had placed himself squarely on the side of the Spanish crown in the diplomacy of colonial affairs. Moreover, he had shown himself ready to use armed force or the threat thereof to achieve specific ends in Spanish and Portuguese America.[30]

Russia's zealous support of the Spanish crown immediately aroused the suspicion of the other powers, causing the courts of London, Vienna, and Berlin to withhold full endorsement of the Russian position on the Banda Oriental.[31] While the Spanish court sought means of conciliation, wrote the Portuguese envoy to St. Petersburg, "the Russian proposal appeared to include measures of force."[32] The tsar, Zea Bermúdez advised his government, was encountering considerable opposition from the other cabinets, "especially those of Vienna and St. James, who have openly expressed surprise that, in response to our initial call, he should have declared himself so clearly and energetically in our favor. . . ."[33] Spain, observed the Austrian ambassador in the Russian capital, had requested "nothing more than the amicable mediation of the allied powers, and not their support in a war against Portugal." Moreover, he added, such support was impractical.[34] "As for the means to render substantive and truly effective the allied powers' support of Spain," the Russian court responded, "it seems hardly necessary to point out that, independent of direct military action in the occupied countries, each power by itself and all the powers collectively can, by simply severing their diplomatic and commercial relations with Brazil and Portugal, obtain the most prompt redress of the legitimate grievances articulated by Spain."[35]

Underlying these mounting tensions in the European alliance was the increasingly pronounced opposition of Anglo-Russian interests, both in Europe and America. "After 1815," writes Manfred Kossok, "this antagonism dominated the entire course of international relations, including the debates on the South American Question."[36] In almost all cases, adds C. K. Webster, tsarist policies were hostile to Britain.[37] At stake was tsarist political hegemony over Europe, briefly attained in the fall of 1814, but lost again following the battle of Waterloo and the second occupation of Paris in July 1815. Great Britain, in concert with Austria and Prussia, had moved to thwart the Russian diplomatic offensive. In response, Alexander I sought to bring the supportive Bourbon courts of France and Spain into the big-power alliance, there to offset the anti-Russian block. It was primarily to this end that Pozzo di Borgo, in Paris, and Tatishchev, in Madrid, now directed their energies.[38] And it was against this backdrop that Alexander increasingly came to view the colonial question, for Great Britain also sought "to eliminate all contending powers" from overseas matters. Russia rejected British pretensions of New World hegemony, however, and endeavored to further its own interests by promoting collective mediation of the Uruguayan dispute.[39] "To a considerable degree," writes L. A. Shur, "Russia's policy in the matter of Spanish America was determined by its efforts to use Spain in the struggle with England."[40]

If Russia and Great Britain had found it possible in March 1817 to adhere to the joint powers' declaration on the Banda Oriental, their ultimate objectives remained diametrically opposed.[41] On the one hand, British diplomacy aimed at weakening the Spanish crown to facilitate the defense of British interests in Portugal and the Mediterranean, while at the same time creating favorable conditions for the abolition of the slave trade and an extension of commercial ties with Spanish America. Russia, on the other hand, sought to restore Spain to great-power status and, in so doing, to undermine British interests in the Mediterranean and Latin America.[42] Both powers wished to see the Spanish colonies opened to foreign commerce. Russia, however, wished this accomplished under Spanish rather than British aegis in order to avoid favored-nation agreements such as the one imposed on the court of Rio de Janeiro by the British in 1810.[43] Free trade in the Spanish colonies with equal opportunity for all interested nations would serve Russian New World interests well. The establishment of such trade by a strong, allied Spanish crown would, in effect, make Russia a favored nation, particularly in those areas of immediate concern to the Russian court. "If Spain, with Russian assistance, could preserve its colonies," notes Shur, "then the conversion of California into a new possession of the Russian-American Company would be only a matter of time."[44]

The allied appeal to the Portuguese court for rectification of its action in the Banda Oriental received the delayed approval of Great Britain in April 1817 and was dispatched forthwith to Rio de Janeiro.[45] It was hoped, Pozzo di Borgo wrote Nesselrode, that Spain would refrain from any hostile action against Portugal until the Portuguese had responded to the appeal. While the Spanish crown was exceedingly irritated over the Uruguayan matter, he observed, Spain's domestic affairs were in such disarray that "destitution would probably take the place of prudence."[46] "For the moment," he reported a short time later, "the Court of Madrid requests no further steps [of the allied powers] and is content to await the outcome of that which we have just taken." Pending a response from the court of Rio de Janeiro, or until such time as that court's silence warranted a reopening of talks on the Banda Oriental, Pozzo advised Nesselrode, he could not prudently pursue the matter further.[47]

At about the same time, Saldanha da Gama addressed a confidential letter on the matter of allied mediation to Nesselrode's colleague, Capo d'Istria.[48] Resting heavily on the rhetorical artifices of the day, he lamented that the tsarist court should have formed "an opinion scarcely worthy of the sense of justice which [the Portuguese] Government has always shown." Saldanha accused the Russian court of overt partiality in the Hispano-Portuguese dispute and of offering Spain assistance surpassing that which had in fact been solicited. Moreover, he suggested, at tsarist instigation the powers were seeking to oblige the Portuguese court "to restore the rights of Spain before ascertaining if those rights had indeed been injured." "The day will come," he concluded, "when complete justice will be done to the noble and loyal views of my government, and when the Allies, informed of the true state of affairs and the real cause of such a hue and cry, recognize the candor of His Most Faithful Majesty's behavior and accord Him the esteem and consideration he so justly deserves."[49]

Capo d'Istria replied to the Portuguese envoy almost immediately. As for the alleged partiality of the tsarist court in favor of Spain, he advised Saldanha, "Russia is indeed Spain's Ally, as she is of all States who accept as the basis of their affairs the principles set forth in the act of 14/26 September 1815."[50] The stand adopted by the court of St. Petersburg in this matter reflected nothing more than a personal and therefore unbinding view of the tsar, which the other powers were free to adopt, modify, or reject. However, Capo d'Istria added, the joint appeal the allied powers had made to the Portuguese court "proves incontestably the identity of views of the intervening Cabinets in this affair, with the sole difference that ours is articulated in positive terms, while that of the other States is perhaps less explicit, although equally determined. . . ." Consequently, the Portuguese government had no cause for complaint, provided it agreed "to explain its actions and to facilitate an arrangement in accord with reason and justice. . . . I share with you," Capo d'Istria assured Saldanha, "the desire and hope for the success of an [allied] intervention which by its impartiality and good intention leaves no room for disquiet, and which above all is beyond reproach because it has as its object justice and the maintenance of the general peace."[51]

By 1817, Russo-Portuguese relations showed clear signs of strain. For some time João VI had looked to Russia as a partial counterweight to British preeminence in Brazil.[52] As discussed earlier, in March 1815 Nesselrode and Saldanha had signed a one-year extension of the 1798 Russo-Portuguese trade treaty, as modified in June 1812, thereby opening the way for the two courts "to establish and consolidate on a permanent basis direct commercial ties between their respective subjects, possessions and states."[53] The stresses and dislocations experienced during the period of continental blockade, however, moved the tsar in 1816 to abandon bilateral trade agreements in favor of a uniform régime of protective tariffs that severely restricted the importation of luxury goods. The Tariff Act of 1816 struck at the very basis of developing Russo-Brazilian trade relations, and the court of Rio de Janeiro made immediate overtures to the tsarist government for a continuation of these relations under the previous terms.[54] Russian reluctance to settle the matter sorely tried Portuguese patience.[55] Indeed, when at last the Russians replied to the Portuguese appeal, an entire year had passed since Saldanha first broached the subject, while seven months had elapsed since the expiration of the Russo-Portuguese treaty. To make matters worse, the Russian reply was in the negative. "Convinced by an intimate familiarity with the grave inconveniences resulting from partial provisions such as those under consideration," Nesselrode informed the Portuguese envoy, the tsar was not able "to undertake a renewal of existing transactions between the two States."[56]

Portuguese displeasure over Russian policy led to a further deterioration of relations between the two empires in the first months of 1817. Tensions shifted from St. Petersburg to Rio de Janeiro, where the new Russian envoy, P. F. Balk-Polev, encountered serious obstacles to the normal dispatch of his responsibilities.[57] The ostensible cause of the difficulty was the claim of certain "irregularities in the official and private comportment" of the Russian diplomat,[58] who, according to

his Spanish counterpart, Andrés Villalba, "is rather strange in some
things and has not always been right in the disputes he has had [with
the Portuguese court]."[59] Some contemporary observers, however, saw
in this incident an attempt by the court of Rio de Janeiro to deflect
Russian protestations over the invasion of the Banda Oriental.[60]

A purely domestic dispute between Balk-Polev, his landlord, and
local workmen hired to make repairs and alterations in the Russian
diplomat's residence provided the occasion for a punitive response by
the court of Rio de Janeiro to tsarist intransigence.[61] Incensed by the
offensive demeanor of these individuals in their dealings with him,
Balk had protested to the Portuguese foreign ministry, at the time
under the direction of the cantankerous Conde da Barca.[62] Rather than
seeking to ameliorate the difficulty, the count seems deliberately to
have aggravated matters by advising Balk to accede to his complain-
ants' demands or abandon the premises. Given the lack of available
diplomatic residences in the Brazilian capital, failure to comply would
necessitate leaving the country.[63]

Matters were further complicated when, in the spring of 1817, the
court of St. Petersburg elevated Balk-Polev to the rank of ambassador
extraordinary, a move undoubtedly designed to placate an annoyed
João VI. The Portuguese foreign ministry, however, failed to take
cognizance of the Russian envoy's new status and it was only through
the intervention of Balk's Dutch and Spanish colleagues that João
finally agreed to receive his credentials.[64] On 20 May 1817, Balk met
with the Portuguese king in private audience, at which time he protested with apparent vehemence the treatment accorded him in Rio de
Janeiro. Two days later, the Conde da Barca informed the Russian
diplomat that in consequence of the disrespect he had shown the king
and until such time as the tsar should rectify the affront, he would no
longer be admitted to court.[65] In a personal letter to Alexander, João
decried Balk's comportment and assured the tsar that only their royal
friendship had dissuaded him from more decisive steps.[66] Balk, for his
part, requested his passports and promptly departed Brazil for Europe.[67]

Pozzo di Borgo, the tsar's senior envoy on the European continent,
viewed this entire incident as particularly vexatious, given the tumultuous state of affairs in America. "We do not have a single individual
of common sense anywhere in the New World," he lamented in August
1817.[68] While Balk-Polev had apparently been the victim of Portuguese resentment toward the court of St. Petersburg, he had nonetheless failed to avoid a situation prejudicial to tsarist interests. Would
it not be possible, Pozzo inquired of Count Nesselrode, to name P. I.

Poletica to an ambassadorial post in the New World, or anyone else of his stature who might be available for such an assignment? At present, he reflected, "we are helpless in this great theater." [69]

After the Bourbon restoration and post-Napoleonic reconstruction in France, it was the colonial question that most concerned Pozzo di Borgo. Already in the summer of 1814 he had called his court's attention to the long-term significance of the American revolutions. The Anglo-Americans, he wrote Nesselrode, sought "to work a complete revolution in the New World's political relations with the Old by destroying all European interests on [the American] continent." An upheaval of such dimensions was hardly desirable, he observed, and wherever feasible Russian influence should be used to quell this, "one of the greatest political revolutions on earth." [70] Pozzo viewed developments in Spanish America with equal apprehension. One fears, he wrote to Nesselrode, "that we are witnessing the destruction of the Spanish colonial system in the New World." [71] "Can you believe," he plaintively asked Capo d'Istria in the spring of 1817, "that insurgent ships control America and blockade Cádiz? . . . What we are about to witness in the other hemisphere is an event of the first magnitude." [72]

News of insurrection in Brazil further disturbed Pozzo. He advised Nesselrode that, although the insurrection had been limited to Pernambuco and was quickly put down by royalist forces, "movements of this sort on a continent where they enjoy almost universal support of the local populace, irrespective of caste, are rarely so erased from the people's memory as to destroy entirely the consequences and, above all, to arrest the contagion of its example." South America had fallen into chaos. [73] "Means other than notes and phrases," Pozzo concluded, "are needed to maintain empires." [74]

The Pernambuco uprising of March 1817 appears to have weighed heavily on the formulation of tsarist New World policy, for it announced more clearly than any single event up to that time the approaching collapse of colonial rule in Latin America. Although as early as 1812 the Russian press had anticipated the spread of revolution from Spanish to Portuguese America, [75] Brazil had shown few symptoms of impending upheaval. Now, suddenly, this New World bulwark of monarchical stability had been shaken to its foundations. "The importance of the revolt in Pernambuco," reported Balk-Polev, "lies in the fact that dissatisfaction has taken root [in Brazil]. A spirit has emerged similar to that which reigns in the Spanish colonies. The political situation in Brazil has changed." [76] "It was not difficult," read an article in the influential *Istoricheskii, statisticheskii i geograficheskii zhurnal*, "for those contemplating independence to fan into flame the spark which had fallen on the inhabitants of Brazil from the torch of independence ignited by their [Spanish American] neighbors."[77] Perhaps now, Pozzo wrote Nesselrode, the court of Brazil would comprehend the folly of pursuing territorial ambitions in the River Plate without first looking to its own internal order.[78]

A rising sense of concern over the course of events in Latin America had stirred the Russian court even before news of the Pernambuco uprising reached St. Petersburg. On one occasion in the spring of 1817, for example, Capo d'Istria expressed dismay to Saldanha da Gama over the apparent inevitability of Spanish American emancipation, to which the Portuguese envoy pointedly replied that Russia, by virtue of its collusion with Napoleon in 1807, had itself "struck the first stone from the Portuguese and Spanish colonial edifice."[79] Tsarist statesmen, of course, were well aware of the intricate interplay of events between the Old World and the New. "The insurrection of a part of His Catholic Majesty's overseas dominions," Tatishchev noted in June 1817, "is not simply a Spanish or American problem."[80] The destiny of South America, elaborated Pozzo, "affects every part of the globe and Europe in particular, for there is not a single government whose relations, well-being and very security are not more or less influenced by the political, moral and commercial state of the new world."[81]

The insurrection in Pernambuco served momentarily to focus tsarist attention on Brazil. This period, reported G. H. von Langsdorff, was "critical" for the Portuguese monarchy.[82] The uprising, added Balk-Polev, had created "confusion and disorder at the [Portuguese] court."[83] The preservation of monarchical order in Brazil, as well as the colonial régime in neighboring Spanish America, Russian diplomats concluded, rested in significant measure on a prompt settlement of hostilities in the River Plate, a view the tsar also shared. Capo d'Istria recalled several years later that Alexander, attaching primary importance to European mediation of the colonial question, felt that such mediation could achieve its ends only after a successful resolution of the dispute between Brazil and Spain.[84]

In addition to the Pernambuco uprising, other events, too, heightened the general sense of urgency surrounding the revolutionary turmoil of Spanish and Portuguese America. The viceroyalty of the River Plate had formally declared its independence from Spain, creating a provisional government under the supreme directorship of monarchist Juan Martín Pueyrredón. In the first weeks of 1817, an insurgent army under the command of General José de San Martín had crossed the Andes from Mendoza and broken the royalist hold on Chile. The speed with which San Martín's forces had effected the difficult march over the mountains and the success of his dramatic campaign of liberation, wrote the Russian envoy in Rio de Janeiro, "demonstrates irrefutably the readiness of Chile's inhabitants to shake off the metropolitan yoke."[85] Thus faced with a crisis of mounting proportions in the overseas dominions and exasperated by Portugal's refusal to rectify seizure of the Banda Oriental, Spain was moved in the summer of 1817 to solicit the collective intervention of the allied powers.[86] Russia endorsed the Spanish petition and, in so doing, openly committed tsarist diplomacy to the cause of colonial pacification.

Having concluded that Russian interests lay in the preservation of the Spanish and Portuguese colonial régimes, the court of St. Petersburg showed growing concern over the inability of the Iberian crowns to administer their vast empires. "Spain and Portugal," noted Pozzo di Borgo, "are weak governments who have just enough strength to sustain the war [in the colonies] without bringing it to a close."[87] "As long as Spain fails to put administrative order into the conduct of state business," he further warned, "her affairs shall be of those dramas that end in catastrophe."[88] Failing reform, or at the very least efficient administration, Spain was lost. *"Mais où sont les hommes?"* queried Pozzo. "Where are the statesmen?"[89] Into this vacuum of administrative indecision Tsar Alexander introduced D. P. Tatishchev, who, as Russian minister plenipotentiary in Madrid, worked diligently to manipulate the Spanish crown in accord with tsarist interests.[90]

The manifest debility of the Spanish crown, coupled with rising British opposition to a concerted intervention by the continental powers in colonial Latin America, forced Russia to pursue a policy of calculated conciliation. The Spanish government, Tatishchev observed to Ferdinand VII's secretary of state, "no doubt recognizes that force alone, unaccompanied by Justice and moderation, would promise nothing more than inconclusive results of brief duration. A Government that seeks only to put down its rebellious subjects by force, without hearing the motives which they give for their excesses," he added, "runs the constant risk of again having to confront them and of exhausting State resources in so detrimental a struggle."[91]

"To pretend to subjugate and to govern America by force of arms," concurred Pozzo, "is to want to silence the tempests and hurricanes of those climes. Instead of persisting in her futile military campaigns," he suggested, "Spain ought to present Europe a plan for colonial pacification based on improved local government, provincial privileges and extensive commercial advantage."[92] The surest way to reestablish peace in the revolted colonies, proposed Tatishchev, "would be to demonstrate the determination of the Mother-country to accord them all the advantages which they might reasonably desire. Why not begin," he asked the Spanish secretary of state, "by spontaneously granting those Colonies which have remained loyal to their legitimate Sovereign such concessions as may be judged sufficient to satisfy the demands of the rebel provinces?" In this way it might be possible to avoid the humiliation of formal negotiations with the insurgents, "be it directly or through the intervention of a foreign power." This last contingency, Tatishchev emphasized, should be avoided, for mediation by another power entailed decided disadvantages.[93] This was especially so from a tsarist perspective, as the power to which Tatishchev alluded was Great Britain.[94]

Conciliation toward the Spanish American insurgents was dictated by a sober evaluation of New and Old World realities. "Spain might object," Pozzo observed, "that a more liberal system of [colonial] administration would gradually lead the colonies to independence. No doubt it will better prepare them for this event in the future," he acknowledged, "but without it they shall gain their independence now and be lost [to the metropolitan governments, as well as to Europe]."[95] Conciliation, however, did not preclude armed force. "Mild manner, persuasion and reconciliation," Tatishchev proposed, "together with demonstrations of vigorous measures, will most surely destroy this fatal delusion which blinds the Insurgents to their true interests."[96]

The use of armed force, too, hinged on the practical exigencies of the moment. The Spanish and Portuguese crowns had proven to be unwilling partners in the enterprise of colonial pacification and neither commanded sufficient military power to guarantee royal authority in their overseas possessions.[97] Great Britain, moreover, had shown itself increasingly hostile to any coercive intervention in Latin America by a coalition of continental powers, and, in August 1817, declared itself unconditionally opposed to mediation by force. Castlereagh advised the allied ambassadors that the prince-regent "cannot consent that his Mediation shall under any circumstances assume an armed character; that whilst he is ready to employ, with the utmost zeal and sincerity, his best exertions to re-establish tranquility and restore harmony between the Crown of Spain and its South American subjects, he can under no circumstances be induced to be a party to any attempt to dictate, by force of arms, the terms of such a reconciliation, nor can H. R. H. become the guarantee of any settlements that may be effectuated to the extent of undertaking the obligation of enforcing its observance by acts of hostility against either of the parties."[98]

Russia, however, seems clearly to have accorded the use of force a place in its strategy for the pacification of Spanish America, as evi-

Дмитрій Павловичъ
Татищевъ,
1767 — 1845

Dmitri Pavlowitch
Tatichtcheff,
1767 — 1845

4. Dmitrii Pavlovich Tatishchev, Russian Minister Plenipotentiary to Spain
(1815–1820)

denced by tsarist efforts to circumvent the British stand on this key matter. Britain's categorical refusal "to sustain with arms what sound policy and the general interest permits us to demand of the [Spanish] American insurgents," declared Pozzo di Borgo with evident annoyance, "is a premature step destined to render useless all others and to compromise the dignity of the greatest sovereigns on earth. . . ."[99] Prudence and actual circumstances ought to determine the means of pacifying the colonies. "Should the continental Allies abstain from any intervention, and should England, as is more than likely, leave [Spanish] America to suffer the ravages of a war of extermination," Pozzo speculated, "the sovereigns of Europe, having witnessed, so to say, a great spectacle of gladiators, will find themselves separated, possibly forever, from the commercial resources and the fruits of civilization of this immense portion of the new world."[100] "It is not my intention," Pozzo advised Nesselrode, "to promise or to grant lightly armed assistance, but only not to base mediation on a contrary policy, since, in the eyes of the [Spanish] American insurgents and of the rest of the world, such a declaration would deprive our efforts of that imposing uncertainty which, behind the just counsels of the great monarchs, reveals the threat of force."[101]

Contrary to the opinions of Kaufmann, Perkins, and others who have written on the subject, there was general agreement between the tsar and his diplomatic agents on the direction of Russian New World policy. Indeed, the views advanced by Tatishchev and Pozzo di Borgo met with approval in St. Petersburg and actually formed the basis of tsarist thinking on the colonial question.[102] This can be seen most clearly in a memorandum on the pacification of America circulated by the Russian court toward the end of November 1817. Apparently issued in response to the British memorandum of late August, this document predicated pacification on three conditions: (1) a prompt and effective settlement of differences between Spain and Portugal in South America; (2) a liberalization of the Spanish colonial régime; and (3) concerted intervention by the European allies on behalf of the Iberian crown, including, should circumstances warrant, the use of force.[103]

Couched in the rhetoric of legitimacy, the Russian memorandum sought to counter British opposition to the possible use of force by the mediating powers. "The declaration issued by the Congress of Vienna on *the abolition of the slave trade* and the acts pertaining thereto," it pointedly recalled, "offer incontrovertible evidence of the legitimacy and efficacy of coercive measures which do not fall within the domain of military force."[104] Alluding to a protocol by which the allied powers had agreed to boycott the colonial produce of those states that refused to abolish the slave trade,[105] the court of St. Petersburg thus hoped to secure British recognition of this same principle in the broader issue of colonial pacification. Once accepted by this the most recalcitrant of the allied courts, Russia might reasonably contemplate an expansion of the principle beyond its original intent. In the meantime, the court of St. Petersburg had moved independently to bolster the Spanish military effort in America.

Russian Warships

On 16 October 1817, a flotilla of eight Russian warships departed the Estonian port of Revel (Tallin) bound for Cádiz.[106] The ships had been ceded to Spain under a shroud of secrecy and were to become the object of considerable speculation on both sides of the Atlantic. In anticipation of adverse British reaction, the tsarist government instructed its ambassador in London to advise Lord Castlereagh of the flotilla's sailing and to assure him that this was a purely commercial transaction without ulterior political motives.[107] Russia pressured Ferdinand VII to offer similar assurances to the British foreign secretary. With little enthusiasm the Spanish crown complied, informing Castlereagh in November 1817 that "by virtue of a private negotiation, and not a political transaction," Spain had just acquired five ships of the line and three frigates from His Majesty the Emperor of All the Russias.[108]

England had little reason to accept these explanations, however, and Spain itself made public the true ends to which the Russian ships would be employed following the flotilla's arrival at Cádiz in February 1818. They would be used, read an official article in the *Gazeta de Madrid*, "to protect Spanish commerce, to put to flight the pirates of our seas, to defend the faithful subjects who in the Colonial dominions are victims of anarchy and disorder, and to restore to Europe the advantage which she has lost on account of the disturbances in America."[109] Indeed, Cádiz had been selected as the preferred port for delivery of the ceded ships because its general situation was considered especially suited to the prompt organization of an expeditionary armada and, equally important, "to concealing the true destination of the [Russian] vessels."[110]

The Russian government also apprised the court of Rio de Janeiro of the impending transfer of warships to Spain. This was "a purely administrative matter," Nesselrode advised the Portuguese envoy, without political significance. Moreover, there were no special arrangements between Russia and Spain and "no territorial concessions anywhere in the world."[111] This clear allusion to rumors—widespread in 1817—that the court of Madrid was about to cede the port of Mahón (Menorca) and possibly other strategic points to Russia,[112] suggests an effort to anticipate Portuguese apprehensions over Russo-Spanish designs in the River Plate. Rather than favoring Russia with territorial concessions, Nesselrode emphasized, Spain was on the contrary contesting territory occupied by the Russian-American Company in northern California. The court of St. Petersburg, he appears to have been saying, had no ambitions in the Banda Oriental.[113]

News of the Russian warships reached the Spanish colonies, too, where it received curious attention. While the strongholds of royalist authority celebrated this event with much optimism, predicting an early end to the insurrection, the effectively independent areas of Spanish America looked upon it with considerable skepticism. *El Sol de Chile*, for example, editorialized that it would be to Russia's advantage "to recognize the independence of America, because in this way her merchants would have a vast open field for their commerce, particularly with opulent Mexico, and the Russian establishments in North America would gain much. . . . The Emperor Alexander," the paper added, "who for two years shared the dangers and fatigues of war with the common soldier in order to defend his country, cannot but show his royal disdain for Ferdinand, who so vilely abandoned his nation's cause."[114] Whatever the situation, cautioned *El Argos de Chile*, "we ought to be prepared to receive these new guests and be certain that they do not take us by surprise in the event these old Russian vessels are not destroyed at Cape Horn, should they have the temerity to attempt the passage in their present state."[115]

As for the United States, the court of St. Petersburg showed little real concern about possible American reactions to the warship affair. It did, however, inform the U. S. envoy to Russia, William Pinkney, of the transfer and, in language identical to that expressed to other governments, disclaimed any political motives in this transaction with the Spanish court. Pinkney, for his part, appears to have been convinced that the matter was as tsarist officials affirmed and so reported to Washington.[116]

Secret talks on the cession of Russian warships to Spain had begun in March 1817, when Ferdinand VII first proposed to Tatishchev the acquisition of four ships of the line and seven or eight frigates from Russia's Baltic fleet.[117] "Without a navy," the king declared, "I am unable to govern in the colonies."[118] Tatishchev reported Ferdinand's request to the tsar in a dispatch of 25 March. In exchange for these vessels, he postulated, "the court of St. Petersburg could demand territorial concessions of Spain, for example in California, which would be exceedingly useful to the Russian-American Company; it might also demand," he added, "exclusive trading rights with Havana, Veracruz, or the ports of Venezuela."[119] The Spanish monarch himself had offered to mortgage "all the revenues from his dominions in Europe and America" in order to pay for the Russian vessels.[120]

Tsar Alexander agreed to the proposed transfer of warships and, at the end of May 1817, instructed his minister in Madrid to work out the details.[121] Tatishchev entered immediately into talks with Ferdinand's private secretary, Antonio de Ugarte, and the Spanish minister of war, Francisco Ramón Eguía, both royal confidants and members of the king's *camarilla* or inner circle.[122] The result was a draft convention, signed by Tatishchev and Eguía on 11 August 1817, that called for the sale to Spain of five ships of the line and three frigates, fully armed and ready for prolonged duty at sea. Spain agreed to pay 13,600,000 rubles for the ships, offering as collateral the £400,000 sterling promised the Spanish crown by the court of St. James in compensation for abolition of the slave trade.[123] Confident of tsarist approval, or perhaps by way of subtle persuasion, the Spanish crown deposited a sizable advance with a London bank to be paid to the court of St. Petersburg once the tsar had ratified the proposed accord.[124]

Historians have made much of the fact that the accord itself has not been located in the state archives of Spain and that the only text available to scholars has, until recently, been an unofficial version published in the London *Morning Chronicle* of 2 December 1823.[125] The disappearance of key documents bearing on this affair suggests collusion by royal officials at the court of Madrid to conceal an irregular and potentially incriminating transaction. It also points to Russian duplicity in the tsar's dealings with the allied powers on the matter of colonial pacification.[126] In searching for the missing document, however, investigating scholars have neglected an important detail: the Russo-Spanish convention of 11 August 1817 was not the actual instrument of cession, but rather a draft accord that the tsar subsequently modified.[127]

Anxious that the pending accord not be interpreted as an act of tsarist foreign policy, Alexander relabeled the document "Act of Sale." At the same time, he purged the treaty's preamble of all reference to a "restoration of the power of the Spanish monarchy," stressing instead the need to protect Spanish commercial shipping from piracy on the high seas. The number and condition of vessels stipulated by the draft accord remained unchanged. The tsar articulated the terms of payment, however, in somewhat greater detail, stressing the financial significance of the warship deal for the Russian treasury.[128] "The principal benefit to be derived by us from this project," he had observed several months before, "consists in the receipt of such an important sum, which would greatly facilitate the revival of our monetary affairs."[129] The tsar also eliminated specific reference to the source of funds with which the Spanish crown would effect the purchase.

These revisions seem designed to counter British displeasure over Russian military assistance to Spain and may well have been drafted for British consumption. Diplomatic dispatches frequently fell into the hands of foreign agents, and there is room to speculate that some official correspondence pertaining to the transfer of Russian warships may have been written with a view to such interception. This seems even more plausible in light of the fact that Alexander did not dispatch a copy of the revised accord to Madrid until two weeks after the Russian flotilla had departed for Cádiz, while the accord was not finally signed and approved by the Spanish court until April 1818.[130] The actual decision to cede the ships, therefore, was made independently of these revised terms of cession.

On 21 February 1818, the Russian warships dropped anchor in the Bay of Cádiz after an exceptionally dilatory voyage of over four months.[131] The *Gazeta de Madrid* reported that the flotilla had arrived "fully armed and ready to undertake long voyages."[132] It soon became apparent, however, that the newly arrived vessels were anything but seaworthy. "Each and every one," declared the minister of the navy, "was totally useless, their hulls more or less rotted, in need of rigging, etc., in a word, unable to sail. . . ."[133] Indeed, only four ever left the Bay of Cádiz and of those only two undertook voyages of any significance. One, the *María Isabel*, sailed for Lima in the spring of 1818, falling prey to the insurgents of Chile that same year; the other, the *Fernando VII*, saw brief service in the Mediterranean, returning to Cádiz again in 1820. By 1823, all but the *María Isabel* had been decommissioned and sold for firewood.[134]

The poor condition of the Russian vessels produced immediate consternation at the Spanish court and quickly led to speculation about the tsar's true intentions.[135] Some suggested, and no doubt others thought, that the scandalous transaction constituted "a treasonous attempt to aid the [Spanish] American separatists."[136] So embarrassing did the incident prove to the court of St. Petersburg that the tsar was moved to cede three more frigates to Spain, albeit at an additional cost of 3.2 million rubles. These vessels, of forty guns each, sailed from Kronshtadt on 11 August 1818, making port at Cádiz nine weeks later.[137] By determination of the tsar, their crews included three officers of the Spanish navy, an apparent attempt to allay further suspicions in Madrid as to tsarist motives.[138] The frigates reached their destination in good order and subsequently all three saw service in the colonies.[139]

The central question in this episode, however, remains unanswered. Was the cession of Russian warships to Spain a calculated act of tsarist foreign policy? Jerónimo Bécker admits the possibility that it was, but at the same time allows for the conspiratorial thesis that identifies Tatishchev and Ugarte as the prime movers in this affair.[140] In W. S. Robertson's view, the warship deal "illustrated the deep interest of the Russian Government in checking the movement for the emancipation of Spanish America,"[141] while Dexter Perkins interpreted the Russo-Spanish accord "as evidence that the Russian autocrat had no intention of interfering directly in the colonial dispute."[142] According to V. M. Miroshevskii, the tsarist government, itself immediately interested in smothering the Spanish-American revolution, "granted the court of Madrid both moral and material support, including the cession of warships in 1817–1818."[143] The primary reason for selling these vessels, responds L. Yu. Slëzkin, was to help replenish badly depleted state coffers. After all, it was abundantly clear "that eight Russian ships would not decide the outcome of a war which embraced a large part of the American continent, as well as the waters of the surrounding seas and of two great oceans."[144]

Slëzkin, however, fails to consider readily available evidence in support of the contrary thesis, namely that the tsarist government did indeed attach decisive military significance to the ceded warships. In the months just prior to the transfer, the question was not one of a continent-wide offensive, as Slëzkin implies, but rather of a single, all-important operation against the insurgent territories of the River Plate. With Hidalgo and Morelos dead in Mexico, Spain appeared to have halted momentarily the revolutionary tide in Middle America. Similarly, crown forces under the command of General Pablo Morillo had managed to hold the principal population centers of northern South America, while Peru continued to show few signs of revolutionary agitation. Chile, on the other hand, had fallen to the insurgent forces of San Martín. To the east across the Andes, the River Plate had by and large thrown off the yoke of crown rule and, as the liberation of Chile dramatically demonstrated, posed an immediate threat to royal authority in the neighboring Spanish territories. Buenos Aires thus acquired strategic importance for the whole of South America.[145]

The courts of Madrid and St. Petersburg agreed on the need to mount an expedition against the River Plate. In effect, recalled the

Spanish secretary of state, "I was persuaded that the Morillo expedition [of 1815] should not have gone to Venezuela, but rather to Buenos Aires, . . . for I believed Buenos Aires to be easier to secure, of greater psychological significance, and above all decisive in settling our differences with Brazil."[146] According to the Spanish naval minister, José Vázquez Figueroa, the king had in fact purchased the Russian vessels for the reconquest of Buenos Aires.[147]

"If Spain, having received the naval assistance which it has pleased Our August Master to grant her, is able to send an imposing expedition against Buenos-Ayres in the River Plate," conjectured Pozzo di Borgo, "this operation will divert the insurgent forces employed in Chile, endanger the major source of insurrection [in South America], blockade the port [of Buenos Aires], and interdict aid received [by the rebels] from different nations."[148] Once Ferdinand VII was again master of Buenos Aires, concurred Tatishchev, "Chile will return to the fold and the dispute over Monte Video and the surrounding territory will cease to be an issue."[149] Spain had, he confirmed, devoted great effort to the organization of an armed incursion designed to restore crown rule on the banks of the River Plate.[150]

An effective resolution of differences between the Spanish and Portuguese crowns in the Banda Oriental seems to have been a key factor in Russian support of the proposed expedition to South America. Should Spain once again assert her authority over the eastern bank of the River Plate, it was reasoned, Brazil would be obliged to withdraw its forces of occupation.[151] From the Russian point of view, it was essential to achieve a unity of political objectives on the part of Spain and Portugal, for the cause of colonial pacification would be decisively advanced by their active collaboration.[152] As late as November 1818, only weeks before Alexander altered the course of tsarist New World policy, Capo d'Istria reiterated to Zea Bermúdez the urgent need to reoccupy Montevideo "at all costs." This, he declared, was "the surest and most effective way to strengthen the diplomatic arguments" by which Spain sought to influence the court of Rio de Janeiro.[153] The prompt dispatch of forces to the River Plate, affirmed Nesselrode, offered "the most effective means to conclude successfully the pending negotiations with Portugal, and, at the same time, to further the important business of pacifying America."[154] Russia, according to the Spanish secretary of state, had in fact demanded that Spain send this expedition to the River Plate.[155]

That the expedition failed to materialize must be explained in large part by administrative ineptitude on the part of Spain, rather than a lack of Russian support or the alleged machinations of tsarist diplomats. "The Court of Madrid is still so far from having an established system of domestic administration," reported Pozzo di Borgo in October 1817, "that one can only hope [the expedition to the River Plate] achieves the desired results." The importance Spain attached to diplomatic posturing, he added, "proves that she continues to ignore the true bases on which rests the power of States."[156] Indeed, José García de León y Pizarro had found the Spanish foreign office in a state of disarray when he became secretary in the fall of 1816. It was, he wrote, "very disorganized in both its material and formal aspects." Its officials manifested "a spirit of ambition and intrigue." There was great laxity in the dispatch of state business, little mental discipline, and no subordination.[157] Much the same situation obtained in the arsenals and shipyards of the Spanish navy. Consequently, when the flotilla of Russian warships arrived at Cádiz in need of major repairs, "there was not a cubit of lumber, nor sufficient workmen, nor even enough money" to accomplish the task at hand.[158]

Force of Arms Abandoned

Tsarist strategy for the restoration of royal authority in Spanish America thus rested on the achievement of three interrelated objectives: (1) the prompt dispatch of a Spanish expeditionary force to the River Plate, (2) an effective resolution of differences between the courts of Madrid and Rio de Janeiro, and (3) acceptance by the allied powers of the principle of collective intervention in colonial Latin America. The cession of warships to Spain thus represented but one dimension of a larger tsarist scheme for the pacification of America and concomitant furtherance of Russian New World interests.

In the first months of 1818, tsarist diplomatic efforts centered on the Luso-Spanish dispute over possession of the Banda Oriental. Spain and Portugal had agreed to talk, Pozzo di Borgo reported on February 7, but the two courts "are very irritated with each other and it is to be feared that, rather than reach an understanding on their common interests, they will continue to berate one another."[159] Two weeks later Pozzo informed Nesselrode that the Portuguese envoy to the Paris talks, Count Palmella, had agreed in principle to a restitution of Uruguay to Spain "as soon as this could be accomplished without compromising the security of Brazil." The allied mediators, however, would have to dissuade the Portuguese from imposing unacceptable conditions on Spain. A permanent and satisfactory settlement, Pozzo concluded, was still a long way off.[160]

The court of St. Petersburg soon began to sense the futility of attempting a resolution of the Uruguayan dispute. Spain, Pozzo reported

in March 1818, "wishes to take possession of Montevideo prior to pacification of the colonies so as to promote through an armed presence
peaceful negotiations on the submission of Buenos Ayres. . . . The
Court of Brazil, for its part, seeks the permanent acquisition of the
Plate." The Portuguese crown, he added, was in contact with the insurgents of Buenos Aires and anxiously awaited the recognition of
Platine independence by the United States, to which it would then
point as evidence of Spain's inability to reestablish its authority in the
region and, consequently, as a justification for continuing Portuguese
occupation of the Banda Oriental.[161] Available intelligence revealed
little chance of reconciling the respective interests of Spain and Portugal in the River Plate.[162]

Despite mounting pessimism in St. Petersburg about the eventual
outcome of the Paris talks, tsarist efforts to promote a settlement in the
Banda Oriental continued throughout the summer of 1818. The tsar
was by no means incognizant of the great difficulties that militated
against a satisfactory conclusion of allied mediation. Perseverance,
wrote Capo d'Istria, "may yet overcome all obstacles."[163] The court of
Rio de Janeiro had, after all, recognized Spain's right to the Banda
Oriental, its only stated precondition for reoccupation by Spanish
forces being the institution of measures to guarantee the security of
Brazil. The next step, therefore, was to determine the precise nature
of Brazil's security requirements and to frame a settlement accordingly.[164]

So anxious was Russia to see the Uruguayan affair settled that it
was even willing to compromise Spanish claims in the interest of furthering the cause of colonial pacification. At this point, observed Pozzo,
"it would be well for Spain to accept some sacrifice, less because Portugal has the absolute right to demand it than because an end to the
differences and quarrels between them is naturally the beginning of
the pacification of the colonies. . . ."[165] Were Spain to enlist the assistance of Portugal in returning order to the insurgent territories, Tatishchev advised the Spanish crown, it would make little difference
whether the Banda Oriental were reoccupied by Spanish forces or held
jointly by Spain and Portugal.[166] Spain rejected this idea, however, and
by mid-July Pozzo again reported that the courts of Madrid and Rio
de Janeiro remained irreconcilably divided.[167] Immersed in "piles of
paper, sophistry and dilatory arguments," he lamented, the allied
mediation was floundering in a "labyrinth of duplicity, foible and
extravagance."[168]

Meanwhile, the court of St. Petersburg was preparing a final diplomatic effort to secure an allied commitment to collective intervention

in Spanish America. The signatories of the Quadruple Alliance had agreed to meet in congress in the fall of 1818 to consider the pending affairs of post-Napoleonic France and the possible withdrawal of allied occupation forces.[169] As the influential Friedrich von Gentz had observed to Count Nesselrode toward the end of 1817, Europe was at the time faced with two major issues—unsettled war claims against France and "the proposed mediation between Spain and America."[170] Accordingly, Tsar Alexander wished to broaden the scope of allied deliberations to include the affairs of Spanish America, a position in which he was supported by the courts of France and Spain. Indeed, he sought actively to gain the admission of Spain to the forthcoming congress, but was blocked by England, Austria, and Prussia. At the same time, he pressured the court of Madrid to submit a realistic plan for the pacification of the colonies to the allied powers.[171] In this endeavor, too, he failed.

Allied representatives gathered at Aix-la-Chapelle in late September 1818. Their august body included the Russian tsar, Frederick William III of Prussia, and Francis I of Austria, as well as the British foreign secretary, Lord Castlereagh, the Duke of Wellington, and numerous other diplomatic personages of the day.[172] The congress convened on 30 September and spent the following three weeks discussing the affairs of France. The matter of the Spanish colonies did not arise until the latter part of October, when Russia again argued in vain for the admission of Spain to the congress proceedings. The Russian position remained essentially unchanged from that articulated in the circular memorandum of November 1817.[173] Now, however, it was vigorously countered by Lord Castlereagh, who insisted that allied intervention in the colonial question be restricted to an offer of good offices that precluded the notion of collective force.

While the discussions of Aix-la-Chapelle on the colonial question proved inconclusive, the British view clearly prevailed. Unable to sway allied opposition to Spain's participation in the discussions and equally unsuccessful in persuading Ferdinand VII to articulate terms of mediation, Russia was obliged to abandon its efforts to bring about a collective agreement on colonial pacification. The final blow to tsarist objectives in the diplomacy of New World colonial affairs came when, rebuffed by the allied powers, Spain itself slammed the door on further consideration of outside mediation.[174]

Tsar Alexander apprised Ferdinand VII personally of Russia's altered stance on colonial pacification in December 1818. Writing from Vienna, where he had repaired following the conclusion of deliberations at Aix-la-Chapelle, the tsar expressed "vivid regrets" at the failure of the allied powers to deal directly and effectively with the pressing affairs of the Spanish empire. "All obstacles to an identity of views on collective intervention," he advised the Spanish monarch, "can be reduced to a single difficulty, namely opposition to *the principle of military cooperation* as an obligation of the intervening Powers." Such cooperation, inasmuch as it implied the use of armed force, was inadmissible to the British government. It was no less so in the eyes of the other powers, the tsar observed, "because it is *in fact* impracticable."[175]

Alexander reiterated these views in a confidential dispatch to Tatishchev three days later.[176] The language of this correspondence, in turn, has led some investigators to see a coincidence of views between Russia and Great Britain and thus to dissociate the Russian court from the bellicose posture of Spain on the colonial question.[177] In actual fact, the tsar's communications to Ferdinand and Tatishchev seem to confirm Russian support of Spanish pretensions in the colonies.

The key word here is "impracticable." What these documents indicate is not a spontaneous adherence to the position of England and certain other of the allied powers, but rather a reluctant resignation to practical circumstances beyond Russian control. Had the principle of military cooperation enjoyed British support and thus been practicable, there is little if any evidence to suggest that Russia would not have pursued just such a course of action on behalf of the Spanish crown. In actuality, a policy of coercion against the Spanish American insurgents proved unworkable and the Russian court responded accordingly. In the closing days of 1818, the tsar abandoned the force of arms as a viable instrument for the attainment of Russian New World objectives.

7. The Final Years: Russian Responses to Colonial Emancipation

The decision of Tsar Alexander I to abandon a policy of force in the matter of colonial pacification only confirmed doubts long held by statesmen of vision about the feasibility of effecting a restoration of crown rule in Spain's New World possessions. As the perceptive Friedrich von Gentz had observed to Count Nesselrode several months prior to the Congress of Aix-la-Chapelle, neither side seemed disposed to conciliation. The Spanish court had for three years pursued a "spurious and disastrous" colonial policy, having made only "meager and insignificant" overtures to the Spanish American insurgents.[1] As for the colonies, Gentz wrote, it might yet be possible to save Mexico and Peru if Spain were to move immediately to implement "an enlightened and liberal system." The River Plate, New Granada, and Venezuela, however, had progressed too far to entertain propositions from the mother country. "Internal civil dissension might one day make it possible to reestablish royal authority in these unfortunate countries," Gentz concluded, but in the meantime "neither a continuation of hostilities nor direct negotiations would serve to recover them."[2]

By the close of 1818, the tsar and his counsellors had in the main come to share Gentz's views on the colonial question. This can be seen in tsarist diplomatic correspondence dating back to 1814 and became increasingly apparent following the Congress of Aix-la-Chapelle.[3] In its official dealings with the other powers, however, the Russian court maintained for yet some time an ambivalent posture on the issue of colonial pacification, while publicly it continued to applaud preparations by the Spanish court to launch an armed invasion of the River Plate.

The decision of Ferdinand VII to reject allied mediation in the colonial question was announced to the powers in the fall of 1818. It was officially communicated to the Russian court in late winter of the following year, together with a reassertion of Spain's unwavering commitment to a restoration of crown rule in the colonies.[4] Responding to

Spanish concern over what in the aftermath of Aix-la-Chapelle had been interpreted as tsarist endorsement of collective mediation under British aegis, Nesselrode assured Zea Bermúdez that it had been neither the tsar's wish nor his intention to pressure Ferdinand to enlist allied assistance in the pacification of the colonies, but rather to suggest the most efficacious manner of attaining positive results from collective mediation should Spain elect to pursue that course of action.[5]

Whereas prior to the Congress of Aix-la-Chapelle Russia had indeed sought to create the conditions necessary for collective intervention in Spanish America, recognition at Aix-la-Chapelle that England, by virtue of her sea power and vested interests, would be the ultimate arbiter in the colonial question moved the tsarist government as a matter of expediency to yield to British terms.[6] Given the impossibility of aiding Spain to recover her colonies by force of arms, the allied powers were now offering her moral support for a colonial system of "peace and pardon" without which no battlefield victory could be more than a passing success.[7] Inasmuch as Spain had finally decided to rely on her own resources to restore crown rule in her overseas possessions, Nesselrode declared, the tsar respected too much "the dignity of the Court of Madrid and the independence of its Councils" not to respect also its decision to decline collective mediation.[8]

Having reluctantly ceded the diplomatic initiative on the colonial question to Great Britain, while at the same time endorsing Spain's independent stance on the pacification of Spanish America, the Russian court sensed the inescapable futility of the entire affair. As noted by Saldanha da Gama in the winter of 1819, Russian hopes for a favorable settlement lay in the dispatch of the River Plate expedition, which it was to be presumed would not be carried out "regardless of last-minute efforts by an indecisive Spanish government."[9] The tsar, reported another Portuguese diplomat, had congratulated the Spanish monarch on his new colonial policy, but also invited him to take careful account of the material means available to him for pacification and to reflect soberly "on the fatal consequences" should those means prove insufficient.[10]

Meanwhile, *Le Conservateur Impartial* heralded the impending departure of the long-awaited expedition to the River Plate. Nothing had been overlooked, it declared in the fall of 1818, "to assure the success of the latest efforts of the Spanish monarchy to reassert its authority in the beautiful and rich countries of South America."[11] The expeditionary forces were in the best of spirits, asserted the paper the following spring, "and everything permitted one to entertain the greatest of hopes." According to news from Buenos Aires, the River Plate was split by internal dissension, while San Martín, for reasons of ill health, had quit his command of the insurgent forces in Chile.[12] By midsummer 1819, *Le Conservateur Impartial* was reporting the imminent departure of the expedition. Arms and provisions were soon to be loaded aboard the waiting vessels, the troops exercised daily, and discipline had been tightened.[13] By year's end, however, the expedition had as yet failed to materialize. Its over sixteen thousand men were still to sail momentarily for Buenos Aires and Montevideo, whence they would proceed overland to Chile and then on to Peru. A second expedition, the paper announced, was being readied for northern South America.[14]

The Russian government found it increasingly difficult to remain optimistic about the outcome of the River Plate expedition. Even as the allied powers met at Aix-la-Chapelle in October 1818, one of the Russian warships ceded to Spain for use in the Platine operation, the *María Isabel*, was seized by insurgent corsairs.[15] The ineptitude of Spanish military planners, reflected in the separation of the *María Isabel* from the expeditionary flotilla and her precipitous dispatch to Peru, was further confirmed by the inordinate delays in implementing the expedition. News of rebellion among the troops stationed at Cádiz disabused tsarist officials of lingering illusions about the prospects for a successful pacification of Spanish South America.[16] While these initial rumblings among the ranks of the expeditionary forces were quickly repressed, they were followed on New Year's Day 1820 by an uprising that would alter the course of European affairs, while assuring the irremediable loss of most of Spain's overseas possessions. Once again, tsarist New World policy was impelled by the rush of events.

Liberal Revolution and the Colonies

On 1 January 1820, in Cabezas de San Juan, General Rafael del Riego proclaimed the Spanish Constitution of 1812, thus initiating an ill-planned but momentarily successful assault against the absolutist régime of Ferdinand VII. By early March, the revolutionary movement had swept the country and Ferdinand was forced to endorse the liberal charter that six years before he had rejected out of hand. The Spanish monarch swore formal allegiance to the Constitution on 9 July 1820 at the opening session of the newly convened *cortes*.[17]

News of the liberal revolt in Spain traveled swiftly. In America, it precipitated the separation of Mexico, whose ruling élites hastened to sever ties with a metropolitian order that threatened their continued survival. In Europe, it marked the beginning of a series of revolutionary events that was to shake the foundations of continental absolutism and produce a hardening of ideological positions on the form and legitimacy of political change. Ferdinand's decision to yield to the constitutional demands of Riego and his followers reached the tsarist court almost immediately. It was reported to the Russian public in the first days of April 1820.[18]

Viewed from St. Petersburg, the Riego uprising was ominously symptomatic of a deeping malaise in the societal relations of Europe. It came against the backdrop of widespread social unrest, the proliferation of secret societies committed to liberal reform, and the shocking assassinations of German writer and publicist August von Kotzebue (23 March 1819)[19] and the Duke of Berry, nephew of Louis XVIII (13 February 1820). It was followed by and in part prompted liberal uprisings in Naples (July 1820), Portugal (August 1820), and Piedmont (March 1821), and was only a year removed from the Greek insurrection against Ottoman rule, itself a product of liberal credos and the agitation of secret societies.

In light of these events Alexander I, himself a "liberal" reformer, found it increasingly difficult to resolve his reformist views with a parallel commitment to order and the traditional loyalties of his own rigidly structured society. His dilemma was shared by others in his imperial service, including the influential Capo d'Istria, who, like the tsar, recognized that social change was inevitable "but hoped it would come peacefully, gradually, and without further revolutionary cataclysms."[20] Those who had precipitated the liberal uprisings in Spain, Naples, and Portugal, "formed in the school of popular despotism during the French Revolution and perfected in the art of overthrowing governments by the despotism of Bonaparte," now sought to seize the power denied them by the congress system of post-Napoleonic Europe.[21]

The Russian tsar was not ideologically opposed to the concept of constitutional rule, having himself imposed a constitution on Poland in 1815 against the almost uniform opposition of allied and tsarist statesmen alike. Moreover, by the Treaty of Velikie Luki he had specifically endorsed the Spanish Constitution of 1812. Indeed, he had consistently recommended a policy of enlightened reform to Ferdinand VII as the only realistic way of preserving the full integrity of the Spanish monarchy in both the Iberian Peninsula and the overseas dominions.

Alexander's position hardened, however, on the question of means. Political reform, while responding to the evolutionary changes of society, remained for him the exclusive responsibility of the duly constituted authority and was therefore legitimate only when instituted by the supreme representative of that authority. At bottom, the tsar was a product of the eighteenth century—an enlightened despot. He could accept a plurality of political régimes provided that basic change within any given régime came from above and was worked in accord with established norms. On his own terms, he was a true *conservateur impartial*.

The tsar's response to events in Spain was consistent with this posture. On 19 April 1820, he was officially informed by Zea Bermúdez of Ferdinand VII's adherence to the new constitutional order. The Spanish envoy recalled tsarist recognition of the legitimacy of the institutions created by the Constitution of 1812 in the Treaty of Velikie Luki and requested a public reaffirmation of that recognition.[22] The tsar replied that while indeed he had endorsed the Constitution of 1812 and had always wished to see the authority of the Spanish monarch preserved in both hemispheres "by means of institutions based on principles generous and pure," he could not endorse the imposition of those institutions on the crown by insurrection. Had they emanated from the throne, he declared, they would have been "conservative" and thus legitimate. Arising, as they did, from a milieu of dissension, they could only be viewed as "subversive."[23]

Ironically, the initial response of the Spanish crown to the revolutionary events of 1820 was to blame the tsarist court for contributing through its minister plenipotentiary, D. P. Tatishchev, to the discontent that had precipitated the Riego uprising. In February of that year, the Duke of San Fernando, newly appointed Spanish secretary of state, informed Capo d'Istria that Tatishchev, then on leave in St. Petersburg, would be ill-advised to return to his post in Madrid. Inasmuch as the rebellious expeditionary army of Cádiz had been the sole responsibility of Antonio Ugarte and in light of the intimate and well-known ties between Ugarte and Tatishchev, the ability of the latter to represent the interests of his sovereign at the Spanish court had been severely compromised. An adverse public opinion that held Ugarte responsible for the military revolt accused the Russian minister of complicity and thus by association made him an object of popular animosity. In the circumstances, San Fernando wrote, the Spanish government could no longer guarantee Tatishchev's personal safety.[24]

Tatishchev had returned to St. Petersburg toward the end of 1819. According to Zea Bermúdez, he was received warmly by the tsar, enjoyed ready access to the imperial cabinet, and was held in great esteem both at court and in the highest circles of Russian society—an image that contrasts markedly with the views of Webster, Kaufmann, and other historians who had depicted Tatishchev as an agent of intrigue working at cross-purposes to the tsar.[25] Although Alexander's response to the Spanish monarch's thinly veiled imputation of detrimental conduct on the part of his ambassador remains unclear, Tatishchev did not in fact return to Spain and was replaced at the court of Madrid by the Russian chargé d'affaires, the talented but inexperienced Count M. N. Bulgari.[26] Thereafter, Russo-Spanish relations gradually deteriorated. That Tatishchev had indeed enjoyed the favor and confidence of his sovereign was demonstrated by his subsequent prominence in tsarist diplomacy on the delicate Eastern Question, in which he overshadowed both Nesselrode and Capo d'Istria.[27]

The gravity of the Spanish situation served to focus tsarist attention once again on the affairs of Europe. While the Russian court continued to pursue its New World interests and at no time retreated from established footholds in the other hemisphere, America slipped noticeably in the order of tsarist priorities. This was reflected in the Russian press, where coverage of events in the Spanish and Portuguese colonies yielded to news from the Iberian Peninsula.

In mid-March 1820, Alexander instructed his diplomatic representatives abroad to raise with the governments to which they were accredited the question of a new congress to consider developments in Spain and a possible collective response should Ferdinand VII request allied assistance. The latter eventuality was temporarily precluded when the Spanish monarch declared his fidelity to the Constitution. Subsequent events in Naples and Portugal, however, added a note of urgency to the tsar's call and, in the fall of 1820, the powers met in congress at Troppau (Opava). After a month of deliberations, Austria, Prussia, and Russia agreed on armed intervention in Naples. In addition, they declared a general policy of nonrecognition of "illegally" constituted régimes, as well as their readiness to suppress such régimes by force of arms should they threaten the vital interests of "legitimate" states. England and France, who had had serious misgivings about the objectives of the other powers and thus participated in the congress only as observers, refused to sign the Troppau protocol. Tsar Alexander, for his part, insisted on the implementation of constitutional reforms in Naples, thereby preserving in part his liberal image.[28]

The powers agreed to complete their deliberations at a second congress to be convened the first of the new year at Laibach (Ljubljana). In the interim, Alexander was badly shaken by developments in his own empire. Even while the powers were meeting at Troppau, the Semënovskii regiment of the imperial guard mutinied. Although the mutiny was symptomatic of a general discontent in the Russian military arising from poor conditions and disciplinary excesses, the tsar nonetheless attributed it to what he came increasingly to view as an international Jacobin conspiracy. Secret societies of revolutionary tendency had appeared in Russia following the return of tsarist troops from the Napoleonic campaigns. The influence of such societies in the political turmoils of Europe's *Mezzogiorno* was manifest, and Alexander quickly drew the parallel with the Semënovskii revolt in St. Petersburg. As the Portuguese envoy to the Russian court observed some time later: "Russia need not fear revolutions bent on changing her form of government so long as her population comprises one free person for every forty serfs. Nevertheless, there can be no doubt that among the military, the youth of the nobility and the small third estate there exists that same spirit of opposition to the constituted authority and the same ideas of reform and constitutionality that have contributed to and even produced the violent commotions in other States. The Emperor cannot ignore this blind tendency toward a premature order, which would be the end of the greatness and preponderance of this Empire and the beginning of its decomposition."[29] At Laibach, Alexander fully endorsed the Austrian intervention in Naples and, upon learning of the rebellion in Piedmont, offered Metternich a Russian army to quell the new uprising.

The Spanish question was not discussed at the Congresses of Troppau and Laibach inasmuch as Austria was totally preoccupied with Italy and England wished to avoid involving the continental powers in the affairs of the Iberian Peninsula. Moreover, the matter of legitimacy presented special problems since Ferdinand VII had in fact declared his intention "to move frankly down the constitutional path."[30] Consequently, in the winter of 1821, the tsar advised his diplomatic representatives that, while Russia could no longer consider Spain an ally, correct relations with the Spanish court would be maintained. The allied powers, he added, had no plans to move against Spain.[31] They had, however, agreed to hold further consultations on the European situation in the fall of 1822, at Verona.

The situation in Spain evolved rapidly. As Ferdinand faced a growing radicalization of the new constitutional régime and felt power slipping inexorably from his hands, he began to treat secretly with the courts of Paris and St. Petersburg in the hope of restoring his royal authority through an allied intervention. In June 1821, he addressed a memorandum to the tsar in which he declared that without powerful armed assistance from abroad, the total destruction of the monarchy was inevitable, "both in the Peninsula and the overseas dominions."[32] In a second letter, he emphasized that recent events in the metropolis and the colonies required the most urgent communication between himself and the tsar and that this could only be accomplished with the immediate return to Madrid of D. P. Tatishchev.[33]

Shortly thereafter, he dispatched the Marquis of Casa Yrujo to Paris to inform Louis XVIII of the degenerating state of affairs in Spain, expressing in the envoy's letter of accreditation his confidence that the French monarch would willingly help "to extricate him from the distressing situation in which he found himself."[34] Toward the end of 1821, Count Bulgari proposed a course of action to Ferdinand designed to prompt a reluctant France to intervene directly on his behalf. In essence, the plan called for material incentives, including commercial advantages in the colonies.[35]

During the following year, the Spanish crown sought incessantly to persuade Louis XVIII to come to its aid—an effort that appears to have had the active support of Russia. Itself preoccupied with events in the Balkans, the tsarist court viewed France as the only member of the Holy Alliance able to mount an armed intervention in Spain. When the four continental powers met at Verona in October 1822, they agreed on this course of action and, despite British opposition, proceeded to take appropriate measures. In concert they each addressed a note to the Spanish government demanding a fundamental revision of the Constitution—a demand they knew would be unacceptable to the *cortes* and by means of which they sought to elicit a response justifying the anticipated intervention. The notes were passed to Spanish authorities in the first days of January 1823. The reply, as expected, obliged the envoys of the continental powers to request their passports and abandon the country. The powers, in turn, severed relations with the Spanish government,[36] and, on 7 April, French forces under the command of the Duke of Angoulême entered Spain. By October, Ferdinand had been restored to full power.

The importance Tsar Alexander I attached to Spanish affairs was reflected in his decision to send Pozzo di Borgo on a special embassy to Madrid following the successful conclusion of the French intervention. At issue was the nature of a restored absolutist régime in Spain and a general consensus that, while the continental powers had been unwilling to tolerate a revolutionary government in that country, they were no less opposed to a restoration of the arbitrary, myopic order that had prevailed there prior to 1820. Indeed, one of the principal reasons why France had resisted Ferdinand's initial appeals for armed assistance was precisely the fear that once he was restored to power the Spanish monarch would revert to his previous unenlightened ways. Russia shared this concern and with good reason. By the time Pozzo arrived in the Spanish capital in late October 1823, Ferdinand had unleashed a wave of repression that threatened to provoke new outbreaks of revolutionary agitation. "'At a time when this infelicitous country is so in need of wisdom and foresight," Pozzo wrote from Madrid, "the public authorities are guided in their actions by passions rather than policy. . . . It would be impossible," he assured Nesselrode, "to give you an accurate picture of the deplorable and all but hopeless state of this monarchy."[37] News of these developments distressed tsarist officials and, according to one foreign diplomat, even caused some to wish for a return to power of the defeated party.[38]

Throughout this troubled period, the colonial question continued to occupy the attention of European statesmen. While the temporary triumph of a liberal constitutional régime in Spain framed the matter of independence in a new light, it produced no essential change in the respective positions of the major powers on this question, nor did it alter the basic posture of the Spanish government. It had a direct impact, however, on the course of events in America, for the victory of Riego and his comrades removed the threat of a major new crown effort in South America and thus opened the way for the decisive patriot actions against the remaining royalist strongholds in Venezuela, New Granada, and Peru. At the same time, it alienated important segments of the royalist camp, as seen most dramatically in the case of Mexico.

The *cortes* of the "liberal triennium" failed entirely to comprehend the situation in the New World and in a real sense sealed the independence of the overseas territories. Insisting blindly that the colonies constituted integral and juridically equal parts of a greater Spain rather than dependencies of a colonialist metropolis, they reduced the colonial question to a simple but false equation of constitutional reform. They were ideologically unequipped to consider independence as a possible historical alternative, and, when the Spanish American separatists persisted in their determination to sever political bonds, reverted to the Fernandine policy of belligerency and nonrecognition.

In the spring of 1822, the Spanish government reaffirmed its unswerving opposition to any dismemberment of the empire. The crown declared its intention "to respect the rights of the Spanish Nation in its American Provinces" and to remain "absolutely passive" while its emissaries sought to reach an understanding with the colonists on the basis of the new constitutional order. Spain's ambassadors to London, Paris, Vienna, Berlin, and St. Petersburg were instructed to request that the powers "not recognize either directly or indirectly the *de facto* Governments that exist in the dissident Provinces"; that they neither send nor receive agents from those provinces and "refrain from establishing all political relations such as normally exist between Nations"; and finally that they give full public support to the crown's position on the colonial matter, including its determination "not to recognize the independence of said Provinces."[39]

The instructions to Spain's new representative at the tsarist court, Pedro Alcántara Argaiz, noted that Russian wishes for a more liberal colonial system had been met "by the equality which the Constitution establishes among all the Provinces of the Monarchy." Argaiz was to remind the tsar that Russia stood to gain major trade advantages by supporting crown interests in the colonies, while those same advantages would be lost were Spanish America to achieve its independence. He was to stress that if Russia wished "to maintain and augment her settlements in America," she would do well to consider "the inevitable prejudice to such expansion promised by an annihilation of Spanish power on that continent."[40] This unmistakable allusion to Russian territorial ambitions in California further attests to the importance of Russia's Pacific settlements in the formulation of tsarist New World policy.

Argaiz's instructions were supplemented with a memorandum addressed to all the European courts concerning the recognition of Spanish American independence by the United States. In an apparent fit of pique and frustration, the Spanish government declared that any power that chose to follow Washington's lead would by that act revoke any and all accords existing between itself and the court of Madrid. At the same time and not without irony, it appealed to the principles of legitimacy and sought assurances that the powers would not abandon their position of hostility to the cause of colonial emancipation.[41]

The Russian response to Argaiz's representations reveals a growing exasperation with Spanish ineptitude in the affairs of state, as well as a basic continuity of tsarist thinking on the entire colonial question. At the end of May 1822, Capo d'Istria informed the Spanish envoy that in his view it would be impossible to induce the overseas territories to recognize crown sovereignty. With whom would crown emissaries treat? he queried. The de facto governments of Spanish America could hardly be expected to renounce the power they had successfully usurped. Moreover, they had little reason to place their faith in a restoration of crown rule when they could readily see that the Peninsula itself faced an uncertain future. The tranquility of America might have been achieved in 1816, Capo d'Istria concluded, by means of those very reforms that in 1822 no longer corresponded to the realities of the New World.[42]

The tsar's official reply to these latest expressions of Spanish concern came through Count Nesselrode, who pointedly suggested to Argaiz that if the Spanish government wished to verify the constancy of Russian support for crown interests in the colonies, it had only to consult its own archives. The record was clear, he implied. There could be no doubt that the allied powers would do nothing to prejudice the manifestly legitimate interests of the Spanish monarchy. The tsar, for his part, "would discard none of the principles of loyalty, justice and moderation" that in the past had determined his policy toward Spain, "under whose laws he wished to see prosper the beautiful and rich territories of Spanish America." This firm position, Nesselrode emphasized, had more than once been expounded to the king.[43]

The restoration of Ferdinand VII to absolute power changed little in the politics of colonial affairs, although for a time there was renewed speculation about a possible intervention in Spanish America by the Holy Alliance. To some it appeared that France might lead such an enterprise, as had occurred in Spain, and in point of fact French statesmen did discuss the feasibility of restoring some semblance of crown authority in the Spanish colonies.[44] Ferdinand, for his part, had again requested collective assistance to recover the overseas territories and the powers had taken that request under consideration. So skeptical were the British of these developments, and in particular of French designs, that foreign secretary George Canning demanded and got an official disclaimer of any intentions on the part of France to intervene in Spain's colonial possessions—the so-called Polignac Memorandum of 9–12 October 1823. At the same time, Canning made it known that England would stand between the colonies and any intervening force from the continent.

The relationship between sedition in the New World and liberal revolution in the Old was apparent to all discerning statesmen of the day and may have been a factor in the blusterous attitude of the United States toward the continental powers enunciated by President James Monroe on 2 December 1823. The image of victorious French armies restoring absolute rule to the Spanish monarch in the name of the Holy Alliance was sufficiently insidious to suggest an expanded effort to extinguish the flames of revolution across the ocean. As shown by the researches of N. N. Bolkhovitinov, however, this was not in fact the case and moreover was so perceived by Monroe and his secretary of state, John Quincy Adams.[45] The immediate target of Monroe's message, the evidence suggests, was rather Great Britain, whose territorial and commercial interests in the Western Hemisphere directly challenged those of the United States as well as any active pursuit of New World ambitions by continental Europe.

While much has been made in this connection of the Russian presence in the Pacific Northwest, recent scholarship has convincingly demonstrated that well prior to the issuance of Monroe's message there was full understanding between Washington and St. Petersburg on the respective territorial interests of each country and that the Russian possessions were of no real concern to the Monroe administration.[46] Even following Tsar Alexander's celebrated decree of 16 September 1821 prohibiting foreign shipping within one hundred Italian miles of the coast of Russian America to fifty-one degrees north latitude, few Americans viewed Russia as a territorial threat. Inasmuch as the United States had no claims north of forty-nine degrees, Adams observed in November 1822, it was immaterial whether Russia extended its claims to fifty-five or fifty-one degrees. That, Adams felt, was a matter that concerned Great Britain.[47] There was, in sum, no sense of a Russian menace "either in Monroe's cabinet or in American public opinion generally in the period from 1818 to 1824."[48]

On the Russian side, there was concern over a possible deterioration in Russo-American relations resulting from a misreading of tsarist intentions in the Pacific Northwest and immediate steps were taken to preclude such an eventuality. Poletica advised Adams in detail of the nature and extent of Russian claims, reassuring the American secretary that those claims extended no further than the fifty-first parallel.[49] Nesselrode and Capo d'Istria reiterated these assurances to the American envoy in St. Petersburg, Henry Middleton, who was informed that the controversial decree on foreign shipping in the waters of Russian American would not be fully implemented.[50] The tsar had concluded, Middleton reported in August 1822, that this matter should not get out of hand and accordingly had issued orders to Russian warships in the area to patrol only the immediate coastal waters of existing Russian settlements.[51]

There appears to have been little connection between tsarist efforts to maintain cordial relations with the United States and the pursuit of Russian objectives in Latin America. Shortly after his arrival in the United States in the spring of 1819, Poletica, in his capacity as newly appointed ambassador, did seek to reassure the American secretary of state that Russia "had no special alliance or peculiarly intimate connection with Spain" and that the tsar had no wish "to take side with Spain in her quarrel with the Colonies."[52] At the same time, and as if to give credence to these assurances, Russia actively supported American claims to Spanish Florida, playing a direct diplomatic role on behalf of the United States in negotiating the final settlement with Spain.[53] Whether or not this policy was consciously designed to facilitate Russian interests elsewhere in the hemisphere is not clear from available sources, although in actual practice it could only serve that end.

The one aspect of Russo-American relations that did impinge on tsarist interests in Latin America was the increasingly problematic issue of recognition. While the United States, in the words of Capo d'Istria, "formed no part whatsoever of the general association [of nations],"[54] its endorsement of independent status for the insurgent territories of Latin America portended grave consequences on both sides of the Atlantic. Should the United States extend recognition to the Spanish colonies, Nesselrode observed in the fall of 1818, it would almost certainly lead to war with Spain, which in all probability "would involve other powers and perhaps turn into a general conflict."[55] Accordingly, tsarist diplomacy sought to dissuade the American government from extending recognition to the insurgent régimes.[56]

The United States in fact delayed official recognition of the Spanish American governments for another three and a half years, during which time the matter occupied a place of only secondary importance within the wider dimensions of Russo-American relations. When that act was at last consummated in the spring of 1822, it elicited an essentially passive response from the tsarist court. Europe, declared Nesselrode, could not view the colonial question in the same light as America; even Great Britain, whose commercial interests ran counter to the Spanish colonial system, supported Spain's proclaimed intention to reestablish metropolitan rule in its overseas possessions. The Russian government, for its part, took satisfaction in the expressed determination of the United States to place no obstacles in the way of a future reconciliation between Spain and Spanish America should such an understanding be achieved free of outside intervention. Adherence to that policy of neutrality, Nesselrode emphasized, would, it was hoped, avert an outbreak of hostilities between Spain and the United States and thus preserve the general peace so beneficial to all.[57]

Tsarist policy toward the Americas in the early 1820s can only be characterized as prudently realistic. It sought to consolidate established Russian interests in the Pacific Northwest, to promote commercial ties throughout the hemisphere, and to avoid entanglements detrimental to the peace and tranquility of Europe. At no time did it pose a military threat to the New World, for Russia was never in a position to challenge the maritime might of Great Britain. Indeed, the tsar had been unable to provide direct material assistance for the Peninsular campaign. Now, on the brink of war in the Balkans, he could hardly contemplate a military involvement halfway around the world. Russian influence, observed Pozzo di Borgo, "was limited to moving others who could offer direct and immediate means of saving the Spanish monarchy."[58] Having drawn the connection between the political upheavals of Europe and America, the tsar was powerless to quell the ominous agitations of the other hemisphere.

The Brazilian Empire

Russia's relations with the Portuguese empire presented a set of considerations quite different from those raised by the separatist struggles of the Spanish colonies. As described in the preceding chapters, the transferral of the Portuguese court to Rio de Janeiro in 1808 and the resultant establishment of direct diplomatic ties with Brazil led to a physical presence in that country that Russia lacked in the neighboring Spanish territories. The prospect of continued crown rule temporarily placed Brazil outside the politics of legitimacy and pacification, a fact that, in combination with the country's strategic and commercial significance, prompted the tsarist court to pursue a permanent presence in this vast region of South America.

The special nature of tsarist interests in Brazil was reflected in the extraordinary activity of the prime agent of those interests—Russia's dynamic consul-general, Georg Heinrich von Langsdorff.[59] Arriving in the Brazilian capital in April 1813, Langsdorff settled easily into his new surroundings and soon enjoyed wide respect among subjects of the Portuguese crown and the foreign community alike. He was "respectably known to the literary world," wrote James Henderson in 1821, while "his pursuit in the obtainment of objects in natural history had been indefatigable."[60] His name, concurred Alexander Caldcleugh, was "well known to all lovers of science."[61] But it was the boundless energy and enthusiasm with which Langsdorff devoted himself to the study of Brazil that most distinguished him from contemporaries of like interests. John Luccock, for example, described him as "active, even restless."[62] German naturalists J. B. von Spix and K. F. P. von Martius found him to be of "uninterrupted good humour," even when faced with the fatigues and "disagreeable adventures" of travel in the interior.[63] Langsdorff, wrote French naturalist Auguste de Saint-Hilaire, "was the most active and indefatigable man I had met in my life." In his company, Saint-Hilaire "learned to travel without

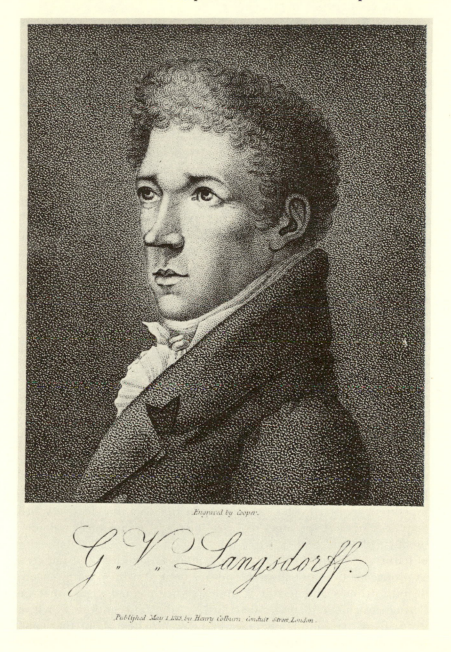

Engraved by Cooper.

G. V. Langsdorff

Published May 1 1813. by Henry Colburn Conduit Street, London.

5. Georg Heinrich von Langsdorff, corresponding, later extraordinary, member of the Russian Academy of Sciences, Russian consul-general in Rio de Janeiro (1812–1829)

wasting a single moment, to be subjected to all manner of privations, and to suffer with cheer every kind of inconvenience."[64]

Three years after his arrival in Brazil, Langsdorff purchased a large tract of land on the main road between Minas Gerais and Pôrto da Estrêla, at the northern extremity of Guanabara Bay.[65] He acquired this property, estimated at ten square miles in area, for under £1,000 and promptly converted it into a prosperous *fazenda*, to which he gave the name Mandioca. By 1819, he had planted some twenty thousand coffee trees and was producing up to a thousand sacks of *farinha* annually from manioc plantings.[66] Physical improvements included "a spacious shed (*rancho*) for the reception of the numerous caravans from Minas, a venda, where brandy was sold, a mill for grinding maize, and a small dwelling-house for the proprietor, in the usual style of the country."[67]

In 1819, Langsdorff petitioned João VI for the same privileges accorded the owners of sugar mills and other agricultural enterprises, specifically exemption of his employees from militia duty, taxation, and all other obligations, civil or military, that might prejudice their labors. By granting these privileges, he assured the Portuguese monarch, "there would emerge in an uncultivated *sertão* at no expense to the State a great establishment, which in a few short years would in various ways enrich that very same State."[68] He was motivated in his endeavors, he assured the king, by a fervent commitment to the "Kingdom of Brazil" and by a desire to contribute to the growth of its agriculture and "territorial opulence." He even envisioned that the products of his *fazenda* would one day form "a basis of national wealth and of State independence."[69]

Dom João granted Langdorff's request, which encouraged the Russian diplomat to implement ambitious plans that for some time had been forming in his mind. In the spring of 1821, he returned to St. Petersburg, where he proposed the organization of a major scientific expedition to Brazil, whose object would be "scientific discovery, geographic, statistical and other research, the study of previously unknown products of trade, and the collection of specimens from all the realms of nature."[70] While in the Russian capital, Langsdorff "did not cease to propagate the most favorable ideas about Brazil, praising its prodigious richness and fertility," attacking with equal vigor what the Portuguese chargé d'affaires described as "the false notions which individuals of passion or ignorance had disseminated about that country."[71] In proposing this expedition, Langsdorff pointed to the numerous foreign scholars then working in Brazil and underscored his desire "that Russia not fall behind the other powers."[72]

The tsar approved Langsdorff's proposal, authorizing for its implementation an initial disbursement of forty thousand rubles, with annual supplements of fifteen thousand rubles for as long as the expedition might last.[73] These monies, in turn, were assigned to the ministry of foreign affairs, under whose authority the proposed expedition fell.[74]

In addition to the scientific expedition, Langsdorff organized at his own expense an ambitious, albeit ultimately abortive, project of immigrant colonization on his Mandioca holdings. He returned to Brazil in early March 1822, accompanied by his son, Karl Georg, expedition members Edouard Charles Ménétries and Johann Moritz Rugendas, eighty-five German colonists, and several persons in his private service.[75] Notwithstanding the distractions of the Mandioca estate and a number of unpleasant problems arising from his immigrant labor,[76] Langsdorff busied himself almost immediately with the affairs of the Russian consulate, including the arrival in late March of the vessels *Otkrytie* and *Blagonamerennyi*, which, bound for Kronshtadt after a protracted voyage to Alaska and the Pacific Northwest, reached Brazil in need of extensive repairs.[77] At the same time, he began to make preparations for the work of the scientific expedition, which under his direction would over the next six years explore wide areas of the Brazilian interior.

Participants in the expedition included the celebrated artists J. M. Rugendas, Amadey Adriane Taunay, and Hercules Florence; French zoologist E. C. Ménétries; German botanist Ludwig Riedel; and Russian astronomer N. G. Rubtsov. The labors of the expedition itself transpired in several stages. The first two years were spent studying the province of Rio de Janeiro; from May 1824 to March 1825, the expedition conducted an extensive investigation of Minas Gerais, and in September 1825, Langsdorff and his colleagues began a prolonged study of São Paulo and Mato Grosso, including a ten-month sojourn in the area of Cuiabá; finally, in December 1827, the expedition set out in two separate parties to explore the Arinos, Guaporé, and other tributaries of the Amazon, reaching Belem do Pará one year later devastated by illness and the extreme rigors of a hostile clime.[78]

While of interest in itself, the Russian scientific expedition to Brazil has a broader significance as an indicator of the deeper sources of tsarist New World involvement. If on the one hand the expedition pursued scientific knowledge, on the other the very quest for such knowledge responded in the final analysis to the needs of nascent industrial capitalism. The conquest of ever wider colonial markets in the course of the eighteenth century had placed an increasing premium on modernization of the means of production, which required a parallel development of technology, itself inextricably tied to advances in the applied, exact, and natural sciences. The development of industrial capitalism in Europe and North America thus contributed significantly to the stimulation of geographic exploration on a worldwide scale.[79]

Although it was peripheral to the main development of industrial capitalism and the related drive for overseas markets, Russia nonetheless participated in that decisive process of modern history and consequently manifested many of its characteristic features. Tsarist preoccupation with colonial expansion and the promotion of Russian maritime power was a prime example. Russian interests in the Spanish and Portuguese colonies likewise derived from needs generated by the gradual development of capitalist relations within Russia. The varied activities of Langsdorff, in turn, responded both directly and indirectly to those needs.

The tsarist court was especially anxious to promote trade relations with Brazil, and the search for new sources of trade occupied Langsdorff from the outset of his tour as consul-general. As previously noted, one of the explicit objectives of the Russian scientific expedition was to investigate hitherto unknown products of trade. The actual development of Russo-Brazilian commercial ties, however, proved uneven, with direct bilateral trade between the two countries declining noticeably after 1816. The tsar's decision to regulate Russian foreign commerce through a uniform régime of protective tariffs greatly prejudiced Portuguese trade with Russian ports, the bulk of which "fell into the hands of the wealthiest or most industrialized nations."[80] Whereas prior to 1816 an average of eighteen to twenty Portuguese merchant vessels had entered the port of Kronshtadt (St. Petersburg) each year, only eight arrived in 1817, three in 1818, and two in 1819. In all probability, lamented the Portuguese chargé d'affaires in St. Petersburg, "this small figure will diminish still further once the accounts of the Portuguese and Russian merchants who deal in this trade are liquidated."[81] The gravity of the situation was highlighted in the fall of 1821 when the formerly prosperous firm of Dionizio Pedro Lopes failed.[82]

This does not, of course, say anything about the actual flow of goods between the Russian and Portuguese empires, which in point of fact appears to have grown. What occurred, as the Portuguese envoy correctly saw, was that an increasing portion of this trade moved in foreign bottoms. In addition, goods were frequently transshipped, making it extremely difficult to determine the true extent of commercial intercourse. Moreover, even direct trade carried in Russian and Portuguese vessels fluctuated markedly, as, for example, in 1821 when Luzo-Brazilian goods imported into Russia were reported to have increased

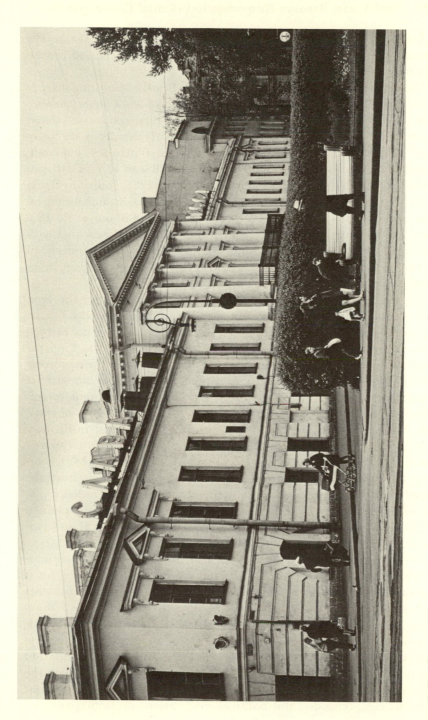

6. Residence of Portuguese merchant Dionizio Pedro Lopes, built on St. Petersburg's Vasil'evskii Island in the years 1808–1810

by 285 percent, while Russian exports to Portugal and Brazil rose 100 percent.[83] The scope of Russo-Portuguese trade in this period can be seen from tables 6–9.

The actual nature of Russian interests in Brazil comes into sharper focus with the declaration of Brazilian independence in September 1822. This act immediately complicated the normal conduct of tsarist affairs in the country, for Alexander I, steadfastly espousing the principles of legitimacy, reaffirmed his loyalty to the Portuguese monarch, João VI. Alexander's minister plenipotentiary, Baron F. V. Tuyll van Serooskerken, had left Rio de Janeiro in May 1821, following Dom João's departure for Portugal.[84] After that date, tsarist ambassadorial representation to the Portuguese court resided in Lisbon, while Brazilian envoys ceased to be received in St. Petersburg and were met with outward hostility by Russian diplomats in other capitals. Indeed, of all the major powers, Russia proved to be the most intransigent in its official support of Portuguese crown rights in Brazil.

Despite official tsarist censure of Brazilian independence, the Russian consulate in Rio de Janeiro continued to function as before, Langsdorff and his vice-consul, P. P. Kielchen, remaining on correct, even amiable terms with the new Brazilian government. Emperor Pedro I, for his part, provided material support to meet the mounting costs of the Russian scientific expedition, as well as to underwrite Langsdorff's own personal ventures in farming and immigrant colonization. Initially, this was facilitated by Dom Pedro's minister of state, José Bonifácio de Andrade e Silva, a scholar and scientist in his own right with whom Langsdorff enjoyed a special bond of mutual understanding. Even after José Bonifácio's removal from office in 1823, however, the Russian consul-general continued to receive favors from the Brazilian court far in excess of the deference normally accorded diplomatic representatives of foreign governments. In part this is explained by Langsdorff's dynamic personality, in part by the political and economic imperatives of the moment.

Tsarist patronage of the Langsdorff expedition likewise ran counter to the legitimist position affirmed by the court of St. Petersburg, for it constituted a commitment to the pursuit of Russian imperial interests in a country whose juridical existence the tsar chose to deny. Moreover, Alexander I was fully apprised of the situation in Brazil at the time he authorized the expedition—an ambitious undertaking of several years' duration that presupposed continuing tsarist representation on its behalf. Langsdorff, for his part, must certainly have foreseen the impending crisis by the time he sailed for Europe in 1820 and without a doubt comprehended the political implications of Dom João's re-

TABLE 6.

PRINCIPAL COMMODITIES IMPORTED INTO ST. PETERSBURG FROM THE PORTUGUESE EMPIRE IN THE YEARS 1814–1819

Goods	Quantity	1814	1815	1816	1817	1818	1819
Almonds	pudy*	5,245	687	2,940	1,736	3,400	2,175
Bay leaves	"	34	300	458	151	362	48
Brazilwood	"	0	2,218	229	786	3,488	250
Cacao	"	756	451	0	0	0	0
Citrus fruits	cases	11,678	11,321	19,671	11,849	9,345	13,003
Citrus rinds	pudy	84	13	0	0	30	32
Coffee	"	582	166	534	203	0	0
Copaiba balsam	"	16	156	72	36	24	0
Cork (pressed)	"	3,222	4,229	2,995	954	7,392	1,617
Cork stoppers	pieces	4,554,000	2,376,000	504,000	216,000	432,000	0
Cotton	pudy	75	580	0	0	0	0
Indigo	cases	0	1	12	1	0	30
Lemons (salted)	casks	249	36	0	0	36	0
Olive oil	pudy	2,285	80	90	13	0	0
Olives	"	75	0	28	0	0	0
Pepper	"	4	1,427	2,064	681	0	0
Piasters	pieces	0	2,026	0	1,000	0	0
Raisins	pudy	178	81	824	0	0	0
Rice	"	384	5,501	7,420	0	0	1,530
Salt	"	42,451	45,597	60,513	53,280	19,724	13,149
Sarsaparilla	"	658	853	777	852	987	1,204
Sugar	"	46,170	22,306	23,409	28,376	28,328	20,026
Tapioca	"	120	27	310	4	0	75
Tea	"	14	4	32	0	0	0
Wine	steekan†	79,866	59,958	47,458	37,287	3,456	10,818

Source: "Marchandises importées a St. Pétersbourg depuis 1814 jusqu'à 1819, tant en vaisseaux portuguais comme étrangers vennant des ports du Royaume du Portugal," ANTT, *caixa* 14.

* 1 *pud* = 36 lbs.

† 1 *steekan* = 5.125 gals. (Amsterdam).

TABLE 7.

PRINCIPAL ITEMS OF EXPORT FROM ST. PETERSBURG TO THE UNITED KINGDOM OF PORTUGAL, BRAZIL, AND THE ALGARVE, 1814–1819

Goods	Quantity	1814	1815	1816	1817	1818	1819
Broadcloth	arshiny*	900	2,601	1,230	0	0	0
Calamanco	pieces	183	250	288	50	11	0
Cordage	pudy	36,233	50,946	27,859	6,021	2,126	5,183
Duck	pieces	7,616	6,970	12,861	6,627	3,026	839
Flax	pudy	39,906	21,730	63,619	28,308	5,184	6,311
Flax tow	"	487	477	193	0	0	84
Flemish linen	pieces	434	417	1,807	80	600	180
Hemp	pudy	33,569	44,096	31,236	25,170	28,181	28,685
Hemp tow	"	2,711	2,843	1,131	146	2,014	861
Hempseed oil	"	4,501	5,029	1,543	2,646	1,273	883
Hides	pieces	700	2,117	106	0	0	0
Hog bristles	pudy	63	338	138	0	18	2
Horsehair	"	38	122	109	4	0	0
Iron (assorted)	"	25,047	13,436	3,323	3,217	5,113	0
Isinglass	"	5	19	6	9	7	0
Linseed oil	"	3,588	351	1,068	4	0	24
Muslin	arshiny	6,250	1,050	13,433	2,700	1,872	0
Pelts (hare)	pieces	114,110	168,646	215,780	0	0	0
Planks	"	2,394	394	16,476	0	0	0
Potash	pudy	0	0	254	736	0	329
Quills	pieces	967,400	0	2,777	0	0	0
Resin	pudy	2,001	393	322	0	18	0
Sailcloth	pieces	10,688	7,509	10,765	1,637	2,704	2,066
Staves	"	1,440	0	6,192	0	0	0
Tallow	pudy	1,754	379	6,421	352	2,493	2,813
Tallow candles	"	5,920	2,430	2,225	552	100	254
Tar	pudy	3,127	1,149	791	0	0	0
Toweling	arshiny	0	5,199	2,065	0	0	0

Water glasses	pieces	338	572	0	4,336	0	0
Wax	*pudy*	673	135	57	61	100	25
Wax candles	"	248	153	129	100	136	4
Wheat	bushels	14,703	62,228	23,035	59,868	55,780	8,654
Window panes	pieces	2,610	4,440	0	13	0	0

Source: "Marchandises exportées de St. Pétersbourg pour le Royaume Uni du Portugal, du Brésil, et des Algarves depuis l'année 1814 jusqu'à l'année 1819," ANTT, *caixa* 14.

* 1 *arshin* = 28 inches.

TABLE 8.

MERCHANT VESSELS SAILING TO ST. PETERSBURG FROM PORTS OF THE PORTUGUESE EMPIRE IN THE YEARS 1814–1819

Registry	1814	1815	1816	1817	1818	1819
Portuguese	15	21	22	6	3	2
Russian	9	10	8	5	1	1
Other	5	4	12	13	15	15
Total	29	35	42	24	19	18

TABLE 9.

MERCHANT VESSELS SAILING FROM ST. PETERSBURG TO PORTS OF THE PORTUGUESE EMPIRE IN THE YEARS 1814–1819

Registry	1814	1815	1816	1817	1818	1819
Portuguese	15	20	22	6	3	2
Russian	8	13	7	1	1	1
Other	5	7	10	18	13	8
Total	28	40	39	25	17	11

Source: As cited for Tables 3–4; and *Considérations sur le Commerce de la Russie avec le Portugal*, St. Pétersbourg, 24 January (5 February) 1820, ANTT, *caixa* 15.

turn to Portugal in the spring of 1821, news of which reached St. Petersburg precisely at the time when he was discussing the proposed expedition with tsarist officials.[85] As early as March 1821, Tuyll had reported that Brazil would soon break its ties with Portugal. Efforts by the Portuguese court to return Brazil to "its former state of colonial dependency," he wrote, would lead to its prompt separation from the metropolis.[86]

Langsdorff's official response to the declaration of Brazilian independence further reveals the contradictory nature of tsarist policy toward this contested colony. Returning to Mandioca in December 1822 from field work with the scientific expedition, he addressed a note to José Bonifácio requesting that his compliments be communicated to the emperor, along with his profound regrets at having missed "so great an event for Brazil, which without a doubt will bring this immense Empire to the highest level of perfection, contentment and prosperity."[87] This initial endorsement of Brazil's new political status, however, was artfully qualified in conformity with the tsar's public stance on the colonial question. "The great interest which H. M. the Emperor my master has always had in the welfare of the House of Bragança," Langsdorff wrote; "the justice of the great cause of peace which the Russian government has always maintained through friendly relations; in sum, the interest of all in the preservation of a legitimate and magnanimous Sovereign, are for me sufficient guarantee that [the tsar] will look favorably upon this grand event."[88]

Langsdorff implied that the tsar would celebrate the independent development of Brazil, whose economy, once freed of its colonial fetters, promised certain advantages to Russian commercial interests. As a firm defender of the principle of autocratic legitimacy, however, he could not openly endorse a revolutionary change in the structure of the Portuguese empire. Indeed, Alexander subsequently advised the Portuguese envoy to St. Petersburg that the matter of Brazil was of the utmost importance, "above all for the principle." "It is my opinion," he asserted, "that the King should never under any circumstances recognize the independence. His Majesty can grant Brazil whatever concessions He may deem appropriate, provided that this country remain subject to His Crown and joined to the Portuguese Monarchy under one and the same Sovereign."[89]

The tsar remained immutably committed to this position until his death in mid-November 1825. As in Russia's previous dealings with colonial Latin America, however, adherence to principle in matters of diplomacy related only tangentially to the pursuit of basic imperial interests in the New World. Thus when the Portuguese crown petitioned the tsarist government in the summer of 1824 to close Russian ports to Brazilian ships, the court of St. Petersburg agreed only to take the request under consideration and in actual fact continued to traffic with vessels of Brazilian registry.[90] In Brazil, meanwhile, Langsdorff and Kielchen devoted special attention to the continued movement of Russian ships through the port of Rio de Janeiro and to securing privileged treatment for those ships while in Brazilian waters.[91]

Post-Independence Perspectives

The accession to the throne of Tsar Nicholas I produced little change in Russian policy toward Latin America. The Decembrist uprising following Nicholas's inauguration may have confirmed the new tsar in his repugnance for the colonial insurgents, who by their revolutionary example had actually inspired certain of the Russian conspirators, but it failed to incline him toward an interventionist policy on behalf of the Iberian crowns.[92] On the contrary, from the outset of his reign he showed a firm grasp of New World realities and a determination to avoid costly entanglements. When, for example, the Spanish ambassador presented his credentials in early April 1826, Nicholas reaffirmed the legitimacy of Ferdinand VII's wish to preserve the overseas territories under crown rule, but quickly added that to contemplate a collective effort by the European powers to recover those territories was totally unrealistic. He then inquired about the status of Cuba and Puerto Rico, expressing satisfaction at the ambassador's assurances that effective measures had been implemented to secure those island against any further acts of sedition.[93]

Nicholas again raised the matter of Cuba and Puerto Rico at a meeting with the Spanish ambassador the following autumn. It was imperative, he insisted, that these islands be secured, for by their good example of enlightened crown rule the disenchanted peoples of Spanish America might yet be drawn back into the metropolitan fold.[94] The tsar's expressed concern for the future of the Greater Antilles, however, appears to have had more to do with Russian interest in Haiti than with a desire to see Spain recover her lost colonies, which in any event he believed irretrievable. At that very time, tsarist officials were considering a proposal by the Russian-American Company to convert the island of Santo Domingo into "a most advantageous commercial entrepôt between the countries of North and South America."[95] With notable vision, the company's board of directors contemplated a thriving trade between the Baltic and the west coast of America by way of the Caribbean "once navigation is opened across the Isthmus of Panama."[96]

Realization of this project hinged on the security of the neighboring islands, which explains in large part Russia's seemingly contradictory support in 1825–1826 of United States efforts to secure Spanish recognition of Gran Colombia.[97] The threatened invasion of Cuba and Puerto Rico by patriot forces from northern South America presaged further turmoil throughout the region, with the probability of additional European involvement arising from British and French designs on the Antilles. Were Spain to desist in its use of the islands as staging points for continued incursions against the South American mainland and to affirm its good faith by formally recognizing the political independence of Gran Colombia, crown rule in Cuba and Puerto Rico might be preserved and a potentially disruptive international scramble for colonial territory avoided.[98]

As Russia and the United States sought jointly to influence the Spanish court in favor of recognition, the Russian government deliberated the ramifications of direct commercial ties with Haiti. Inasmuch as France had recognized Haitian independence, stated Nesselrode in the fall of 1826, the Russian-American Company "could be permitted to trade with the inhabitants of that island and to establish storage facilities there for its goods."[99] Appraisals of the benefits to be derived from such trade, however, differed widely, and not all quarters of the tsarist government responded positively to the Russian-American Company proposal.

Objections centered on the matter of fiscal incentives. The cabinet of ministers, which endorsed the proposal in January 1827, favored a policy of limited customs exemptions to offset initial risks. The ministry of finance, on the other hand, strenuously opposed such a policy, holding that there was no justification for underwriting the envisioned trade "with a gift from state coffers."[100] At the same time, local sugar refiners and private merchant interests expressed concern over what some felt would be unacceptable competition from a state-supported monopoly.[101]

The most ardent and articulate advocate of direct Russo-Haitian trade was Admiral N. S. Mordvinov, who argued forcefully that any European power "that did not promote and expand trade and which failed to pursue new commercial opportunities ran the inevitable risk of losing its established markets."[102] He rejected out of hand the view advanced by some merchants that colonial imports could be secured more advantageously through foreign shippers trading with Brazil, Cuba, and North America.[103] He likewise dismissed the argument that there was no market for Russian goods in Haiti "because people there go barefoot and there are no railroads."[104] When one realizes, he responded,

> that in Haiti the supreme ruler, ministers, senators, generals, counts, marquis, and various other officials wear embroidered caftans, while their wives wear muslin dresses with white silk lace, one can suppose they are in need of shirts and shoes, and therefore of linen, sackcloth, and leather. Haiti, it is true, has no railroads, but its inhabitants need axes, knives, pitchforks, nails, wheel rims, caldrons, locks, hinges, and many other items of hardware, all of which are supplied by numerous English and French ships. Among the Antilles, the island of Haiti is itself one of the largest and, due to its geographic situation, is perhaps the most valuable as an entrepôt for trade.[105]

It was not a question, Mordvinov emphasized, of promoting the particular interests of the Russian-American Company, but rather of stimulating Russian trade in general.[106] There simply were too few private merchants in Russia with sufficient capital to engage in the trans-Atlantic trade. Indeed, neither the Russian-American Company nor any private individual could afford to undertake commercial relations with America in the absence of a minimum guaranteed profit.[107]

Mordvinov accordingly proposed that trade with Haiti be exempted from all customs obligations for the first six years of operations, during which time the company could "accommodate its shipments to the tastes and needs of the Haitians" and "initiate dealings with the neighboring islands and the inhabitants of the mainland." The future opening of navigation across the Isthmus of Panama, he reiterated, would make Haiti especially valuable as a convenient source of supply for Russian America.[108]

These arguments, however, failed to convince a majority of the council of state, which in May 1827 voted not to recommend approval of the requested customs exemptions. The tsar accepted the council's recommendation and thus brought the matter to a close. Held to established tariff schedules, the Russian-American Company abandoned its plans for direct commercial intercourse with the Caribbean.[109] Although it produced no material results, the affair is instructive as another example of the intricate relationship between tsarist diplomacy and the multiple, often conflicting interests of imperial expansion.

Concern with securing a viable base of supply for Russian America likewise underlay the continuing Russian presence in Alta California. The Ross settlement had developed slowly since its founding in 1812 and, while achieving a modest level of self-sufficiency, never produced enough staples to meet the needs of the Alaskan settlements.[110] Moreover, its value as a source of seal and sea otter pelts declined sharply in the 1820s, with the result that it actually became a financial liability.[111]

Primarily because of these difficulties the place of California in the larger panorama of Russian imperial interests became the object of renewed discussion in the 1820s. There was general agreement within the Russian-American Company that the failure of the Ross settlement to service the basic needs of Russian America stemmed from its not entirely felicitous location—a failure, some suggested, that could be remedied by the acquisition of additional territory. Serious attention was given to extending Russian claims south to San Francisco Bay, north to the forty-second parallel, and eastward to the Sacramento River.[112] The port of San Francisco itself, argued I. F. Kruzenshtern, could be secured from Spain through formal cession.[113]

Rumors of new Russian designs on California circulated widely during this period. Allusions to territorial concessions appear in the diplomatic correspondence of Spain and Russia, as noted earlier, while from its founding in the fall of 1821 the newly independent government of Mexico expressed deep concern over anticipated Russian incursions against the northwestern frontier.[114] By the close of 1821, however, the political and diplomatic coordinates of the colonial map had been decisively altered and it was no longer possible to frame the territorial question in terms of outstanding Spanish obligations to the court of St. Petersburg.[115] There was no reason to pursue the matter with Spain, the tsar observed in October 1824, because Spanish dominion over California had in fact ceased. As for the revolutionary government of Mexico, Nesselrode added, "we shall have no dealings with them and consequently are unable to approach them on the issue of our rights to the Ross settlement and to the land which it occupies."[116] While Russia continued for a while to promote its interests in California and in time dealt directly with Mexican authorities, the permanent severance of ties between Mexico and Spain effectively removed the problem of territorial expansion from the scope of Russo-Spanish relations.[117]

In South America, Nicholas I adhered strictly to the policy line set by his predecessor, refusing even to recognize the ceremonial title "Emperor of Brazil," which João VI had bestowed upon himself when at the close of 1825 he formally endorsed Brazilian independence.[118] It was another three years before Russia at last followed the lead of the other powers and reestablished full diplomatic relations with Rio de Janeiro. In October 1828, as Langsdorff, delirious with tropical fever, made his way painfully toward Santarem at the juncture of the Tapajos and Amazon rivers, the tsar appointed F. F. Borel ambassador to Brazil.[119]

The initial phase of Russian involvement in Latin America thus drew to a close. For several decades the tsarist empire had probed and explored the Western Hemisphere in search of viable relationships. As foreseen in the 1760s by a Spanish Jesuit, these approaches were to proceed "along obscure paths of more or less prudent conjecture, blindly groping through the dark, testing many directions until at last reaching the desired objective."[120] They led, following the collapse of the Spanish and Portuguese New World empires, to a modest but permanent presence in the former colonial territories.

For the remainder of the nineteenth century, Russian interests in Latin America centered on Brazil, described suggestively by a tsarist diplomat of the period as "the largest, most accessible and productive part of South America's Atlantic seaboard."[121] Contacts were maintained as well with the neighboring Spanish American republics and by 1890 Russia had established formal diplomatic relations with the governments of Mexico, Argentina, and Uruguay. While these ties scarcely indicated a Russian "opening" to Latin America, they did evidence a continuity of interests in the region consonant with the global perspectives of a major world power.

Notes

Abbreviations Used

ADPT   Arkhiv Dmitriia Pavlovicha Tatishcheva [D. P. Tatishchev papers], Saltykov-Shchedrin State Public Library, Leningrad, USSR.

AGI   Archivo General de Indias, Seville.

AGS   *Arkhiv Gosudarstvennogo soveta* [Council of state papers]. 5 vols. in 16. St. Petersburg, 1869–1904.

AHI   Arquivo Histórico do Itamaratí, Rio de Janeiro.

AHN   Archivo Histórico Nacional, Madrid.

AM   *Arkhiv grafov Mordvinovykh* [Mordvinov papers]. 10 vols. St. Petersburg, 1901–1903.

AN SSSR   Akademiia nauk SSSR [USSR Academy of Sciences].

ANTT   Arquivo Nacional Tôrre do Tombo, Lisbon.

AVMM   Arkhiv Vladimira Mikhailovicha Miroshevskogo [V. M. Miroshevskii papers], Lenin State Library, Moscow.

BL   Hubert Howe Bancroft Library, University of California, Berkeley.

BMN   Biblioteca del Museo Naval, Madrid.

BNM   Biblioteca Nacional, Madrid.

IVGO   *Izvestiia Vsesoiuznogo Geograficheskogo Obshchestva* [Transactions of the All-Union Geographical Society].

o. s.   old style, i.e., according to the Julian calendar.

PSZRI   *Polnoe sobranie zakonov Rossiiskoi imperii* [Complete collection of laws of the Russian Empire]. 1649 to 12 December 1825 [o. s.]. 49 vols. St. Petersburg, 1830.

RAC   Russian-American Company.

Sbornik   *Sbornik Imperatorskogo Russkogo Istoricheskogo Obshchestva* [Collection of the Imperial Russian Historical Society]. 148 vols. St. Petersburg, 1867–1917.

VLU   *Vestnik Leningradskogo Universiteta* [Bulletin of the University of Leningrad], history, language, and literature series.

VPR   *Vneshniaia politika Rossii XIX i nachala XX veka. Dokumenty Rossiiskogo Ministerstva inostrannykh del* [Russian foreign policy in the nineteenth and early twentieth centuries. Documents from the Russian ministry of foreign affairs]. First series, 1801–1815. 8 vols. Moscow, 1960–1972.

Chapter 1: Introduction

1. See R. A. Humphreys, "The Historiography of the Spanish American Revolutions," in *Relazioni del X Congresso Internazionale di Scienze Storiche*, I, 207–233; also published in *The Hispanic American Historical Review* 36, no. 1 (February 1956): 92–105. See, also, R. A. Humphreys and John Lynch (eds.), *The Origins of the Latin American Revolutions, 1808–1826*. For Soviet views, see M. S. Al'perovich, V. I. Ermolaev, I. R. Lavretskii, and S. I. Semënov, "Ob osvoboditel'noi voine ispanskikh kolonii v Amerike (1810–1826)," *Voprosy istorii* 11 (1956): 52–71; and N. M. Lavrov, "Osnovnye problemy voiny za nezavisimost' v Latinskoi Amerike," in: N. M. Lavrov, A. I. Shtrakhov, and B. I. Koval (eds.), *Voina za nezavisimost' v Latinskoi Amerike (1810–1826)*, pp. 15–43.

2. See, for example, Charles C. Griffin, *The United States and the Disruption of the Spanish Empire, 1810–1822. A Study of the Relations of the United States with Spain and with the Rebel Spanish Colonies*; William F. Kaufmann, *British Policy and the Independence of Latin America, 1804–1828*; J. Fred Rippy, *Rivalry of the United States and Great Britain Over Latin America (1808–1830)*; William S. Robertson, *France and Latin-American Independence*; and Arthur P. Whitaker, *The United States and the Independence of Latin America, 1800–1830*.

3. See Theo P. M. de Jong, *Nederland en Latijns-Amerika (1816–1826)*; Manfred Kossok, *Im Schatten der Heiligen Allianz. Deutschland und Lateinamerika, 1815–1830*; William Spence Robertson, "Metternich's Attitude toward Revolutions in Latin America," *The Hispanic American Historical Review* 21, no. 4 (November 1941): 538–558; and Sven Ola Swärd, *Latinamerika i svensk politik unde 1810-och 1820-talen* (Uppsala: Almqvist and Wiksells Boktryckery AB, 1949).

4. Federico Chabod, *Storia della politica estera italiana dal 1870 al 1896* (Bari: Laterza, 1962), pp. xi–xii.

5. Ibid., p. xii.

6. See Dexter Perkins, "Russia and the Spanish Colonies, 1817–1818," *The American Historical Review* 28, no. 4 (July 1923): 656–672; and William Spence Robertson, "Russia and the Emancipation of Spanish America, 1816–1826," *The Hispanic American Historical Review* 21, no. 2 (May 1941): 196–221. Both authors rely heavily on the important *Correspondence diplomatique des ambassadeurs et ministres de Russie en France et de France en Russie avec leurs gouvernements de 1814 à 1830*, compiled by A. A. Polovtsov and published as part of the Imperial Russian Historical Society series (*Sbornik*, vols. 112, 119, and 127). Robertson makes use of a variety of other diplomatic sources as well, including manuscript materials housed in the Petrograd archives of the tsarist ministry of foreign affairs. Like Perkins, however, he fails to move beyond a face value reading of purely diplomatic documentation.

7. Conde Emanuel de Bennigsen, "Nota acêrca de alguns projetos de colonização russa na América do Sul durante o século XVIII," *Revista de História* 4, no. 15 (July-September 1953): 169–177; A. Béthencourt, "Proyecto de un establecimiento ruso en Brasil (1732–1733)," *Revista de Indias* 10, nos. 37–38 (July-December 1949): 651–668; R. A. Humphreys, "Richard Oswald's Plan for an English and Russian Attack on Spanish America, 1781–1782," *The Hispanic American Historical Review* 18, no. 1 (February 1938): 95–101; and Lewis A. Tambs, "Anglo-Russian Enterprises Against Hispanic South

America, 1732–1737," *The Slavonic and East European Review* 48, no. 112 (July 1970): 357–372.

8. See, for example, Clarence L. Andrews, "Russian Plans for American Dominion," *The Washington Historical Quarterly* 18, no. 2 (April 1927): 83–92; O. E. Essig, "The Russian Settlement at Ross," *Quarterly of the California Historical Society* 12, no. 3 (September 1933): 191–209; A. P. Kashevaroff, "Fort Ross. An Account of the Russian Settlement in San Francisco Bay," *Alaska Magazine* 1, no. 5 (May 1927): 235–242; Anatole G. Mazour, "Dimitry Zavalishin: Dreamer of a Russian-American Empire," *Pacific Historical Review* 5, no. 1 (February 1936): 26–37; idem, "Doctor Yegor Scheffer: Dreamer of a Russian Empire in the Pacific," *Pacific Historical Review* 6, no. 1 (February 1937): 15–20; Richard A. Pierce, "Georg Anton Schäffer, Russia's Man in Hawaii, 1815–1817," *Pacific Historical Review* 32, no. 4 (November 1963): 397–405; A. E. Sokol, "Russian Expansion and Exploration in the Pacific," *The American Slavic and East European Review* 11, no. 2 (April 1952): 85–105; Stuart R. Tompkins and Max L. Moorhead, "Russia's Approach to America," *The British Columbia Historical Quarterly* 13 (1949): 55–66, 231–255.

9. A useful introductory volume to the literature on the Monroe Doctrine is Donald Marquand Dozer (ed.), *The Monroe Doctrine. Its Modern Significance.*

10. See Dexter Perkins, "Europe, Spanish America, and the Monroe Doctrine," *The American Historical Review* 27 (January 1922): 207–218; and idem, *The Monroe Doctrine, 1823–1826.* On the Russian presence in the Pacific Northwest, see Irby C. Nichols, "The Russian Ukase and the Monroe Doctrine: A Re-evaluation," *Pacific Historical Review* 36, no. 1 (February 1967): 13–26.

11. Dozer, *The Monroe Doctrine*, pp. 3–4. Dozer recognizes, however, that the possibility of European intervention "has been variously estimated" and "was not so serious as Monroe and Adams believed it to be." (Ibid., p. 5)

12. Federico G. Gil, *Latin American–United States Relations*, p. 57.

13. Perkins, "Russia and the Spanish Colonies," p. 672.

14. On the Monroe Doctrine, see N. N. Bolkhovitinov, *Doktrina Monro (proiskhozhdenie i kharakter)*; idem, "Russkaia Amerika i provozglashenie doktriny Monro," *Voprosy istorii*, no. 9 (September 1971): 69–84.

15. N. N. Bolkhovitinov, "K voprosu ob ugroze interventsii Sviashchennogo soiuza v Latinskuiu Ameriku (iz predystorii doktriny Monro)," *Novaia i noveishaia istoriia*, no. 3 (May-June 1957): 46.

16. Ibid., p. 65.

17. Ibid., pp. 65–66. A brief discussion of Bolkhovitinov's analysis of the Monroe Doctrine is found in Basil Dmytryshyn and Jesse L. Gilmore, "The Monroe Doctrine: A Soviet View," *Bulletin: Institute for the Study of the USSR* 11 (May 1964): 3–14; reprinted in Dozer, *The Monroe Doctrine*, pp. 197–204.

18. S. B. Okun, *Rossiisko-amerikanskaia kompaniia*; L. S. Berg, *Otkrytie Kamchatki i ekspeditsii Beringa (1725–1742)*; A. I. Andreev (ed.), *Russkie otkrytiia v Tikhom okeane i Severnoi Amerike v XVIII–XIX vekakh. Sbornik materialov*; A. V. Efimov, *Iz istorii velikikh russkikh geograficheskikh otkrytii.*

19. A. V. Efimov, *Iz istorii velikikh russkikh geograficheskikh otkrytii*, 2nd rev. ed.

20. D. M. Lebedev and V. A. Esakov, *Russkie geograficheskie otkrytiia i issledovaniia s drevnykh vremën do 1917 goda*. See, also, Dimitri M. Lebedev and Vadim I. Grekov, "Geographical Exploration by the Russians," in Herman R. Friis (ed.), *The Pacific Basin. A History of Its Geographical Exploration* (New York: American Geographical Society, 1967), pp. 170–200.

21. S. G. Fedorova, *Russkoe naselenie Aliaski i Kalifornii. Konets XVIII veka-1867 g.*

22. Hubert Howe Bancroft, *History of Alaska, 1730–1885*; idem, *History of California*, vol. 2; idem, *History of the Northwest Coast*, vol. 2.

23. P. Tikhmenev, *Istoricheskoe obozrenie obrazovaniia Rossiisko-amerikanskoi kompanii i deistvii eë do nastoiashchego vremeni.*

24. N. N. Bolkhovitinov, *Stanovlenie russko-amerikanskikh otnoshenii, 1775–1815*; idem, *Russko-amerikanskie otnosheniia, 1815–1832 gg.* For a survey of Soviet scholarship in United States history, see idem, "The Study of United States History in the Soviet Union," *The American Historical Review* 74, no. 4 (April 1969): 1221–1242.

25. Ekkehard Völkl, *Russland und Lateinamerika, 1741–1841.*

26. L. Yu. Slëzkin, *Rossiia i voina za nezavisimost' v Ispanskoi Amerike.*

27. Ibid., p. 223.

28. Ibid., p. 225.

29. Ibid., p. 223. See, also, Ya. M. Svet and L. A. Shur, "Russko-latino-amerikanskie otnosheniia XVI–XIX vv. v osveshchenii zarubezhnykh issledovatelei," *Latinskaia Amerika*, no. 6 (November-December 1970): 138–159; and idem, "Pis'mo v redaktsiiu," *Latinskaia Amerika*, no. 5 (September-October 1971): 222–223.

30. Slëzkin, *Rossiia i voina za nezavisimost'*, p. 354.

31. Ibid., pp. 354–355.

32. Ibid., p. 355.

33. M. S. Al'perovich, *Sovetskaia istoriografiia stran Latinskoi Ameriki*, pp. 35–36; B. N. Komissarov, "Spor o russko-ispanskoi konventsii," *Voprosy istorii*, no. 6 (June 1966): 195–197. A Spanish-language version of the Al'perovich study was published in Prague under the title, "La historia de los países latinoamericanos y su estudio en la Unión Soviética," *Ibero-Americana Pragensia* 2 (1968): 181–207; 3 (1969): 241–264.

34. B. N. Komissarov, "Ob otnoshenii Rossii k voine Ispanskoi Ameriki za nezavisimost'," *Vestnik Leningradskogo Universiteta*, no. 8, vyp. 2 (1964): 62–63, 70–71; L. A. Shur, *Rossiia i Latinskaia Amerika. Ocherki politicheskikh, ekonomicheskikh i kul'turnykh otnoshenii*, pp. 42–50.

35. Slëzkin, *Rossiia i voina za nezavisimost'*, pp. 142–143.

36. Komissarov, "Ob otnoshenii Rossii k voine Ispanskoi Ameriki za nezavisimost'," pp. 62–63, 70–71; Shur, *Rossiia i Latinskaia Amerika*, pp. 42–50.

37. Komissarov, "Spor o russko-ispanskoi konventsii," p. 197.

38. Of primary significance is the diplomatic correspondence housed in the Arquivo Histórico do Itamaratí (Rio de Janeiro) and the Arquivo Nacional Tôrre do Tombo (Lisbon). None of this material has been used in previous investigations of the present topic.

39. Slëzkin, "Voina Ispanskoi Ameriki za nezavisimost' v otsenke russkikh diplomatov (1810–1816 gg.)," in V. V. Vol'skii (ed.), *Latinskaia Amerika v proshlom i nastoiashchem*, pp. 370–371.

40. N. N. Bolkhovitinov (comp.), "Otnoshenie Rossii k nachalu voiny Latinskoi Ameriki za nezavisimost'," *Istoricheskii arkhiv*, no. 3 (1962): 120.

41. Slëzkin, "Voina Ispanskoi Ameriki za nezavisimost'," p. 371.

42. Bolkhovitinov, "Otnoshenie Rossii k nachalu voiny Latinskoi Ameriki za nazavisimost'," p. 120.

43. Saldanha da Gama to Agiar, No. 82, São Petersburgo, 19 April 1817, AHI, Vol. 338/3/4.

44. Long-standing ties with Greece and Eastern Orthodoxy would normally have placed Russia on the side of Greek independence from the Ottoman Empire. The particular political configuration of Congress Europe, however, and the related danger of reopening the so-called Eastern Question moved Tsar Alexander I to abandon the Greek cause in an effort to preserve stability in the European system. See Barbara Jelavich, *A Century of Russian Foreign Policy, 1814–1914*, pp. 64–69.

45. On Langsdorff and Russo-Brazilian relations in the early nineteenth century, see Russell H. Bartley, "The Inception of Russo-Brazilian Relations (1808–1828)," *The Hispanic American Historical Review* 56, no. 2 (May 1976): 217–240; idem, "G. I. Langsdorf i russko-brazil'skie otnosheniia v pervoi treti XIX v.," *Latinskaia Amerika*, no. 3 (1976): 164–169; B. N. Komissarov, "Akademik G. I. Langsdorf i ego ekspeditsiia v Braziliiu v 1821–1829 gg.," in D. E. Bertel's, B. N. Komissarov, and T. I. Lysenko (comps.), L. A. Shur (ed.), *Materialy ekspeditsii akademika Grigoriia Ivanovicha Langsdorfa v Braziliiu v 1821–1829 gg.*, pp. 7–43.

Chapter 2: The Awakening of Russian Interest in America

1. Ya. M. Svet and L. A. Shur, "Russko-latinoamerikanskie otnosheniia XVI–XIX vv. v osveshchenii zarubezhnykh issledovatelei," *Latinskaia Amerika*, no. 6 (November-December 1970): 143.

2. L. S. Berg, *Istoriia russkikh geograficheskikh otkrytii*, p. 51.

3. For a concise account in English, see Avrahm Yarmolinsky, *Russian Americana. Sixteenth to Eighteenth Centuries*.

4. The suggestion that Russian interest in Latin America dates from the time of Macarius the Greek is at variance with the facts and appears to have been made for popular rather than scholarly consumption. See, for example, Victor V. Vol'skii, "The Study of Latin America in the U. S. S. R.," *Latin American Research Review* 3, no. 1 (Fall 1967): 77.

5. B. H. Sumner, *Peter the Great and the Emergence of Russia*, p. 42.

6. Ibid.

7. Yarmolinsky, *Russian Americana*, p. 30.

8. Ibid.

9. Ibid., pp. 30–32.

10. Yuri Semyonov, *Siberia. Its Conquest and Development*, pp. 140–141.

11. Ibid.; Yarmolinsky, *Russian Americana*, p. 32.

12. Alfred Hulse Brooks, "History of Explorations and Surveys," in Morgan B. Sherwood (ed.), *Alaska and Its History*, pp. 26–28.

13. A. Pokrovskii (ed.), *Ekspeditsiia Beringa. Sbornik dokumentov*, p. 21.

14. T. K. Krylova, "Otnosheniia Rossii i Ispanii v pervoi chetverti XVIII veka," in A. M. Deborin et al. (eds.), *Kul'tura Ispanii*, pp. 338 ff. A German

account of early Russo-Spanish relations based in part on the Krylova article is found in: Ana María Schop Soler, *Die spanisch-russischen Beziehungen im 18. Jahrhundert*, pp. 29–43.

15. *Colección de documentos y manuscritos compilados por Fernández de Navarrete*, 32 vols. (Nendeln, Liechtenstein, 1971), I, Foreword. See, also, M. P. Alekseev, *Ocherki istorii ispano-russkikh literaturnykh otnoshenii XVI–XIX vv.*, p. 33.

16. Krylova, "Otnosheniia Rossii i Ispanii," p. 341.

17. Ibid., p. 344.

18. Ibid., pp. 341–342.

19. Ibid., p. 344.

20. Ibid., pp. 346–351.

21. Pokrovskii, *Ekspeditsiia Beringa*, p. 21. See, also, Stuart R. Tompkins and Max L. Moorhead, "Russia's Approach to America," *The British Columbia Historical Quarterly* 13 (1949): 55.

22. Pokrovskii, *Ekspeditsiia Beringa*, p. 25.

23. A. V. Efimov, *Iz istorii velikikh russkikh geograficheskikh otkrytii*, p. 35.

24. Conde Emanuel de Bennigsen, "Nota acêrca de alguns projetos de colonização russa na América do Sul durante o século XVIII," *Revista de História* 4, no. 15 (July-September 1953): 170–171; L. A. Shur, *Rossiia i Latinskaia Amerika*, pp. 10–11.

25. "Proekt zavoevaniia Ameriki, podannyi Petru Velikomu," *Moskvitianin* 1 (1851): 121–124.

26. Ibid., p. 121.

27. Ibid., pp. 123–124.

28. A. Béthencourt, "Proyecto de un establecimiento ruso en Brasil (1732–1733)," *Revista de Indias* 10, nos. 37–38 (July-December 1949): 655. Much of this article is based on a manuscript account written by da Costa and preserved in the AGI. The article itself is carelessly written and many points are confused by poor documentation. The years given in the title, for example, do not correspond to the period covered.

29. Ibid., pp. 655–666.

30. Ibid., pp. 663–664.

31. Bennigsen, "Nota acêrca de alguns projetos de colonização russa," pp. 174–175.

32. Shur, *Rossiia i Latinskaia Amerika*, p. 10.

33. Efimov, *Iz istorii velikikh russkikh geograficheskikh otkrytii*, p. 131.

34. Ibid., pp. 128–129.

35. Shur, *Rossiia i Latinskaia Amerika*, pp. 12, 25–26; Yarmolinsky, *Russian Americana*, pp. 38–39.

36. Yarmolinsky, *Russian Americana*, pp. 34–36.

37. Shur, *Rossiia i Latinskaia Amerika*, pp. 14–17.

38. Ibid., pp. 22–24, 26–29.

39. V. A. Divin, "Russkie moreplavaniia k beregam Ameriki posle Beringa i Chirikova," in I. R. Grigulevich et al. (eds.), *Ot Aliaski do Ognennoi Zemli*, p. 89.

40. *Azbuchnyi ukazatel' imën russkikh deiatelei dlia russkogo biograficheskogo slovaria*, I, 127, 451, 470; *Bol'shaia sovetskaia entsiklopediia*, XXIII, 511–513; *Russkii biograficheskii slovar'*, IV, 95–96; X, 37–40.

41. Narrative accounts of Miranda's sojourn in Russia can be found in

Joseph O. Baylen and Dorothy Woodward, "Francisco de Miranda in Russia," *The Americas* 6, no. 4 (April 1950): 431–446; Joseph F. Thorning, *Miranda. World Citizen,* pp. 47–61; and William Spence Robertson, *The Life of Miranda,* I, 71–81. See, also, I. R. Lavretskii, *Miranda.*

42. Baylen and Woodward suggest that Miranda's departure from Russia in early September 1787 was occasioned at least in part by the expressed resentment of certain foreign diplomats toward the tsarina's favorite. See their "Francisco de Miranda in Russia," p. 437 n.

43. V. M. Miroshevskii, *Osvoboditel'nye dvizheniia v amerikanskikh koloniiakh Ispanii ot ikh zavoevaniia do voiny za nezavisimost' (1492–1810 gg.),* pp. 91–94.

44. Ibid., p. 86.

45. Ibid., p. 88; Stuart Ramsay Tompkins, *Alaska. Promyshlennik and Sourdough,* p. 85.

46. Miroshevskii, *Osvoboditel'nye dvizheniia,* p. 88.

47. Ibid., p. 89.

48. F. Giuseppe Torrubia, *I Moscoviti nella California.* In the period under consideration, the toponym "California" signified the entire coastal region of the American Northwest.

49. P. Miguel Benavente, "Reflexiones sobre los establecimientos que podían hacer los rusos en las Californias" [1764], BNM, Mss. 3101, fols. 314–336.

50. C. Alan Hutchinson, *Frontier Settlement in Mexican California. The Híjar-Padrés Colony and Its Origins, 1769–1835,* pp. 3–4; Warren L. Cook, *Flood Tide of Empire. Spain and the Pacific Northwest, 1543–1819,* pp. 45–46.

51. Benavente, "Reflexiones," fols. 316–317.

52. Cook, *Flood Tide of Empire,* pp. 47–48 ff.; Hutchinson, *Frontier Settlement in Mexican California,* pp. 5–10 ff.

53. Miroshevskii, *Osvoboditel'nye dvizheniia,* pp. 90–91. Available evidence relative to the "Kamchatka project" is limited to oblique references in Miranda's later correspondence. See, for example, Pownall to Miranda, 30 April 1790, *Archivo del General Miranda,* VI, 45. Miranda related in a diarial note how in the spring of 1799 Count S. R. Vorontsov, Russian ambassador at the court of St. James, had assisted him in procuring a passport to Trinidad; Vorontsov, wrote Miranda, had assured him that, were it not for the odd disposition of Tsar Paul I, or were Catherine II still alive, he should quickly secure two Russian frigates and two thousand troops for the anticipated move against northern South America. ("Notas de diario, 1799–1800," *Archivo del General Miranda,* XV, 355–356.) In reply, Miranda declared that although it might one day be said that both the Old World and the New owed a debt of gratitude to Russia, the partisans of Spanish American independence already owed more to that country than to any other. (Miranda to Woronzow, 27 May 1799, *Archivo del General Miranda,* XV, 367.)

54. Tompkins, *Alaska,* p. 85; Miroshevskii, *Osvoboditel'nye dvizheniia,* p. 91.

55. See St. O. Gulishambarov, *Vsemirnaia torgovlia v XIX v. i uchastie v nei Rossii,* pp. 20–55; P. A. Khromov, *Ekonomicheskoe razvitie Rossii v XIX–XX vekakh, 1800–1917,* pp. 93–102; Evdokim Ziablovskii, *Statisticheskoe opisanie Rossiiskoi Imperii v nyneshnem eë sostoianii,* II, Pt. 5, pp. 93–126;

M. F. Zlotnikov, *Kontinental'naia blokada i Rossiia*, pp. 9–48. The best statistical synthesis of Russian foreign trade in this period is found in Zlotnikov's
study of the continental blockade. A wholly accurate accounting of colonial
goods absorbed by the Russian market during the early years of the nineteenth century is not possible. Despite marked improvements in the compila-
tion of official statistics following the ministerial reforms of 1802, fundamental
inadequacies persisted throughout most of the period under study. In addition
to incomplete data, the researcher is faced with an annoying lack of uniform-
ity in basic units of quantification. Imports, exports, total commercial turn-
overs, and trade balances are given variously in metallic and paper values,
and occasionally measures of bulk are arbitrarily interspersed with monetary
units. Figures for total weights and volumes of imported goods are incomplete
and of only relative accuracy. In those instances where reasonably complete
statistics have been compiled, monetary values are given in paper notes, thus
introducing the exceedingly complex factor of inflation. See, for example,
V. I. Pokrovskii (ed.), *Sbornik svedenii po istorii i statistike vneshnei torgovli
Rossii*, I, 1–212.

56. François Crouzet, *L'économie britannique et le blocus continental
(1806–1813)*, I, 155; Bertrand Gille, *Histoire économique et sociale de la
Russie du moyen-âge au vingtième siècle*, p. 129.

57. Zlotnikov, *Kontinental'naia blokada i Rossiia*, pp. 42–44.

58. N. N. Bolkhovitinov, *Stanovlenie russko-amerikanskikh otnoshenii,
1775–1815*, pp. 191–196.

59. Ibid., pp. 193–198. See, also, Dorothy Burne Goebel, "British Trade to
the Spanish Colonies, 1796–1823," *The American Historical Review* 43 (January 1938): 291–296; Gulishambarov, *Vsemirnaia torgovlia*, pp. 22–24; Alan
K. Manchester, *British Preëminence in Brazil, Its Rise and Decline. A Study
in European Expansion*, pp. 51–53; Grigorii Nebol'sin, *Statisticheskoe obozrenie vneshnei torgovli Rossii*, I, 29–30; Roberto C. Simonsen, *História econômica do Brasil*, pp. 346–348.

60. Crouzet, *L'économie britannique et le blocus continental*, I, 157–161.

61. Ibid., pp. 144–145; Jorge de Macedo, *O bloqueio continental. Economia e guerra peninsular*, pp. 43–45; Manchester, *British Preëminence*, pp.
47–53.

62. Crouzet, *L'économie britannique et le blocus continental*, I, 156–157;
Khromov, *Ekonomicheskoe razvitie Rossii*, pp. 100–101; Zlotnikov, *Kontinental'naia blokada*, pp. 28–29.

63. "Preço corrente das producções de Portugal e suas colônias em São
Petersburgo aos 30 Nov. de 1806," AHI, Vol. 338/3/2.

64. Jerome Blum, *Lord and Peasant in Russia from the Ninth to the Nineteenth Century*, p. 278.

65. Ibid., pp. 278–279. The actual causes of this rapid population growth
remain obscure. All that can be said with certainty is that it paralleled a
similar pattern elsewhere in Europe.

66. P. I. Liashchenko, *Istoriia narodnogo khoziaistva SSSR*, I, 396; Khromov, *Ekonomicheskoe razvitie Rossii*, p. 79.

67. Blum, *Lord and Peasant*, pp. 280–281; Liashchenko, *Istoriia narodnogo
khoziaistva*, I, 396; P. Miliukov, *Ocherki po istorii russkoi kul'tury*, I, 79;
A. G. Rashin, *Formirovanie promyshlennogo proletariata v Rossii*, pp. 82–83.
Scholars are not agreed on the extent of urban growth in eighteenth- and

nineteenth-century Russia. Perhaps the most widely cited figures are those given by Miliukov: 1724—328,000; 1782—802,000; 1796—1,301,000; 1812—1,653,000. Rashin, on the other hand, has strongly differed, revising these estimates upward to a total of 2,279,000 for 1794 and 2,851,000 for 1811.

68. Alexander Baykov, "The Economic Development of Russia," *The Economic History Review*, 2nd ser., 7, no. 2 (1954): 86.

69. A. G. Rashin, *Naselenie Rossii za 100 let (1811–1913)*, p. 86.

70. Blum, *Lord and Peasant*, p. 281.

71. Rashin, *Naselenie Rossii*, pp. 89–91.

72. Ibid., p. 119.

73. Ibid., p. 127.

74. The ministerial reforms of 1802 brought an end to the ineffective Petrine boards or *kollegii* of the eighteenth century, replacing them with modern state ministries and their attendant bureaucracies.

75. Rashin, *Naselenie Rossii*, p. 124.

76. Gille, *Histoire économique et sociale de la Russie*, p. 132.

77. Ibid., p. 125; Liashchenko, *Istoriia narodnogo khoziaistva*, p. 408; Khromov, *Ekonomicheskoe razvitie Rossii*, p. 100.

78. Nebol'sin, *Statisticheskoe obozrenie vneshnei torgovli Rossii*, I, 302.

79. Rumiantsev to Alexander I, circa 9 January 1807, VPR, III, 459.

Chapter 3: The Continental System and Russian Commercial Interests in the New World

1. S. B. Okun, *Ocherki istorii SSSR. Konets XVIII–pervaia chetvert' XIX veka*, pp. 158–161.

2. F. de Martens, *Recueil des Traités et Conventions, conclus par la Russie avec les Puissances étrangères* (15 vols. St. Petersburg: Impr. du Ministère des Voies de Communication, 1874–1909), XIII, 322–326.

3. Rumiantsev to Alexander I, 16 May 1806, VPR, III, 149–150.

4. Ibid., p. 151; AGS, IV, Pt. 2, 1469–1479.

5. Rumiantsev was at once a stockholder in and active patron of the growing Russian-American Company.

6. Rumiantsev to Alexander I, 16 May 1806, VPR, III, 151.

7. Ibid.

8. Rumiantsev to Alexander I, circa 9 January 1807, VPR, III, 446, 459–460.

9. S. K. Viazmitinov to St. Petersburg city *duma*, 19 November 1807, VPR, IV, 112.

10. The term *obyvateli*, here rendered as "residents," also signifies members of the urban petty bourgeoisie.

11. T. I. Tutolmin to N. P. Rumiantsev, 23 November 1807, VPR, IV, 113–114.

12. "Razmyshlenie o sovremennom bezdeistvii morskoi torgovli v Evrope," *Vestnik Evropy* 40, no. 16 (August 1808) : 333.

13. Ibid., pp. 333–334.

14. Ibid., p. 335.

15. M. F. Zlotnikov, *Kontinental'naia blokada i Rossiia*, pp. 335–345.

16. Ibid., pp. 337–338.

17. Ibid., p. 337.

18. Ibid.
19. Gur'ev to Council of State, 12 November 1810, VPR, V, 583–588.
20. Ibid., p. 583.
21. Ibid., p. 584.
22. Ibid.
23. Committee of St. Petersburg Merchants to Council of State, 3 December 1810, VPR, V, 605–611. For further discussion of this committee, see Zlotnikov, *Kontinental'naia blokada*, pp. 229–235.
24. As already noted, "basic necessities of life" varied significantly from one social stratum to another. Thus a number of luxury items were considered by the Russian nobility and urban bourgeoisie to be articles of prime necessity.
25. Committee of St. Petersburg Merchants to Council of State, 3 December 1810, VPR, V, 610.
26. PSZRI, XXXI, no. 24.464, pp. 486–492; PSZRI, *Kniga tarifov*, Pt. III (obshchee dopolnenie k tarifam), 1810—k no. 24.464, pp. 58–61.
27. PSZRI, XXXI, 486.
28. Zlotnikov, *Kontinental'naia blokada*, p. 241.
29. "Preço corrente das producções de Portugal e suas colônias, em São Petersburgo ao 1.º de Jan.ʳᵒ de 1809," AHI, Vol. 338/3/2.
30. PSZRI, XLV, 58–61; Zlotnikov, *Kontinental'naia blokada*, pp. 242–243.
31. PSZRI, XLV, 58–61.
32. "Braziliia i eë zhiteli," *Politicheskii, statisticheskii i geografcheskii zhurnal* 1, Bk. 1 (January 1808): 52–53.
33. Ibid., p. 55.
34. See, for example: "Izvestiia o torgovle Portugalii," *Sanktpeterburgskie kommercheskie vedomosti*, no. 28 (11 July 1807): 110–112, and no. 29 (18 July 1807): 113; "Rio Yaneiro (Nyneshniaia rezidentsiia Printsa Brazil'-skogo)," *Vestnik Evropy*, no. 11 (June 1808): 185–188.
35. *Sanktpeterburgskie kommercheskie vedomosti*, no. 27 (2 July 1808): 107.
36. At the time of his petition for official government endorsement of this proposed commercial venture in South America, Kremer had only recently secured the release of eight vessels owned by him that had been impounded the previous year by the British in response to Russia's announced embargo on British goods. See AGS, III, Pt. 2, 763–764.
37. Kremer to Rumiantsev, 4 June 1808, VPR, IV, 272.
38. Ibid.
39. Ibid., pp. 272–273.
40. Rumiantsev had been instrumental in promoting I. F. Kruzenshtern's trial voyage of supply from the Baltic to Russian America in the years 1803–1806. See I. F. Kruzenshtern, *Puteshestvie vokrug sveta v 1803, 4, 5 i 1806 godakh*, I, xxiii–xxiv.
41. VPR, IV, 618, n. 169.
42. Andrade to Souza Coutinho, no. 203, São Petersburgo, 18 January 1809, AHI, Vol. 338/3/2 (copy).
43. Ibid.
44. Ibid.
45. Ibid.
46. Open letter signed by Dionizio Pedro Lopes, 1 January 1809, São Petersburgo, AHI, Vol. 338/3/2.

47. Ibid.

48. Andrade to Azevedo, S. Petersburgo, 17 (29) March 1808, ANTT, *caixa* 12, fol. 7. The success of Lopes's commercial establishment, as well as the reality of expanding Russo-Portuguese trade in the early nineteenth century, is strikingly reflected in the palatial residence Lopes built for himself on St. Petersburg's Vasil'evskii Island. Completed in 1810, this impressive structure is today one of the architectural monuments of contemporary Leningrad. See *Pamiatniki arkhitektury Leningrada* (Leningrad: Izdatel'stvo literatury po stroitel'stvu, 1972), pp. 370–371.

49. "Declaração do Consul Portuguez na Rússia," *Correio Braziliense* (June 1812) : 697–698.

50. Andrade to Azevedo, S. Petersburgo, 14 (26) January 1808, ANTT, *caixa* 11, fol. 2.

51. See PSZRI, XXV, no. 18.779, pp. 471–483.

52. Andrade to Azevedo, no. 182, São Petersburgo, 3 March 1808, AHI, Vol. 338/3/2 (copy). Implicit in Rumiantsev's statement was a fundamental alteration in the terms of the existing agreement, namely that ships sailing from points along the coast of the Portuguese mainland would no longer be permitted to enter Russian ports. This change was formally decreed by Alexander I some fifteen months later, at which time it became a source of considerable friction between the Russian and Portuguese courts.

53. Ibid.

54. N. Ivashintsov, *Russkie krugosvetnye puteshestviia, s 1803 po 1849 god,* pp. 18–22.

55. Ibid., pp. 16–17.

56. V. M. Golovnin, *Puteshestvie Rossiiskogo Imperatorskogo shliupa Diana, iz Kronshtadta v Kamchatku,* I, 159–172.

57. Andrade to Azevedo, no. 182, São Petersburgo, 3 March 1808.

58. Andrade to Souza Coutinho, no. 215, São Petersburgo, 7 May 1809, AHI, Vol. 338/3/2 (copy).

59. Ibid.

60. Rumiantsev to Alexander I, 22 December 1809, VPR, V, 323.

61. Alexander I to Pahlen, 8 January 1810, VPR, V, 339.

62. Rumiantsev to Andrade, St. Pétersbourg, 21 December 1809 (2 January 1810), ANTT, *caixa* 12. Published in VPR, V, 328; see also ibid., p. 684, n. 204.

63. Rumiantsev to Andrade, St. Pétersbourg, 21 December 1809 (2 January 1810) , ANTT, *caixa* 12, fol. 3.

64. Rumiantsev here referred to the Russo-Portuguese Treaty of Friendship, Navigation, and Trade, concluded on 27 December 1798, and the Russo-Portuguese Mutual Defense Treaty, concluded on 18 September 1799, texts of which appear in PSZRI, XXV, 471–483 and 784–788.

65. Rumiantsev to Andrade, St. Pétersbourg, 21 December 1809 (2 January 1810), ANTT, *caixa* 12, fol. 4.

66. Andrade to Linhares, São Petersburgo, 26 January 1810, AHI, Vol. 338/3/2 (copy).

67. Rumiantsev to Council of State, circa 12 February 1810, VPR, V, 359–361.

68. Ibid., p. 359.

69. These advantages explicitly accorded Russian merchants the same rights

and privileges granted their British counterparts. The treaty further stated that Russian merchants would be party to any future tariff reductions affecting goods exchanged directly between Portugal and the Russian Empire. Clearly, an extension of these privileges to Brazil at a time when Great Britain sought actively to dominate Brazilian foreign trade signified much more than the execution of a simple bilateral accord. It was to this point that Count Rumiantsev addressed himself before the council of state and to this point that he wished to draw the council's attention. See PSZRI, XXV, 471–483.

70. Rumiantsev to Council of State, circa 12 February 1810, VPR, V, 361. This direct proposal to tap the illicit traffic of diamonds and precious metals in the Spanish colonies reflects the basic pragmatism with which Rumiantsev approached matters of commerce and national interest. His reference to Peru as a source of mineral wealth anticipated later Russian-American Company activity along the west coast of South America.

71. Ibid., p. 361.

72. AGS, IV, Pt. 2, 1135–1137.

73. Rumiantsev to Andrade, St. Pétersbourg, 15 March 1810, AHI, Vol. 338/3/2 (copy).

74. Article six of the Russo-Portuguese Treaty of Friendship, Navigation, and Trade of 1798 established a duty of 4 rubles 50 kopeks on every 240 bottles of wine imported into Russia from Madeira and the Azores on ships of Russian or Portuguese registry by subjects of the Russian or Portuguese courts. Article eight of this treaty provided for a 50 percent reduction in existing tariffs on Brazilian indigo and tobacco imported directly from the Portuguese Empire in conformity with the conditions stipulated in Article six. The treaty made no mention of sugar, cacao, dyewood, rice, or medicinals. See PSZRI, XXV, no. 18.779, pp. 473–475.

75. Russian goods enumerated in Articles seven and eight included hempseed oil, linseed oil, iron, barrel staves, anchors, military ordnance, sailcloth, and linens. See PSZRI, XXV, no. 18.779, pp. 473–475.

76. Rumiantsev to Andrade, St. Pétersbourg, 15 March 1810, AHI, Vol. 338/3/2.

77. Rumiantsev to Andrade, 22 March 1810, VPR, V, 399–400.

78. Ibid.

79. Kommercheskie vedomosti, no. 20 (19 May 1810): 77. During the year 1810 the Sanktpeterburgskie kommercheskie vedomosti appeared under this abbreviated title.

80. Repeated references in this statement to "Brazil and its colonies" suggest the significance tsarist officialdom already attached to Portuguese America. Formally, the presence of João VI in Rio de Janeiro could only be viewed as temporary, yet in the spring of 1810 the Russian court publicly revealed a contrary appraisal of Portuguese imperial affairs.

81. Rumiantsev to Council of State, 3 March 1811, VPR, VI, 83–84.

82. Ibid., p. 83.

83. VPR, VI, 692, n. 93.

84. Rumiantsev to Council of State, 3 March 1811, VPR, VI, 84.

85. Although Bezerra was named envoy extraordinary and minister plenipotentiary to the court of St. Petersburg in August 1809, he apparently did not arrive in the Russian capital until late winter or early spring 1811. See

Brazil, Secretaria de Estado das Relações Exteriores, *Relações Diplomáticas do Brazil*, p. 98.

86. Bezerra to Linhares, no. 558, São Petersburgo, 9 November 1811, AHI, Vol. 338/3/3 (copy).

87. "Convention," AHI, Vol. 338/3/3 (copy).

88. Ibid., Article two.

89. Ibid., Article four.

90. Ibid., Article two.

91. Bezerra to Linhares, no. 558, São Petersburgo, 9 November 1811, AHI, Vol. 338/3/3.

92. Bezerra to Linhares, no. 563, São Petersburgo, 11 October [sic] 1811, AHI, Vol. 338/3/3 (copy). As with other correspondence in this volume, the dispatch appears to be incorrectly dated, suggesting carelessness on the part of the copyist. While no. 561 is dated 26 November, no. 562 is dated 4 October. Number 562, however, includes a copy of a note from Count Rumiantsev dated 19 November 1811!

93. Bezerra to Linhares, no. 570, São Petersburgo, 8 February 1812, AHI, Vol. 338/3/3 (copy).

94. Gur'ev to Rumiantsev, 7 April 1812, VPR, VI, 328.

95. PSZRI, XXXII, no. 24.960, pp. 17–18.

96. Bezerra to Linhares, no. 570, São Petersburgo, 8 February 1812, AHI, Vol. 338/3/3.

97. Bezerra to Linhares, no. 575, São Petersburgo, 11 March 1812, AHI, Vol. 338/3/3 (copy).

98. Rumiantsev to Bezerra, St. Pétersbourg, 9 April 1812, AHI, Vol. 338/3/3; ANTT, *caixa* 13 (copies). See, also, Rumiantsev to Bezerra, 21 April 1812, VPR, VI, 365–366.

99. Reference to Lopes's appointment is made in Bezerra to Linhares, no. 575, São Petersburgo, 11 March 1812, AHI, Vol. 338/3/3.

100. Rumiantsev to Bezerra, St. Pétersbourg, 9 April 1812, VPR, VI, 366.

101. "Deklaratsiia o prodlenii sroka deistviia russko-portugal'skogo dogovora o druzhbe, torgovle i moreplavanii ot 16(27) dekabria 1798 g.," 10 June 1812, VPR, VI, 420. See, also, *Correio Braziliense* (August 1812): 180–183.

102. Alexander I to Pahlen, 8 January 1810, VPR, V, 339.

103. N. N. Bolkhovitinov, comp., "Otnoshenie Rossii k nachalu voiny Latinskoi Ameriki za nezavisimost'," *Istoricheskii arkhiv*, no. 3 (1962): 121.

104. N. N. Bolkhovitinov, *Stanovlenie russko-amerikanskikh otnoshenii*, p. 422.

105. Idem, "Otnoshenie Rossii k nachalu voiny Latinskoi Ameriki za nezavisimost'," p. 122.

106. Rumiantsev to Council of State, 28 September 1811, *Istoricheskii arkhiv*, no. 3 (1962): 126; also VPR, VI, 172.

107. Ibid.

108. Ibid. At this time, Russia maintained consular agents in Boston, Charleston, New Orleans, and Savannah. See VPR, VI, 357.

109. Ministry of Foreign Affairs to Kozlov, 24 August 1811, VPR, VI, 148 (Article three).

110. Ibid. (Article four).

111. Rumiantsev to Council of State, 28 September 1811, *Istoricheskii arkhiv*, no. 3 (1962): 125–127; also VPR, VI, 171–172.

112. Ibid., *Istoricheskii arkhiv*, p. 126; VPR, VI, 172.

113. Rumiantsev here referred to the *mezzogiorno* of America (*poludennaia Amerika*), by which he appears to have meant continental South America. He must further have meant Spanish South America, as the way had already been cleared for direct trade relations between Russia and Portuguese America. Geographical imprecisions of this kind occur frequently in the Russian source materials of the period.

114. "Proekt ukaza ministru finansov D. A. Gur'evu ob otkrytii russkikh portov dlia korablei iz Latinskoi Ameriki," n.d., *Istoricheskii arkhiv*, no. 3 (1962): 127.

115. Although twenty-five council members are said to have voted on Rumiantsev's proposal, the official protocol issued by the council carries only fifteen signatures. At the same time, this document has numbered spaces for thirty-six names. Some council members, therefore, appear deliberately not to have signed the protocol, perhaps indicating deeper divisions of opinion than suggested by the recorded vote.

116. "Protokol obshchego sobraniia Gosudarstvennogo soveta ob ustanovlenii torgovykh snoshenii s byvshimi ispanskimi koloniiami," 21 October 1811, *Istoricheskii arkhiv*, no. 3 (1962): 128. Also VPR, VI, 202.

117. "Mnenie Gosudarstvennogo soveta po voprosu ob ustanovlenii torgovykh snoshenii s byvshimi ispanskimi koloniiami," 8 November 1811, *Istoricheskii arkhiv*, no. 3 (1962): 129. Also VPR, VI, 216–217.

118. Bolkhovitinov, *Stanovlenie russko-amerikanskikh otnoshenii*, pp. 426–429.

119. Harris to López Méndez, St. Petersburg, 31 March 1812, and Harris to Monroe, St. Petersburg, 13 May 1812, *Istoricheskii arkhiv*, no. 3 (1962): 129–130.

120. Ibid.

121. Bolkhovitinov, *Stanovlenie russko-amerikanskikh otnoshenii*, p. 429.

122. Kozlov to Russian consular agents in Boston, Charleston, New Orleans, and Savannah, 14 April 1812, VPR, VI, 357–358.

123. "Instructions pour M. Antonio Lynch, agent commercial de Russie dans l'île de Cuba," 8(20) February 1813, VPR, VII, 59–61.

124. Kozlov to Rumiantsev, 8(20) February 1813, VPR, VII, 58.

125. Ibid.

126. Bolkhovitinov, *Stanovlenie russko-amerikanskikh otnoshenii*, p. 436.

127. Rumiantsev to Kozlov, 24 August 1811, VPR, VI, 147–154.

Chapter 4: The Russian Presence in America

1. G. H. von Langsdorff, *Voyages and Travels in Various Parts of the World During the Years 1803, 1804, 1805, 1806, and 1807*, II, 70. A participant in the first Russian circumnavigation of the world (1803–1806), Langsdorff visited the principal settlements of Alaska and the Aleutian Islands, as well as Spanish California.

2. Hector Chevigny, *Russian America. The Great Alaskan Venture, 1741–1867*, p. 74.

3. Anatole G. Mazour, "The Russian-American Company: Private or Gov-

ernment Enterprise?" *Pacific Historical Review* 13, no. 2 (June 1944): 168–169; S. B. Okun, *Rossiisko-amerikanskaia kompaniia*, p. 90.

4. A. A. Preobrazhenskii, "O sostave aktsionerov Rossiisko-Amerikanskoi Kompanii v nachale XIX v.," *Istoricheskie zapiski*, no. 67 (1960): 290–292.

5. Mazour, "The Russian-American Company," p. 169; Okun, *Rossiisko-amerikanskaia kompaniia*, p. 91.

6. Mazour, "The Russian-American Company," pp. 169–170.

7. Okun, *Rossiisko-amerikanskaia kompaniia*, p. 91.

8. Mazour, "The Russian-American Company," pp. 169–170; Okun, *Rossiisko-amerikanskaia kompaniia*, pp. 92–93.

9. Okun, *Rossiisko-amerikanskaia kompaniia*, p. 91.

10. Ibid., p. 96. A. A. Baranov, chief administrator of the Russian-American Company's New World holdings since the company's founding, was relieved of his responsibilities in the fall of 1818 by Lieutenant-Captain L. A. Hagemeister of the imperial Russian navy.

11. Okun, *Rossiisko-amerikanskaia kompaniia*, pp. 49–50.

12. "Zapiska G. I. Shelikhova o privilegiiakh ego kompnaii," in A. I. Andreev (ed.), *Russkie otkrytiia v Tikhom okeane i Severnoi Amerike v XVIII–XIX vekakh*, p. 84.

13. Rumiantsev to Alexander I, 4 March 1803, VPR, I, 386.

14. Rezanov to Alexander I, Unalashka, 18 July 1805 (o. s.), in P. Tikhmenev, *Istoricheskoe obozrenie obrazovaniia Rossiisko-amerikanskoi kompanii i deistvii eë do nastoiashchego vremeni*, II, 193–194.

15. Rezanov to RAC Board of Directors, Secret, Unalashka, 15 February 1806 (o. s.), in Tikhmenev, *Istoricheskoe obozrenie*, II, 235.

16. "Sostoianie Kompanii k 1819 godu," AGM, VI, 638.

17. Okun, *Rossiisko-amerikanskaia kompaniia*, p. 94.

18. Ibid., p. 95.

19. I. F. Kruzenshtern, *Puteshestvie vokrug sveta v 1803, 4, 5 i 1806 godakh*, I, xviii–xix.

20. Ibid., pp. xix–xx.

21. See chapter 1, above.

22. A. J. von Krusenstern, *Voyage Round the World, in the Years 1803, 1804, 1805, & 1806*, I, xxix.

23. Ibid., pp. xxvii–xxviii.

24. Ibid., pp. 2–3.

25. Chevigny, *Russian America*, p. 107.

26. I. P. Magidovich (comp.), "Izvestnye russkie moreplavateli (spravka)," in V. S. Lupach (ed.), *Russkie moreplavateli* (Moscow: Voennoe izdat'stvo Ministerstva oborony Soiuza SSR, 1953), pp. 479–480, 513–514.

27. Krusenstern, *Voyage Round the World*, I, 22–51.

28. Langsdorff, *Voyages and Travels*, I, 28–29.

29. Krusenstern, *Voyage Round the World*, I, 67.

30. Langsdorff, *Voyages and Travels*, I, 77.

31. Ibid., p. 41.

32. Ibid., p. 43.

33. Lisianskii, however, took exception to Langsdorff's view of Brazilian slavery, which he considered far less brutal than did the German naturalist. See Urey Lisiansky, *A Voyage Round the World, in the Years 1803, 4, 5, & 6*, p. 35 n.

34. Ibid., p. 36.

35. Krusenstern, *Voyage Round the World*, I, 71.

36. Seized in March 1777 by a large Spanish force under the command of Pedro de Cevallos, governor of Buenos Aires and first viceroy of the River Plate. This was one of numerous episodes in a protracted struggle between Spain and Portugal over Colônia do Sacramento and control of the so-called Eastern Bank or Banda Oriental. By the treaty of San Ildefonso (La Granja), signed in October 1777, Spain relinquished Santa Catarina to Portugal in return for permanent jurisdiction over the disputed Uruguayan territory.

37. Krusenstern, *Voyage Round the World*, I, 72.

38. N. Ivashintsov, *Russkie krugosvetnye puteshestviia, s 1803 po 1849 god*, pp. 1–15.

39. "We gained no new advantages," wrote Kruzenshtern of the embassy, "but even lost those we had possessed, namely, the written permission which Laxmann [previous emissary sent by Catherine II] had procured for us to visit Nangasaky [*sic*]. All communication is now at an end between Japan and Russia. . . ." Krusenstern, *Voyage Round the World*, p. 286.

40. Langsdorff, *Voyages and Travels*, II, 1–80.

41. Ibid., p. 98.

42. The best account of this episode in English remains Hubert Howe Bancroft, *History of California*, II, 66–75.

43. RAC Board of Directors to Baranov, no. 190, Sankt-Peterburg, 18 April 1802 (o. s.), BL, RAC, Korrespondentsiia, reel 1.

44. Rezanov to RAC Board of Directors, 15 February 1806, in Tikhmenev, *Istoricheskoe obozrenie*, II, 233–234. See, also, C. Alan Hutchinson, *Frontier Settlement in Mexican California*, p. 23.

45. Rezanov to Rumiantsev, Novoarkhangel'sk, 17 June 1806 (o. s.), in Tikhmenev, *Istoricheskoe obozrenie*, II, 254–256; Bancroft, *History of California*, II, 66–68.

46. This calculated ploy appears to have produced the desired results and became standard procedure in subsequent Russian dealings with Spanish California. See, for example, RAC Board of Directors to Rumiantsev, 15(27) May 1814, VPR, VII, 697.

47. Rezanov to Rumiantsev, 17 June 1806 (o. s.), in Tikhmenev, *Istoricheskoe obozrenie*, II, 257.

48. Bancroft, *History of California*, II, 71; Langsdorff, *Voyages and Travels*, II, 178–179; RAC Board of Directors to Rumiantsev, 15(27) May 1814, VPR, VII, 696.

49. Bancroft, *History of California*, II, 73.

50. Langsdorff, *Voyages and Travels*, II, 183.

51. Rezanov to Rumiantsev, 17 June 1806 (o. s.), in Tikhmenev, *Istoricheskoe obozrenie*, II, 265.

52. Langsdorff, *Voyages and Travels*, II, 183.

53. Rezanov to Alexander I, Novo-Arkhangel'sk, 29 June 1806 (o. s.), VPR, III, 209.

54. Rezanov to Rumiantsev, 17 June 1806 (o. s.), in Tikhmenev, *Istoricheskoe obozrenie*, II, 266.

55. Ibid., p. 267.

56. Ibid.

57. Okun, *Rossiisko-amerikanskaia kompaniia*, p. 115.

58. Ibid., p. 119; Hubert Howe Bancroft, *History of Alaska, 1730–1885*, pp. 482–483.

59. Bancroft, *History of Alaska*, pp. 476–481.

60. Ibid., pp. 481–482.

61. Ibid., pp. 482–483. Kuskov had embarked on a second expedition to California in 1810 but got only as far as the Queen Charlotte Islands, where an encounter with hostile Indians forced him to return to Sitka.

62. The best single account of the Ross colony remains Bancroft, *History of California*, II, 294–320, and IV, 158–189.

63. Callejo to Ministro de Estado, México, 9 September 1813, AHN, *legajo* 6124, *caja* 1 (copy).

64. Luyando to Bardaxí, Madrid, 3 January 1814, AHN, *legajo* 6124, *caja* 1.

65. Bardaxí to Luyando, Petersburgo, 20 May 1814, AHN, *legajo* 6124, *caja* 1.

66. "Koloniia Ross," AGM, VI, 668.

67. Okun, *Rossiisko-amerikanskaia kompaniia*, p. 120.

68. L. Yu. Slëzkin, *Rossiia i voina za nezavisimost'*, p. 97.

69. Zea Bermúdez to Pizarro, San Petersburgo, 4 May 1817, AHN, *legajo* 6126, *caja* 1.

70. Zea Bermúdez to Pizarro, San Petersburgo, 22 July 1817, AHN, *legajo* 6126, *caja* 1.

71. Zea Bermúdez to Pizarro, San Petersburgo, 9 September 1817, AHN, *legajo* 6126, *caja* 2.

72. Weakened by illness and the excesses of winter, Rezanov died in the Siberian town of Krasnoiarsk, where he was buried in March 1807. See Chevigny, *Russian America*, p. 124; Tikhmenev, *Istoricheskoe obozrenie*, I, 162.

73. Krusenstern, *Voyage Round the World*, II, 44–256.

74. Lisiansky, *A Voyage Round the World*, pp. 138–244.

75. Krusenstern, *Voyage Round the World*, II, 256–404; Lisiansky, *A Voyage Round the World*, pp. 245–319. In April 1806, the *Nadezhda* and *Neva* became separated off the Cape of Good Hope. Kruzenshtern put in at the island of St. Helena in the hope of encountering the *Neva*, but Lisianskii had resolved to make straight for Portsmouth. At St. Helena, Kruzenshtern thought it remarkable to find only a single British merchantman in that normally busy harbor of the South Atlantic. "We learnt," he wrote in his journal, "that only twenty-four hours previous to our arrival Sir Home Popham had sailed with a considerable fleet to the conquest of Buenos Ayres, an expedition much condemned by the people of this island." See Krusenstern, *Voyage Round the World*, II, 387.

76. Rezanov to Rumiantsev, 17 June 1806 (o. s.), in Tikhmenev, *Istoricheskoe obozrenie*, II, 266–267.

77. Krusenstern, *Voyage Round the World*, I, xxviii n.

78. Even in the case of vessels bound for the Cape of Good Hope, prevailing sea currents determined that on the outward passage the most convenient route lay along the eastern coast of South America. Ships returning to Europe via the Cape of Good Hope, on the other hand, rode the northerly currents prevailing off the west coast of subequatorial Africa.

79. Krusenstern, *Voyage Round the World*, I, 142–143.

80. Budberg to Vasil'ev, 26 August 1806, VPR, III, 271.

81. Ivashintsov, *Russkie krugosvetnye puteshestviia*, pp. 16–22. In 1813, the

Neva was shipwrecked in the Alexander Archipelago. (Ibid., pp. 16–17.) That same year, the *Diana* was decommissioned at Petropavlovsk, no longer fit for service. (V. M. Golovnin, *Voyage de M. Golownin . . . pendant les années 1811, 1812 et 1813*, 2 vols., II, 443–444.)

82. Ivashintsov, *Russkie krugosvetnye puteshestviia*, pp. 1–87; Lupach, *Russkie moreplavateli*, pp. 137–225, 235–266; N. N. Zubov, *Otechestvennye moreplavateli-issledovateli morei i okeanov*, pp. 142–196.

83. Records of such voyages are more difficult to uncover than those of official sailings inasmuch as they eluded deposit in state or ministerial archives. The problem is further complicated by the apparent fact that many, perhaps most, of these ships were manned by non-Russian crews and, in some cases, were simply chartered from foreign shipmasters.

84. Zubov, *Otechestvennye moreplavateli-issledovateli*, p. 148.

85. *Gaceta de Buenos Ayres* (6 December 1820), 140; *Gaceta de Buenos Ayres* (11 April 1821), 236; Ekkehard Völkl, *Russland und Lateinamerika*, p. 173. In the summer of 1816, the Spanish envoy in St. Petersburg advised his home government of "daily arrivals at Cronstadt of Anglo-American vessels direct from Havana." (Pérez de Lema to Pedro Cevallos, Petersburgo, 15 August 1816, AHN, *legajo* 6125, *caja* 1.) See, also, Langsdorff to Conde dos Arcos, Rio de Janeiro, 28 March 1818, ANTT, *caixa* 2; "Mappa das embarcaçoens, que entraram e sahiram do porto do Rio-de-Janeiro no anno de 1819," *Correio Braziliense* (September 1820): 267.

86. Certificate of safe conduct for the *Suvorov*, signed and sealed by Eusebio de Bardaxí y Azara, San Petersburgo, 23 September 1813, AHN, *legajo* 6124, *caja* 2.

87. "Ob"iasneniia Leitenanta Lazareva," in Russia, Glavnoe arkhivnoe upravlenie MVD SSSR, *M. P. Lazarev. Dokumenty*, I, 72. [Cited hereafter as *Dokumenty*.]

88. "Iz 'Istinnykh zapisok moei zhizni' leitenanta S. Ya. Unkovskogo," in *Dokumenty*, p. 47.

89. Some confusion surrounds the precise movements of the *Suvorov* during this part of its voyage. Ivashintsov wrote in his generally authoritative volume on Russian circumnavigations of the world that Lazarev "stopped for four days at the Spanish town of Santa Rosa, on the coast of Colombia, near the equator. . . ." (*Russkie krugosvetnye puteshestviia*, p. 24.) B. N. Komissarov adds that the town of Santa Rosa was "on the Pacific coast of New Granada . . . in the territory of modern-day Ecuador." ("Russkie moreplavateli o voine Ispanskoi Ameriki za nezavisimost'," in N. M. Lavrov et al [eds.], *Voina za nezavisimost' v Latinskoi Amerike, 1810–1826*, p. 302 n.) Zubov, in turn, simply notes that Lazarev "visited the town of Santa Rosa," without further elaboration. (*Otechestvennye moreplavateli-issledovateli*, p. 160.)

Ivashintsov, himself a career officer in the imperial Russian navy, presumably based his account on documents preserved in the naval archives. It remains unclear, however, whether Lazarev's journal of this voyage has survived to the present, for it has not been published, nor is it cited in the available literature. The problem is further confused by the fact that S. Ya. Unkovskii, one of Lazarev's officers, makes no mention of Santa Rosa in the part of his journal that has been published. (See *Dokumenty*, pp. 11–60.)

90. *Dokumenty*, p. 47.

91. Ivashintsov, *Russkie krugosvetnye puteshestviia*, pp. 23–24.

92. *Dokumenty,* p. 42.

93. Ibid., p. 72.

94. *Dokumenty,* pp. 47–48.

95. Ibid., p. 48.

96. The Royal Philippine Company was chartered by Charles III, on 10 March 1785, for the purpose of stimulating direct trade between Spain and the Philippine Islands. The company's initial charter was for a period of twenty-five years, but was subsequently extended until its final demise in 1834. The company maintained agents or factors, as they were known, in the principal urban centers of Spanish America so as to handle goods brought from Europe on the outbound voyage. (William Lytle Schurz, *The Manila Galleon,* pp. 412–416.)

"The Philippine Company," observed a Russian contemporary, "has two Factors in Lima, Calcutta, Canton and other cities where they are sent for six years, a period beyond which they seem unwilling to remain." (V. M. Golovnin, *Puteshestvie vokrug sveta . . . na voennom shliupe Kamchatke, v. 1817, 1818 i 1819 godakh,* I, 86 n.)

97. *Dokumenty,* p. 48.

98. Although ships of the Royal Philippine Company might carry European merchandise to Spanish American ports on the outbound voyage, there to exchange that merchandise for cargoes of colonial products to be sold or traded in the Far East, the company's charter prohibited all traffic in the opposite direction. To enforce this regulation, the crown compelled all vessels sailing to the Philippines to return to Spain via the Cape of Good Hope. (Schurz, *The Manila Galleon,* pp. 413–414.)

99. "Ob"iasneniia Leitenanta Lazareva," in *Dokumenty,* p. 73.

100. *Dokumenty,* p. 49.

101. Marqués de la Concordia to Ministro de la Corte de España cerca de S. M. el Emperador de todas las Rusias, Lima, 25 February 1816, AHN, *legajo* 6125, *caja* 2.

102. *Dokumenty,* p. 49.

103. Ibid., p. 59.

104. Unkovskii's curious reference to mulattoes as an identifiable revolutionary group points again to the need for further research on the social components of the independence movement. His reference to Chile, however, suggests an uncritical projection of perceived Peruvian realities to other areas of Spanish America where in fact quite different conditions prevailed.

105. *Dokumenty,* p. 51.

106. Ibid., pp. 51–52.

107. Nesselrode to Pérez de Lema, St. Pétersbourg, 10 August 1816, AHN, *legajo* 6125, *caja* 1.

108. Pérez de Lema to Cevallos, Petersburgo, 15 August 1816, AHN, *legajo* 6125, *caja* 1.

109. Pérez de Lema to Cevallos, Petersburgo, 23 August 1816, AHN, *legajo* 6125, *caja* 1.

110. Ministry of Foreign Affairs to Pérez de Lema, St. Pétersbourg, 9 May 1815, AHN, *legajo* 6125, *caja* 1. The primary object of this voyage was in fact to search for a northern passage from the Pacific to the Atlantic, to which end the *Riurik* spent the summer of 1816 exploring Kotzebue Sound and the northern coast of the Seward Peninsula.

111. Pérez de Lema to Cevallos, Petersburgo, 27 May 1815, AHN, *legajo* 6125, *caja* 1.

112. Otto von Kotzebue, *A Voyage of Discovery, into the South Sea and Beering's Straits, for the Purpose of Exploring a North-East Passage, undertaken in the Years 1815–1818*, I, 117.

113. Ibid., p. 132.

114. Ibid., III, 21.

115. Otto von Kotzebue, *A New Voyage Round the World, in the Years 1823, 24, 25, and 26*, I, 77–78.

116. Nesselrode to Pérez de Lema, St. Pétersbourg, 25 May 1816, AHN, *legajo* 6125, *caja* 1.

117. Certificate of safe conduct issued by Pérez de Lema, San Petersburgo, 25 May 1816, AHN, *legajo* 6125, *caja* 1 (copy).

118. Nesselrode to Pérez de Lema, St. Pétersbourg, 2 August 1816, AHN, *legajo* 6125, *caja* 1.

119. Certificate of safe conduct issued by Pérez de Lema, San Petersburgo, 6 August 1816, *legajo* 6125, *caja* 1 (copy).

120. Pérez de Lema to Cevallos, 15 August 1816, AHN, *legajo* 6125, *caja* 1.

121. Pérez de Lema to Cevallos, 23 August 1816, AHN, *legajo* 6125, *caja* 1.

122. Pérez de Lema to Marqués de la Concordia, Petersburgo, 29 August 1817, AHN, *legajo* 6125, *caja* 2.

123. Ivashintsov, *Russkie krugosvetnye puteshestviia*, p. 35.

124. Ibid., pp. 35–36.

125. Semën Ivanovich Yanovskii, "Zapiski," prilozhenie k *Izvestiiam Kaluzhskoi uchënoi arkhivnoi komissii, vyp.* 5–6 (1898): 98. To date, this is the only journal from the voyage of the *Kutuzov* and *Suvorov* to have been published. As Soviet scholars have cited no other accounts in their published research, it remains unclear whether such accounts have indeed survived to the present.

126. Ivashintsov, *Russkie krugosvetnye puteshestviia*, p. 36.

127. Yanovskii, "Zapiski," p. 111.

128. Ibid.

129. Ivashintsov, *Russkie krugosvetnye puteshestviia*, p. 36. Ivashintsov's reference to "Spanish ships" could signify either royalist or insurgent vessels, as well as noninsurgent ships engaging in the contraband trade.

130. Slëzkin, *Rossiia i voina za nezavisimost' v Ispanskoi Amerike*, pp. 117–118 n. Slëzkin erroneously suggests that contrary winds and dwindling supplies of water and firewood brought the *Kutuzov* to Ecuador, not trade. Hagemeister anchored 160 miles from Guayaquil, he writes, at a place devoid of inhabitants, thereby precluding any exchange of goods. Since Hagemeister had accomplished the difficult ten-week voyage from Rio de Janeiro to Callao without need for midcourse provisioning, however, it seems doubtful that "contrary winds" should occasion such a need in less than ten degrees of latitude. The *Kutuzov* did stop to replenish its on-board water supply at the mouth of the Tumbes River, on the southern bank of the Gulf of Guayaquil, but only after spending six weeks in the estuary of the Guayas River, where, according to Ivashintsov, Hagemeister effected the supposed exchange of goods. When the *Kutuzov* reached Tumbes, it was over two months out of Callao and faced with an additional two-month voyage to Alta California, more than sufficient reason to replenish on-board water. Slëzkin is also incor-

rect in suggesting that the *Kutuzov*'s watering place was uninhabited, for the town of Tumbes dates from pre-Columbian times and was already a thriving settlement when Pizarro arrived there in 1527.

131. Golovnin, *Puteshestvie vokrug sveta*, I, 110.
132. Ibid., p. 112.
133. Ibid.
134. Ibid., p. 107.
135. Ibid., p. 125.
136. Ibid., p. 108.
137. Kotzebue, *A New Voyage Round the World*, I, 81–99.
138. In point of fact, Kruzenshtern's grand design remained partially functional as late as the mid-1830s. In times of severe shortages, for example, ships were sent to Chile to procure needed foodstuffs for the Russian colonies in the Pacific Northwest. (Tikhmenev, *Istoricheskoe obozrenie*, I, 344–347.) To place these seemingly extraordinary contacts in historical perspective, it is perhaps instructive to note that maritime ties of an analogous nature existed in roughly the same period between Chile and Australia. (Thomas M. Bader, "Before the Gold Fleets: Trade and Relations between Chile and Australia, 1830–1848," *Journal of Latin American Studies* VI, 1 [May 1974]: 35–58.)

Chapter 5: Initial Responses to Political Change in the Spanish and Portuguese Empires

1. *Sanktpeterburgskie kommercheskie vedomosti*, no. 1 (3 January 1807): 1; ibid., no. 2 (10 January 1807): 8.
2. Ibid., no. 10 (7 March 1807): 38. Inasmuch as the initial invasion force numbered 1,200 men and, though defeated, the intruders were not annihilated, this casualty figure is clearly inflated.
3. *Vestnik Evropy*, XXXVII, no. 2 (January 1808), 155–156.
4. Ibid., pp. 168–169. Reference to João VI as "ex-regent" undoubtedly recalls Junot's declaration upon taking Lisbon in late November 1807 that the House of Bragança had ceased to reign. The alleged stationing of British forces in Brazil, on the other hand, was mere speculation about future British actions, as the Portuguese court had not yet reached South America when this article appeared. Although little evidence has come to light documenting the presence of British land forces on Brazilian soil immediately following the transfer of the Portuguese court to Rio de Janeiro, the Russian ambassador in Paris referred several years later to English soldiers serving in the Portuguese expeditionary army that, in the summer of 1816, occupied the eastern bank of the River Plate. (Pozzo di Borgo to Nesselrode, Paris, 3 October 1817, *Sbornik*, CXIX, no. 189, p. 395.)
5. L. Yu. Slëzkin, *Rossiia i voina za nezavisimost' v Ispanskoi Amerike*, p. 40.
6. Quoted ibid.
7. Quoted ibid.
8. Ibid., pp. 40–41.
9. What appears to have been the first such directive was issued in August 1808 to A. Ya. Dashkov, Russian chargé d'affaires and consul-general in Philadelphia.
10. Slëzkin, *Rossiia i voina za nezavisimost'*, p. 42.

11. The authority that enlightened Russians posited in Humboldt's writings is further evidenced by the fact that in 1814 Tsar Alexander I himself ordered eight copies of the multivolume *Voyage aux régions équinoxiales*. ("Pis'ma Imperatora Aleksandra I i drugikh osob tsarstvuiushchego doma k F. Ts. Lagarpu," *Sbornik*, V, 1–21, no. 49.)

12. *Vestnik Evropy*, no. 18 (September 1809): 148.

13. Ibid., p. 151. It is interesting that these particular observations should have been published in Russia at such an early date, for the principal work in which Humboldt treats this theme did not appear until 1811, i.e., *Essai politique sur le royaume de la Nouvelle Espagne*.

14. *Vestnik Evropy*, no. 18 (September 1809): 148.

15. Ibid., pp. 148–149.

16. Ibid., no. 7 (May 1811): 77. "No city of the new continent," Humboldt wrote, "without even excepting those of the United States, can display such great and solid scientific establishments as the capital of Mexico." (Alexander von Humboldt, *Political Essay on the Kingdom of New Spain*, I, 212.)

17. *Vestnik Evropy*, no. 7 (May 1811): 77–78.

18. Ibid., no. 3 (February 1811): 242.

19. Ibid., no. 5 (March 1811): 81.

20. *Istoricheskii, statisticheskii i geograficheskii zhurnal* 2, Bk. 1 (April 1811): 47.

21. Ibid., 2, Bk. 2 (May 1811): 99.

22. Ibid., pp. 111–112.

23. Ibid., 2, Bk. 3 (June 1811): 205. This report was basically accurate and reflects the improving quality of information about Latin America available to the Russian reading public by the second decade of the nineteenth century.

24. Ibid., pp. 207–208.

25. Ibid., 4, Bk. 1 (October 1811): 53.

26. Ibid., p. 53.

27. Ibid., 1, Bk. 1 (January 1812): 34–35.

28. Ibid., pp. 36–37.

29. Ibid., p. 40.

30. Ibid., p. 45.

31. Quoted by Slëzkin, *Rossiia i voina za nezavisimost'*, p. 42.

32. V. O. Kliuchevskii, *Sochineniia*, V, 226.

33. Ibid., pp. 226–227.

34. This paper was first published in January 1813 under the direction of A. Pluchart, a French printer and lithographer retained by the Russian ministry of foreign affairs to manage the ministry press.

35. *Le Conservateur Impartial*, Supplément au no. 72 (9 September 1813): 382.

36. Slëzkin, *Rossiia i voina za nezavisimost'*, pp. 90–91.

37. Ibid., p. 91.

38. *Le Conservateur Impartial*, no. 77 (25 September 1814): 435. Two renowned perpetrators of carnage in Venezuela were José Tomás Boves and his lieutenant, Francisco Tomás Morales, who sought to introduce racial strife into the rebel camp as a weapon against the largely white insurgent leadership. Having defeated Bolívar in August 1812 at Aragua de Barcelona, Morales reportedly butchered all captured prisoners, as well as much of the civilian populace.

39. Slëzkin, *Rossiia i voina za nezavisimost'*, p. 91.
40. *Le Conservateur Impartial*, no. 72 (8 September 1814): 410.
41. Ibid., no. 71 (4 September 1814): 406.
42. Ibid., no. 78 (29 September 1814): 441.
43. Slëzkin, *Rossiia i voina za nezavisimost'*, pp. 91–92.
44. *Le Conservateur Impartial*, no. 71 (4 September 1814): 406.
45. Slëzkin, *Rossiia i voina za nezavisimost'*, p. 91. Royalist authority was temporarily restored in Chile as a result of the battle of Rancagua, fought in the first days of October 1814.
46. *Le Conservateur Impartial*, no. 77 (25 September 1814): 435.
47. Ibid., no. 79 (2 October 1814): 447.
48. Slëzkin, *Rossiia i voina za nezavisimost'*, pp. 90–91.
49. Founded in October 1812 in response to the crisis of that year, as suggested by its name.
50. *Syn otechestva* 19, no. 5, 2nd pribavlenie (8 February 1815): 4.
51. Ibid., 20, no. 7 (March 1815): 34–35.
52. Ibid., p. 35. In the usage of the time, "Spanish West Indies" referred to the whole of Spanish America.
53. Ibid., pp. 35–36.
54. N. N. Bolkhovitinov, *Stanovlenie russko-amerikanskikh otnoshenii*, pp. 348–349.
55. Ibid., p. 357.
56. Ibid., pp. 349–350.
57. Ministry of Foreign Affairs to Dashkov, 30 August 1808, VPR, IV, 326.
58. Bolkhovitinov, *Stanovlenie russko-amerikanskikh otnoshenii*, p. 366.
59. John Quincy Adams, *Memoirs*, II, 3.
60. Bolkhovitinov, *Stanovlenie russko-amerikanskikh otnoshenii*, pp. 363–364. Russian desire to expand ties with the New World is reflected in the determination with which the tsar pursued the establishment of a diplomatic legation in Philadelphia, despite delays on the American side sufficient in other circumstances to have occasioned a corresponding response on the Russian side. Failure of the U. S. Senate in February 1809 to confirm William Short, President Thomas Jefferson's nomination for minister plenipotentiary to the court of St. Petersburg, did not deter Alexander I from dispatching his newly appointed envoy extraordinary, Count Pahlen, to Paris, there to await authorization from American representatives to proceed to his post in the United States.
61. "Zapiska F. P. Palena," Paris, circa 26 November 1809, VPR, V, 294.
62. Ibid.
63. See, for example, *Vestnik Evropy*, no. 7 (May 1811): 75–80.
64. "Zapiska F. P. Palena," VPR, V, 294.
65. Ibid., pp. 294–295.
66. Alexander I to Pahlen, 8 January 1810, VPR, V, 339.
67. *National Intelligencer* (13 June 1810): 3.
68. L. Yu. Slëzkin, "Voina Ispanskoi Ameriki za nezavisimost' v otsenke russkikh diplomatov (1810–1816 gg.)," in V. V. Vol'skii et al. (eds), *Latinskaia Amerika v proshlom i nastoiashchem*, p. 375.
69. Pahlen to Rumiantsev, Philadelphia, 7 September 1810, VPR, V, 501.
70. Pahlen to Rumiantsev, Philadelphia, 25 October 1810, VPR, V, 552.
71. Ibid., pp. 552–553.

72. Pahlen to Rumiantsev, Washington, 28 November 1810, VPR, V, 596.

73. Ibid., p. 597.

74. Adams, *Memoirs*, II, 102.

75. "The opening of the trade to South America and the Spanish West Indies," observed Adams on another occasion, "had naturally much increased the trade between the United States and Russia. Those countries consumed great quantities of the Russian manufactures," he added, "more even than North America." (Adams, *Memoirs*, II, 197.)

76. Adams, *Memoirs*, II, 182.

77. Ibid., pp. 182–185.

78. Slëzkin, "Voina Ispanskoi Ameriki za nezavisimost'," p. 376 n.

79. Bolkhovitinov, *Stanovlenie russko-amerikanskikh otnoshenii*, p. 429.

80. Ibid., p. 432.

81. Ibid., p. 429.

82. Adams, *Memoirs*, II, 280–281.

83. Ibid., p. 281.

84. Bolkhovitinov, *Stanovlenie russko-amerikanskikh otnoshenii*, p. 429 n.

85. Alexander I to Pahlen, 3 September 1811, VPR, VI, 156. According to the terms of the Anglo-Portuguese trade agreement of 1810, duties on goods imported into Brazil by British merchants were reduced to 15 percent of their market value. Goods imported by Portuguese merchants were subject to a 16 percent duty, while all others were obliged to pay 24 percent market value. See, for example, V. I. Ermolaev et al. (eds.), *Ocherki istorii Brazilii* (Moscow: Izdatel'stvo sotsial'nof ekonomicheskoi literatury, 1962), p. 72.

86. Alexander I to Pahlen, 3 September 1811, VPR, VI, 156.

87. Ibid., p. 157.

88. Ibid.

89. Ibid.

90. Ibid., pp. 157–158. "Il faut, en attendent les circonstances qui décideront du parti qu'il conviendra de prendre à leur égard, caresser leur amour-propre par une perspective adroitement ménagée des facilités qu'ils rencontreront probablement ici à faire reconnaître leur nouvelle existence politique et sourtout de celles lesquelles ils peuvent déjà compter en faveur de leur commerce quelle que soit l'autorité qui les gouvernera."

91. B. N. Komissarov, "Arkhiv ekspeditsii G. I. Langsdorfa v Braziliiu (1821–1829)," in I. R. Grigulevich et al. (eds.), *Ot Aliaski do Ognennoi Zemli*, p. 275.

92. Slëzkin, *Rossiia i voina za nezavisimost' v Ispanskoi Amerike*, p. 67.

93. Rumiantsev to Bezerra, St. Pétersbourg, 9(21) April 1812, ANTT, *caixa* 13 (copy).

94. Ibid.; Bezerra to Linhares, S. Petersburgo, 16(28) April 1812, ANTT, *caixa* 13.

95. Borel to Foreign Trade Department, Ministry of Finance, "Rapports de commerce avec la Russie," 1(13) April 1813, VPR, VII, 154–159; Pahlen to Galvéas, Rio de Janeiro, 13(25) May 1813, VPR, VII, 217; Borel to Pahlen, Madeira, 18(30) June 1813, VPR, VII, 272–273; Pahlen to Galvéas, Rio de Janeiro, 18(30) August 1813, VPR, VII, 362.

96. Bolkhovitinov, *Stanovlenie russko-amerikanskikh otnoshenii*, p. 432; Slëzkin, *Rossiia i voina za nezavisimost'*, p. 43.

97. Pahlen to Galvéas, Rio de Janeiro, 3 August 1812, ANTT, *caixa* 1.

98. Pahlen to Galvéas, Rio de Janeiro, 8 August 1812, ANTT, *caixa* 1.

99. Bezerra to Linhares, S. Petersburgo, 3(15) July 1811, ANTT, *caixa* 12, fol. 5; Bezerra to Linhares, 20 July (1 August) 1811, ANTT, *caixa* 12, fols. 1–2.

100. Ibid.

101. B. N. Komissarov to the author, Leningrad, 26 March 1976; Bezerra to Galvéas, S. Petersburgo, 14(26) September 1812, ANTT, *caixa* 13.

102. On Langsdorff, see Roderick J. Barman, "The Forgotten Journey: Georg Heinrich Langsdorff and the Russian Imperial Scientific Expedition to Brazil, 1821–1829," *Terrae Incognitae* 3 (1971): 67–96; Russell H. Bartley, "G. I. Langsdorf i russko-brazil'skie otnosheniia v pervoi treti XIX v.," *Latinskaia Amerika*, no. 3 (May-June 1976): 164–169; idem, "Akademik G. I. Langsdorf i stanovlenie russko-brazil'skikh otnoshenii (1804-1828 gg.)"; B. N. Komissarov, "Akademik G. I. Langsdorf i ego ekspeditsiia v Braziliiu v 1821–1829 gg.," in D. E. Bertel's et al. (comps.), *Materialy ekspeditsii akademika Grigoriia Ivanovicha Langsdorfa v Braziliiu v 1821–1829 gg.*, pp. 7–43; G. G. Manizer, *A expedição do acadêmico G. I. Langsdorff ao Brasil (1821–1828)* (São Paulo: Companhia Editora Nacional, 1967).

103. Komissarov, "Akademik G. I. Langsdorf i ego ekspeditsiia v Braziliiu," pp. 12–13.

104. Langsdorff to Ministry of Foreign Affairs, Rio de Janeiro, 7(19) May 1813, VPR, VII, 207.

105. Langsdorff to Ministry of Foreign Affairs, Rio de Janeiro, 24 July (5 August) 1813, VPR, VII, 333.

106. B. F. Sukhomlinov, "Ob ustanovlenii russko-brazil'skikh otnoshenii," *Novaia i noveishaia istoriia*, no. 2 (March-April 1965): 90.

107. Ibid.

108. Slëzkin, *Rossiia i voina za nezavisimost'*, pp. 79–80.

109. Ibid., p. 79.

110. Ibid., p. 80.

111. Alexander I to Stroganov, 24 May 1805, VPR, II, 416.

112. Ibid., p. 420.

113. Ibid., p. 425.

114. William Spence Robertson, *France and Latin-American Independence*, pp. 22–28.

115. Andrade to Souza Coutinho, no. 215, São Petersburgo, 7 May 1809, AHI, Vol. 338/3/2 (copy).

116. Andrade to Linhares, no. 227, São Petersburgo, 30 August 1809, AHI, Vol. 338/3/2.

117. This unnamed agent of the central *junta*, described by the Portuguese chargé d'affaires as "a man of great propriety, intelligence and loyalty to his legitimate sovereign" and "a long-time resident" in the Russian capital (see ibid.), was almost certainly Antonio Colombí y Payet. Having gone to Russia in 1775 as Spanish consul-general, Colombí later founded a successful commercial house that imported produce from Spain and the Spanish colonies for sale on the Russian market. Of established reputation among St. Petersburg society, Colombí enjoyed access to the imperial family and was instrumental in facilitating subsequent contacts between the Spanish regency and the Russian court. (See Eduardo R. Eggers and Enrique Feune de Colombí, *Francisco de Zea Bermúdez y su época, 1779-1850*, pp. 22–45.)

118. Andrade to Souza Coutinho, 7 May 1809, AHI, Vol. 338/3/2.
119. Rumiantsev to Stroganov, 5 July 1808, VPR, IV, 287. Stroganov informed St. Petersburg of his decision to remain in Madrid just two days after the bloody uprising of 2 May 1808 against the occupation forces of Marshal Joachim Murat.
120. Stroganov to Rumiantsev, 19 August 1808, VPR, IV, 312.
121. Stroganov to Rumiantsev, 12 August 1808, VPR, IV, 307.
122. Ibid.
123. Alexander I to Repnin, 1 June 1810, VPR, V, 450.
124. Ibid., pp. 450–451.
125. Repnin to Rumiantsev, Paris, 8 November 1810, VPR, V, 579–580.
126. Ibid., p. 580.
127. Eggers and Feune, *Francisco de Zea Bermúdez y su época*, pp. 41–42.
128. Ugarte rose from relative insignificance to a position of considerable influence at the Spanish court. Prior to the French invasion of the Iberian Peninsula, he had come to enjoy the confidence of the Russian minister, Stroganov, who, upon departing Spain for Portugal in the fall of 1808, entrusted his belongings to Ugarte for safekeeping. Ugarte's diligence in this matter appears to have won him the confidence of D. P. Tatishchev, tsarist minister plenipotentiary and master of intrigue at the Spanish court in the post-Napoleonic period. Both Ugarte and Tatishchev penetrated Ferdinand VII's inner circle of confidants, where they influenced diverse affairs of state.
129. I. Zvavich, "Ispaniia v diplomaticheskikh otnosheniiakh Rossii v 1812 godu," *Istoricheskii zhurnal*, nos. 3–4 (1943): 45.
130. Eggers and Feune, *Francisco de Zea Bermúdez y su época*, p. 42.
131. Zvavich, "Ispaniia v diplomaticheskikh otnosheniiakh Rossii," p. 45. Once the inevitability of war with France became apparent, Alexander I increasingly pursued a double-faceted policy of overtly appeasing Napoleon while covertly seeking potential alliances against the French emperor. Rumiantsev, whose pro-French sentiments were well known, served as the tsar's principal instrument of appeasement. Koshelev, opposed personally as well as politically to Rumiantsev, became the tsar's main channel of contact with Napoleon's enemies. (See Patricia Kennedy Grimsted, *The Foreign Ministers of Alexander I*, pp. 180–182.)
132. Eggers and Feune, *Francisco de Zea Bermúdez y su época*, pp. 43–44.
133. Ibid., p. 49; Real orden de la Regencia to Zea Bermúdez, 29 June 1811, AHN, *legajo* 6123, *caja* 2.
134. Zvavich, "Ispaniia v diplomaticheskikh otnosheniiakh Rossii," p. 46.
135. "Pamiatnaia zapiska Aleksandra I," 7 February 1812, VPR, VI, 271.
136. Eggers and Feune, *Francisco de Zea Bermúdez y su época*, p. 49.
137. [Zea Bermúdez] to Bardaxí, San Petersburgo, 19 February 1812, AHN, Estado: Rusia, Embajada de España, *legajo* 6123, *caja* 2. Prior to the signing of a formal Russo-Spanish treaty of alliance, dispatches filed by Zea Bermúdez from St. Petersburg carried an illegible but clearly stylized signature to protect his identity.
138. Ibid.
139. Grimsted, *The Foreign Ministers of Alexander I*, p. 188.
140. [Zea Bermúdez] to Bardaxí, 19 February 1812, AHN, *legajo* 6123, *caja* 2.

141. Eggers and Feune, *Francisco de Zea Bermúdez y su época*, p. 50.

142. Ibid., pp. 51–52. For texts of the Treaty of Velikie Luki, see *Gazeta de Madrid*, no. 16 (19 September 1812): 149–150; PSZRI, XXXII, 390–391; VPR, VI, 495–496.

143. VPR, VI, 495.

144. Zvavich, "Ispaniia v diplomaticheskikh otnosheniiakh Rossii," pp. 48–49.

145. Bardaxí's initial instructions noted that conclusion of a formal alliance between Spain and Russia had been deferred indefinitely by the court of St. Petersburg because of the Spanish regency's inability to provide the requisite monetary gratification. Bardaxí was thus instructed "to employ all his energy, talent and sagacity" to circumvent the material obstacles to the desired accord. (Pezuela to Bardaxí, Cádiz, 9 August 1812, AHN, *legajo* 6123, *caja* 1.)

146. Bardaxí to Labrador, San Petersburgo, 6 January 1813, AHN, *legajo* 6124, *caja* 3.

147. Ibid.

148. Ibid.

149. Quoted by Slëzkin, "Voina Ispanskoi Ameriki za nezavisimost'," p. 384.

150. Quoted ibid., p. 385.

Chapter 6: Colonial Pacification and the Dilemma of Intervention

1. Andrei A. Lobanov-Rostovsky, *Russia and Europe, 1789–1825*, p. 358.

2. Barbara Jelavich, *A Century of Russian Foreign Policy, 1814–1914*, p. 43.

3. Dexter Perkins, "Russia and the Spanish Colonies, 1817–1818," *The American Historical Review* 28, no. 4 (July 1923): 662.

4. William W. Kaufmann, *British Policy and the Independence of Latin America, 1804–1828*, pp. 92 ff.

5. V. M. Miroshevskii, "Velikie derzhavy i voina za nezavisimost' Ispanskoi Ameriki" (unpublished doctoral dissertation), AVMM, *karton* 1, fol. 137.

6. William Spence Robertson, "Russia and the Emancipation of Spanish America, 1816–1826," *The Hispanic American Historical Review* 21, no. 2 (May 1941): 220.

7. Lobanov-Rostovsky, *Russia and Europe*, p. 389.

8. L. Yu. Slëzkin, *Rossiia i voina za nezavisimost' v Ispanskoi Amerike*, p. 355.

9. C. K. Webster (ed.), *Britain and the Independence of Latin America, 1812–1830*, I, 14.

10. Perkins, "Russia and the Spanish Colonies," p. 658. For a criticism of Perkins's view, see Slëzkin, *Rossiia i voina za nezavisimost'*, p. 125 n.

11. Kaufmann, *British Policy and the Independence of Latin America*, p. 109.

12. Robert M. Slusser, "The Role of the Foreign Ministry," in Ivo J. Lederer (ed.), *Russian Foreign Policy. Essays in Historical Perspective*, p. 200.

13. Hajo Holborn, "Russia and the European Political System," in Lederer, *Russian Foreign Policy*, p. 383. Even C. K. Webster, who attaches considerable significance to the alleged independence of Pozzo di Borgo and Tatishchev, recognizes "something of a consistent plan" in the tsar's foreign policy. See C. K. Webster, *The Foreign Policy of Castlereagh, 1815–1822*, p. 90.

14. Patricia Kennedy Grimsted, *The Foreign Ministers of Alexander I. Political Attitudes and the Conduct of Russian Diplomacy, 1801–1825*, pp. 188–197.

15. Otto von Kotzebue, *A Voyage of Discovery, into the South Sea and Beering's Straits, for the Purpose of Exploring a North-East Passage, undertaken in the Years 1815–1818* . . . , I, 6–7 ff. See, also, "Nouvelles de l'intérieur," *Le Conservateur Impartial*, no. 61 (11 August 1815).

16. Slëzkin, *Rossiia i voina za nezavisimost'*, pp. 117–118.

17. C. K. Webster, *The Congress of Vienna, 1814–1815*, p. 128.

18. "Actes du Congrès de Vienne," *Le Conservateur Impartial*, no. 65 (13 August 1815): 317–334. See, also, Russia, Ministerstvo inostrannykh del, *Dokumenty dlia istorii diplomaticheskikh snoshenii Rossii s zapadnymi derzhavami, ot zakliucheniia vseobshchego mira v 1814 do kongressa v Verone v 1822 godu*, I, 165–255.

19. [Alvaro] Teixeira Soares, *Diplomacia do Império no Rio da Prata (até 1865)*, pp. 43–46. Although the Portuguese managed to hold Montevideo and other population centers, they failed to secure the outlying areas.

20. João VI to Fernando VII, Palácio do Rio de Janeiro, 15 February 1817, AGI, *legajo* 99.

21. Nesselrode to Pozzo di Borgo, Saint-Pétersbourg, 30 December 1816, *Sbornik*, CXII, no. 581, p. 730.

22. Nesselrode to Zea Bermúdez, St. Pétersbourg, 15 December 1816 [o. s.], AHN, *legajo* 6125, *caja* 3.

23. Ibid.

24. Nesselrode to Pozzo di Borgo, Saint-Pétersbourg, 30 December 1816, *Sbornik*, CXII, no. 581, pp. 731–732.

25. Jerónimo Bécker, *Historia de las relaciones exteriores de España durante el siglo XIX*, I, 413.

26. Ibid., pp. 414–416.

27. Pozzo di Borgo to Nesselrode, Paris, 15 March 1817, *Sbornik*, CXIX, no. 40, p. 85.

28. See Nesselrode to Pozzo di Borgo, Saint-Pétersbourg, 30 December 1816, *Sbornik*, CXII, no. 581, pp. 731–732.

29. Webster, *Britain and the Independence of Latin America*, I, 68.

30. Contrary to Perkins's view that "down to the middle of 1817 Tsar Alexander does not seem to have concerned himself directly with the restoration of peace and Spanish dominion in the New World," it is clear from the relevant correspondence that by the close of 1816 the tsar had already given considerable thought to the problem of colonial pacification. Material examined thus far in the present study reveals Alexander to have been more conversant in the affairs of Spanish and Portuguese America than scholars have hitherto recognized. (See Perkins, "Russia and the Spanish Colonies," p. 657.)

31. Nesselrode to Pozzo di Borgo, Saint-Pétersbourg, 17 April 1817, *Sbornik*, CXIX, no. 62, p. 134.

32. Saldanha to Aguiar, S. Petersburgo, 8(20) March 1817, ANTT, *caixa* 14, fol. 2.

33. Zea Bermúdez to Pizarro, San Petersburgo, 7 May 1817, AHN, *legajo* 6126, *caja* 1.

34. "Mémoire en réponse aux communications de la Cour d'Autriche," Saint-Pétersbourg, 15 April 1817, *Sbornik*, CXIX, no. 61, p. 131.

35. Ibid., p. 132.

36. Manfred Kossok, *La Santa Alianza y la política de los estados alemanes ante la emancipación latinoamericana (1815–1830)*, p. 5.

37. Webster, *The Foreign Policy of Castlereagh*, p. 88.

38. Ibid., pp. 92–93; Lobanov-Rostovsky, *Russia and Europe*, pp. 360–374.

39. Kossok, *La Santa Alianza*, p. 6.

40. L. A. Shur, *Rossiia i Latinskaia Amerika*, p. 43.

41. That stand was made possible by the fact that it served at one and the same time the otherwise opposing interests of Russia and Great Britain. On the one hand, the Portuguese occupation of Uruguay prejudiced British commercial interests in the region. In addition, the expansion of Brazil to the eastern bank of the River Plate promised to strengthen the Portuguese position in South America and thereby undermine British influence in Rio de Janeiro. Russia, on the other hand, seized the occasion to enhance Spain's standing among the allied powers, with a view to ultimately advancing Russian interests in Spanish North America. Having already secured access to the ports and products of Brazil through normal diplomatic channels, Russia remained by and large invulnerable to Portuguese reprisals for its outspoken support of Spain, clearly the injured party in the Uruguayan dispute. Finally, Russia and Great Britain avoided a military confrontation, which almost certainly would have ensued had Spain sparked a new European conflict by invading Portugal in retaliation for the Portuguese occupation of the Banda Oriental. See Kaufmann, *British Policy and the Independence of Latin America*, p. 115; Slëzkin, *Rossiia i voina za nezavisimost'*, pp. 128–129.

42. Slëzkin, *Rossiia i voina za nezavisimost'*, p. 130.

43. On this point, Pozzo di Borgo informed his government that according to various sources it appeared that the British, "although aware for some time of Portuguese designs on the Spanish territory of La Plata," had hesitated to intervene in the matter "in the hope of profiting from Spain's difficulties by inducing her to sign a trade treaty which would open the ports of [Spanish] America to [Great Britain]." (Pozzo di Borgo to Nesselrode, Paris, 12 April 1817, *Sbornik*, CXIX, no. 60, p. 128.)

44. Shur, *Rossiia i Latinskaia Amerika*, p. 43.

45. Pozzo di Borgo to Nesselrode, Paris, 12 April 1817, *Sbornik*, CXIX, no. 60, p. 128.

46. Ibid., pp. 128–129.

47. Pozzo di Borgo to Nesselrode, Paris, 19 May 1817, *Sbornik*, CXIX, no. 92, p. 185.

48. From 1816 to 1822, the Russian ministry of foreign affairs offered the curious spectacle of joint direction shared by German-born Count Karl Robert Nesselrode and Greek-born Count Ioannes Capo d'Istria. Of the two, Capo d'Istria appears to have been the more dynamic, often revealing a highly refined sense of Russian imperial interests. Unable to abandon entirely his commitment to the Greek struggle against Ottoman domination, however, he withdrew from the tsar's service in the summer of 1822, leaving the administration of Russian diplomatic affairs in the hands of the industrious but always subservient Nesselrode. Capo d'Istria would later become the first president of independent Greece (1827–1831), in which capacity he again served tsarist interests abroad. (See, for example, C. M. Woodhouse, *Capodistria. The Founder of Greek Independence*.)

49. Saldanha to Capo d'Istria, St. Pétersbourg, 18 May 1817, AHN, *legajo* 6126, *caja* 2 (copy).

50. Capo d'Istria to Saldanha, St. Pétersbourg, 25 May 1817, AHN, *legajo* 6126 *caja* 2 (copy). See, also, *Sbornik*, CXIX, p. 260 n. Reference to the act of 14(26) September is to the Act of Holy Alliance, signed on that date in 1815 by Austria, Prussia, and Russia.

51. Ibid. Saldanha also protested the fact that the Russian ministry of foreign affairs had prepared official copies of tsarist correspondence with the Portuguese government for Spanish authorities, pointing to this as further evidence of tsarist partiality on behalf of Spain. (See Saldanha to Capo d'Istria, St. Pétersbourg, 18 May 1817, AHN, *legajo* 6126, *caja* 2.) As the correspondence in question bore directly on the matter of mediation solicited by Spain, Capo d'Istria responded, the Spanish court was entitled to know its contents. In such a delicate affair, he added, the allied powers, and notably Russia, had conducted themselves in an exemplary manner. (Capo d'Istria to Saldanha, St. Pétersbourg, 25 May 1817, AHN, *legajo* 6126, *caja* 2.) In point of fact, however, the Russian ministry made a practice of informing the Spanish court of pertinent diplomatic exchanges on the colonial question and even provided copies of the Saldanha–Capo d'Istria correspondence of 18 and 25 May, despite its supposedly confidential character. (See Zea Bermúdez to Pizarro, San Petersburgo, 24 June 1817, AHN, *legajo* 6126, *caja* 2.)

52. B. F. Sukhomlinov, "Ob ustanovlenii russko-brazil'skikh otnoshenii," *Novaia i noveishaia istoriia*, no. 2 (March-April 1965): 91–92.

53. "Deklaratsiia o prodlenii sroka deistviia russko-portugal'skogo dogovora o druzhbe, torgovle i moreplavanii ot 16(27) dekabria 1789 g.," S.-Peterburg, 10 June 1812, VPR, VI, 420.

54. Saldanha to Aguiar, São Petersburgo, 17 February 1816, AHI, Vol. 338/3/4 (copy).

55. Portuguese patience was further tried by the cumbersome dispatch of tsarist diplomatic affairs under the joint direction of Counts Nesselrode and Capo d'Istria, neither of whom proved readily accessible to foreign diplomats resident in St. Petersburg. "I see no possibility of concluding any business whatsoever," Saldanha reported in the winter of 1816, "so long as this state of uncertainty continues in the Department of Foreign Affairs; nor do I see a probability of change in this Department. In response to those who have had occasion to inquire whether they should address themselves to Count Nesselrode or to Count Capodistrias," he added, "H. M. the Emperor has replied that they should address themselves to both. Meanwhile, all Official Notes have until now been addressed to Count Nesselrode, and he has been responsible for attending to such papers. Passports and other papers of this nature, however, are the responsibility of M. Weydemeyer. The Ministry of Foreign Affairs, therefore, finds its authority divided among three different individuals: imagine, then, the confusion which results from this and the visible embarrassment in which the Diplomatic Corps finds itself." (Saldanha to Aguiar, São Petersburgo, 17 February 1816, AHI, Vol. 338/3/4.)

56. Nesselrode to Saldanha, St. Pétersbourg, 21 January 1817, AHI, Vol. 338/3/4 (copy).

57. Balk-Polev replaced Count Pahlen as head of the Russian legation in Rio de Janeiro in August 1816. (Sverchkov to Aguiar, Rio de Janeiro, 11 August 1816, ANTT, *caixa* 2.)

58. Ricardo Piccirilli, *Argentinos en Rio de Janeiro, 1815–1820. Diplomacia. Monarquía. Independencia,* p. 60.

59. Villalba to Pizarro, Río de Janeiro, 28 April 1817, AGI, *legajo* 99. "It cannot be denied," Villalba asserted in a later dispatch, "that [Balk-Polev] has talent; but, in honor of the truth, it is necessary to confess forthrightly that he is ill-suited to carry out such high responsibilities," for he lacked the requisite "delicacy, prudence and levelheadedness." All the other members of Rio's diplomatic corps, Villalba added, shared this opinion of the Russian envoy. (Villalba to Pizarro, Río de Janeiro, 19 June 1817, AGI, *legajo* 99.)

60. *Correio Braziliense* (August 1817): 224; Piccirilli, *Argentinos en Rio de Janeiro,* pp. 60–61.

61. Villalba to Pizarro, Río de Janeiro, 28 April 1817, AGI, *legajo* 99.

62. The Spanish envoy in Rio de Janeiro advised his home government that all foreign legations in the Brazilian capital were treated with a minimum of deference by the Portuguese court and that the individual most responsible for mounting frictions was "the half-paralytic Conde da Barca." (Villalba to Pizarro, Río de Janeiro, 28 April 1817, 20 and 23 June 1817, AGI, *legajo* 99.)

63. Villalba to Pizarro, Río de Janeiro, 28 April 1817, AGI, *legajo* 99.

64. Ibid.

65. Villalba to Pizarro, Río de Janeiro, 24 May 1817, AGI, *legajo* 99.

66. João VI to Alexander I, Rio de Janeiro, 24 May 1817, AHI, Documentos Autógrafos de D. João VI (copy).

67. Balk-Polev was apparently reluctant to take this step, doing so largely at the insistence of the Spanish and Dutch envoys in Rio de Janeiro, who persuaded him that the gravity of the Portuguese affront left no alternative. (Villalba to Pizarro, Río de Janeiro, 24 May 1817, AGI, *legajo* 99.) The tsar, for his part, disapproved of Balk's conduct and ordered him to return at once to St. Petersburg. (*Sbornik,* CXIX, 315 n.) Even before Balk's departure from Brazil, the Russian government appears to have had doubts about his actions at the Portuguese court. The Portuguese envoy to St. Petersburg, in turn, had cautioned his government against improprieties in its official dealings with the Russian envoy lest the tsar take personal affront. (Saldanha to Conde da Barca, São Petersburgo, 17 April (1 May) 1817, AHI, Vol. 338/3/4; ANTT, *caixa* 14.) Following his return to St. Petersburg, Balk-Polev was severed from imperial service, barred from court, and ostracized from the capital. (Abreu to Villanova Portugal, S. Petersburgo, 19(31) October 1819, ANTT, *caixa* 14.)

68. Pozzo di Borgo to Nesselrode, Paris, 2 August 1817, *Sbornik,* CXIX, no. 153, p. 315. Pozzo no doubt referred to representatives of ambassadorial rank, for in Brazil the tsar continued to be represented by his talented and experienced consul-general, G. H. von Langsdorff. In the United States, A. Ya. Dashkov was at that moment preparing to return to Europe, while his replacement, F. V. Tuyll van Serooskerken, had not yet arrived in America.

69. Ibid. The tsar heeded Pozzo's suggestions. In the fall of 1817, he named Poletica Russian ambassador to the United States, reassigning Tuyll to Rio de Janeiro to replace Balk-Polev.

70. Pozzo di Borgo to Nesselrode, Paris, 9 August 1814, *Sbornik,* CXII, no. 49, pp. 60–61.

71. Pozzo di Borgo to Nesselrode, Paris, 26 September 1814, *Sbornik,* CXII, no. 78, p. 92.

72. Pozzo di Borgo to Capo d'Istria, Paris, 20 May 1817, *Sbornik*, CXIX, no. 97, pp. 192–193.

73. Pozzo di Borgo to Nesselrode, Paris, 14 June 1817, *Sbornik*, CXIX, no. 111, p. 228.

74. Pozzo di Borgo to Capo d'Istria, Paris, 20 May 1817, *Sbornik*, CXIX, no. 97, p. 192.

75. *Istoricheskii, statisticheskii i geograficheskii zhurnal*, 1, Bk. 1 (January 1812), 34–35.

76. Quoted by V. I. Ermolaev, "Dvizhenie za nezavisimost' Brazilii (1789–1822 gg.)," in: N. M. Lavrov et al. (eds.), *Voina za nezavisimost' v Latinskoi Amerike (1810–1826)* (Moscow: Nauka, 1964), p. 186. See, also, idem, "Nekotorye voprosy osvoboditel'noi bor'by amerikanskikh kolonii Ispanii i Portugalii (K 150-letiiu nachala voiny za nezavisimost' 1810–1826 gg.)," *Novaia i noveishaia istoriia*, no. 3 (May–June 1960): 29.

77. *Istoricheskii, statisticheskii i geograficheskii zhurnal*, 3, Bk. 2 (August 1817): 137–138.

78. Pozzo di Borgo to Nesselrode, Paris, 14 June 1817, *Sbornik*, CXIX, no. 111, p. 228.

79. Saldanha to Aguiar, São Petersburgo, 19 April 1817, AHI, Vol. 338/3/4 (copy). Also ANTT, *caixa* 14.

80. Tatishchev to Pizarro, Madrid, 18 June 1817, AGI, *legajo* 88.

81. Pozzo di Borgo to Nesselrode, Paris, 2 August 1817, *Sbornik*, CXIX, no. 153, p. 315.

82. Ermolaev, "Nekotorye voprosy osvoboditel'noi bor'by amerikanskikh kolonii Ispanii i Portugalii," p. 28.

83. Ibid.

84. "Zapiska grafa Ioanna Kapodistrii ob ego sluzhebnoi deiatel'nosti," *Sbornik*, III, 221–222.

85. Slëzkin, *Rossiia i voina za nezavisimost'*, pp. 134–135.

86. Pozzo di Borgo to Nesselrode, Paris, 2 August 1817, *Sbornik*, CXIX, no. 147, pp. 304–305.

87. Pozzo di Borgo to Nesselrode, Paris, 14 June 1817, *Sbornik*, CXIX, no. 111, p. 229.

88. Pozzo di Borgo to Capo d'Istria, Paris, 20 May 1817, *Sbornik*, CXIX, no. 97, p. 192.

89. Pozzo di Borgo to Capo d'Istria, Paris, 14 June 1817, *Sbornik*, CXIX, no. 115, p. 239.

90. "Although it appears true that Tatishchev meddled in some affairs that were not within his province," writes Jerónimo Bécker, "it is more to the point that he used his influence to support, against the clergy and against the Court, the minister of finance, D. Martín de Garay, whose plans for severe economy and capital reforms encountered stiff opposition from the privileged. For this Tatishchev does not deserve the censure of which he is sometimes the object, and even less from Spanish liberals if, as is believed, he worked energetically for the granting of a broad amnesty and a constitutional charter to the insurgent countries of America." (Bécker, *Historia de las relaciones exteriores de España*, I, 419.)

91. Tatishchev to Pizarro, Madrid, 18 June 1817, AGI, *legajo* 88.

92. Pozzo di Borgo to Nesselrode, Paris, 14 June 1817, *Sbornik*, CXIX, no. 111, p. 230.

93. Tatishchev to Pizarro, Madrid, 18 June 1817, AGI, *legajo* 88. Pozzo di Borgo outlined an almost identical plan to the Russian ministry of foreign affairs just five days before Tatishchev advanced this proposal to the Spanish secretary of state. (See Pozzo di Borgo to Nesselrode, Paris, 14 June 1817, *Sbornik*, CXIX, no. 111, pp. 230–231.)

94. British interest in mediating between the Spanish crown and Spain's revolted American colonies actually dated from 1812. (See, for example, Castlereagh to Wellesley, no. 13, 1 April 1812, in Webster, *Britain and the Independence of Latin America*, II, 309–316.

95. Pozzo di Borgo to Nesselrode, Paris, 14 June 1817, *Sbornik*, CXIX, no. 111, p. 231.

96. Tatishchev to Pizarro, Madrid, 18 June 1817, AGI, *legajo* 88.

97. On the Spanish army in America, see Margaret L. Woodward, "The Spanish Army and the Loss of America, 1810–1824," *The Hispanic American Historical Review* 48, no. 4 (November 1968): 586–607.

98. Foreign Office, "Confidential Memorandum," 20 August 1817, in Webster, *Britain and the Independence of Latin America*, II, 356.

99. Pozzo di Borgo to Nesselrode, Paris, 3 October 1817, *Sbornik*, CXIX, no. 188, p. 393.

100. Pozzo di Borgo to Nesselrode, Paris, 2 August 1817, *Sbornik*, CXIX, no. 147, p. 304.

101. Pozzo di Borgo to Nesselrode, Paris, 3 October 1817, *Sbornik*, CXIX, no. 188, p. 393.

102. Pozzo's proposals for pacification, remarked Nesselrode in the summer of 1817, "appear to offer the means of success. They are, moreover, entirely analogous to the principles professed by the Emperor. . . ." (Nesselrode to Pozzo di Borgo, Saint-Pétersbourg, 24 August 1817, *Sbornik*, CXIX, no. 168, p. 335.)

103. "De la négotiation relative à la question du Rio de la Plata, et, en général, de la pacification des colonies. (Mémoire à communiquer aux puissances intéressées, ainsi qu'aux cabinets des puissances médiatrices.)," Moscou, 29 November 1817, *Sbornik*, CXIX, no. 223, pp. 474–482.

104. Ibid., p. 481.

105. Perkins, "Russia and the Spanish Colonies," p. 664.

106. The ships were the *Tri Sviatitelia* (renamed *Velasco*), *Nord-Adler* (renamed *España*), *Neptunus* (renamed *Fernando VII*), *Drezden* (renamed *Alejandro I*), and *Liubek* (renamed *Numancia*), of seventy-four guns each, and the fifty-gun frigates *Mercurius* (*Mercurio*), *Patritsii* (renamed *María Isabel*), and *Avtroil* (*Astrolabio*). (*Estado general de la Armada para el año de 1849*, Apéndice, pp. 59–61.) There is a discrepancy in the renaming of two of the Russian vessels. Vásquez Figueroa, then minister of the Spanish navy, states that the *Nord-Adler* became the *Numancia*, while the *Liubek* was renamed the *España*. (José Vázquez Figueroa, "Navíos rusos y mi salida del segundo ministerio . . . ," 14 September 1818, BMN, Ms. 433, doc. 30, fol. 634.)

107. Slëzkin, *Rossiia i voina za nezavisimost'*, p. 141.

108. San Carlos to Pizarro, Londres, 19 November 1817, AHN, *legajo* 5469. Copy of Spanish note to Castlereagh attached.

109. Wellesley to Castlereagh, no. 25 (most secret and confidential), Madrid, 1 March 1818, in Webster, *Britain and the Independence of Latin America*, II, 365. Includes English translation of the article from the *Gazeta de Madrid*.

110. "Contestación a las observaciones hechas sobre el apronto y venta de cierto número de buques de guerra que necesita S. M. C." (Kontrzamechaniia na proekt prodazhi Rossiei voennykh korablei Ispanii), Madrid, [1817], ADPT (copy).

111. Saldanha to Conde da Barca, S. Petersburgo, 17(29) September 1817, ANTT, caixa 14, fol. 1.

112. Saldanha to Aguiar, S. Petersburgo, 20 February (4 March) 1817, ANTT, caixa 14, fols. 9–10.

113. Saldanha to Conde da Barca, S. Petersburgo, 17(29) September 1817, ANTT, caixa 14, fol. 1.

114. El Sol de Chile (18 December 1818), CAPCH, I, 263.

115. El Argos de Chile (23 July 1818), CAPCH, I, 31.

116. N. N. Bolkhovitinov, Russko-amerikanskie otnosheniia, 1815–1832 gg., p. 53.

117. V. M. Miroshevskii, "Pokupka Ispaniei russkikh voennykh korablei," typescript, AVMM, karton 1. Published posthumously with an introductory note by B. N. Komissarov under the title, "Ob otnoshenii Rossii k voine Ispanskoi Ameriki za nezavisimost' (po materialam arkhiva V. M. Miroshevskogo)," VLU, no. 8, vyp. 2 (1964): 60–70. Subsequent references are to the original typescript.

118. Ibid., fol. 1. Ferdinand had at first considered soliciting permission to build several warships annually in Russian yards, "but had then concluded that to rebuild the Spanish navy in this way would be too complicated and too slow to have any effect." He therefore decided to request the immediate delivery of a dozen warships already in service. (See ibid., fols. 1–2). Although Tatishchev's role in this affair remains clouded, there is reason to suspect that the Russian minister may have been instrumental in Ferdinand's decision to pursue this latter course.

119. Quoted ibid., fol. 2.

120. "Contestación a las observaciones hechas sobre el apronto y venta de cierto número de buques de guerra," Madrid, [1817], ADPT.

121. Miroshevskii, "Pokupka Ispaniei russkikh voennykh korablei," AVMM, karton 1, fol. 2.

122. The Spanish ministry of the navy took no part in these negotiations, nor was the ministry's head, Vázquez Figueroa, advised of the proposed transactions until after the Russian vessels had reached Cádiz. (Vásquez Figueroa, "Navíos rusos y mi salida del segundo ministerio," Ms. 433, doc. 30, fols. 607–634.) Vázquez Figueroa further indicates that Zea Bermúdez may have been party to the secret warship deal. (Ibid., fol. 614.) José García de León y Pizarro, then Spanish secretary of state, likewise alludes to the involvement of Zea Bermúdez in transacting the Russo-Spanish accord. (See García de León y Pizarro, Memorias, I, 270.)

123. That Russia should have accepted the British indemnizations as adequate collateral suggests the political significance the tsar attached to the bolstering of Spain's naval forces, for in point of fact there was no guarantee that the sum in question would actually be paid. The Anglo-Spanish treaty abolishing the slave trade had not yet been signed, nor would it be until the fall of 1817. (See Cesáreo Fernández Duro, Armada española desde la unión de los reinos de Castilla y de Aragón, IX, 136; and Webster, The Foreign Policy of Castlereagh, p. 459.) Moreover, Spain had thus far been notably

unsuccessful in pressing its demands for financial compensation as a precondition of abolition. In the spring of 1816, the Spanish court had sought a total of £1.5 million sterling in indemnities from the British government. The British having rejected such a sum out of hand, Spain subsequently reduced the figure to £500,000. Failing to obtain this sum as well, the Spanish court proposed a cash indemnity of £400,000, plus a British government loan of £700,000. The court of St. James agreed to pay the £400,000, but refused to guarantee the loan. In return for a one-year extension of the date of total abolition, Spain finally accepted the reduced indemnity and signed a formal accord with Great Britain on 23 September 1817. (Bécker, *Historia de las relaciones exteriores de España*, I, 423–430.)

124. Slëzkin, *Rossiia i voina za nezavisimost'*, p. 141.

125. See, for example, Bécker, *Historia de las relaciones exteriores de España*, I, 420 n; Fernández Duro, *Armada española*, IX, 135–136; Perkins, "Russia and the Spanish Colonies," pp. 657–658. An original copy of the Russo-Spanish accord has been located in the historical archives of the USSR Ministry of Foreign Affairs in Moscow. (See Bolkhovitinov, *Russko-amerikanskie otnosheniia*, pp. 51–52, n. 104.)

126. In the view of V. M. Miroshevskii, a dispatch addressed to Nesselrode on 7 March 1820 by M. N. Bulgari, tsarist chargé d'affaires in Madrid, "explains why no traces remain in Spanish archives of the convention concluded by Tatishchev. The only copy was held by the king's favorite, Antonio Ugarte. Shortly after the outbreak of the Spanish [Liberal] revolution the king was obliged (on 4 March 1820) to order Ugarte's arrest. Having learned of this, Bulgari secretly asked Ferdinand to remove all documents relating to the sale of the [Russian] squadron from his favorite's archive, for otherwise they would be confiscated by the court and receive wide publicity. The king granted this request and the appropriate documents were secretly transferred to his private office. Their subsequent fate is unclear; one can suppose that after a time, fearing discovery, [Ferdinand] destroyed the only official text of the convention. As for its publication in the 'Morning Chronicle,' this was probably based on a copy of the convention in the Russian [embassy] archives which fell into the hands of English secret agents." (Miroshevskii, "Pokupka Ispaniei russkikh voennykh korablei," p. 5.)

127. Slëzkin, *Rossiia i voina za nezavisimost'*, pp. 141–142.

128. Ibid., p. 142.

129. Quoted ibid., p. 143.

130. Ibid., pp. 141–142.

131. Russian vessels sailing to the New World in this period normally accomplished the somewhat longer voyage from the Baltic to the Canary Islands in about ten weeks. The principal variable was the length of time spent in port at Falmouth or Portsmouth, England.

132. Quoted in Bécker, *Historia de las relaciones exteriores de España*, I, 421.

133. Vázquez Figueroa, "Navíos rusos y mi salida del segundo ministerio," Ms. 433, doc. 30, fol. 616.

134. Ibid., fol. 624; *Estado general de la Armada*, Apéndice, pp. 59–61.

135. Miroshevskii, "Pokupka Ispaniei russkikh voennykh korablei," fol. 12.

136. Fernández Duro, *Armada española*, IX, 138.

137. Slëzkin, *Rossiia i voina za nezavisimost'*, pp. 164–165; Miroshevskii,

"Pokupka Ispaniei russkikh voennykh korablei," fol. 14; Zea Bermúdez to Pizarro, San Petersburgo, 25 and 30 July and 12 August 1818, AHN, Embajada de España, *legajo* 6127, *caja* 3. The three frigates were the *Lëgkii* (*Ligera*), *Provornyi* (*Viva*), and *Pospeshnyi* (*Pronta*).

138. Nesselrode to Zea Bermúdez, St. Pétersbourg, 11 July 1818 [o. s.], AHN, Estado: Rusia, Embajada de España, *legajo* 6127, *caja* 1; Zea Bermúdez to Pizarro, San Petersburgo, 25 July 1818, AHN, Estado: Rusia, Embajada de España, *legajo* 6127, *caja* 3.

139. *Estado general de la Armada*, Apéndice, pp. 59–61.

140. Bécker, *Historia de las relaciones exteriores de España*, I, 419–420.

141. Robertson, "Russia and the Emancipation of Spanish America," p. 199.

142. Perkins, "Russia and the Spanish Colonies," p. 658.

143. Miroshevskii, "Velikie derzhavy i voina za nezavisimost' Ispanskoi Ameriki," p. 140.

144. Slëzkin, *Rossiia i voina za nezavisimost'*, pp. 143–144.

145. Miroshevskii, "Velikie derzhavy i voina za nezavisimost' Ispanskoi Ameriki," pp. 156–157.

146. García de León y Pizarro, *Memorias*, I, 265.

147. Vázquez Figueroa, "Navíos rusos y mi salida del segundo ministerio," Ms. 433, doc. 30, fols. 616–617.

148. Pozzo di Borgo to Nesselrode, Paris, 20 October 1817, *Sbornik*, CXIX, no. 197, p. 142.

149. Tatishchev to Nesselrode, Madrid, 10(22) September 1818, ADPT, fol. 2 (copy).

150. Tatishchev to Ferdinand VII, draft letter approved by the tsar, St. Pétersbourg, December 1819 (January 1820), ADPT, fol. 3.

151. Capo d'Istria to Zea Bermúdez, Varsovie, 30 March 1818, AHN, *legajo* 6127, *caja* 1; Tatishchev to Nesselrode, Madrid, 10(22) September 1818, ADPT, fol. 2 (copy).

152. Capo d'Istria to Tatishchev, Moscou, 28 November 1817, ADPT, fols. 6–7.

153. Zea Bermúdez to Casa Yrujo, Aquisgrán, 25 November 1818, AHN, *legajo* 6127, *caja* 3.

154. Zea Bermúdez to Casa Yrujo, París, 28 December 1818, AGI, *legajo* 88.

155. García de León y Pizarro, *Memorias*, I, 268.

156. Pozzo di Borgo to Nesselrode, Paris, 20 October 1817, *Sbornik*, CXIX, no. 197, p. 412.

157. García de León y Pizarro, *Memorias*, I, 206–207.

158. Vázquez Figueroa, "Navíos rusos y mi salida del segundo ministerio," Ms. 433, doc. 30, fol. 610.

159. Pozzo di Borgo to Nesselrode, Paris, 1 February 1818, *Sbornik*, CXIX, no. 262, p. 577.

160. Pozzo di Borgo to Nesselrode, Paris, 15 February 1818, *Sbornik*, CXIX, no. 266, p. 591.

161. Pozzo di Borgo to Nesselrode, Paris, 25 March 1818, *Sbornik*, CXIX, no. 283, pp. 621–622.

162. Capo d'Istria to Zea Bermúdez, Varsovie, 30 March 1818, AHN, *legajo* 6127, *caja* 1.

163. Capo d'Istria to Pozzo di Borgo, Varsovie, 8 April 1818, *Sbornik*, CXIX, no. 297, p. 658.

164. Capo d'Istria to Pozzo di Borgo, Varsovie, 8 April 1818, *Sbornik*, CXIX, no. 296, pp. 656–657. Also AHN, *legajo* 6127, *caja* 1; and ANTT, *caixa* 14.

165. Pozzo di Borgo to Nesselrode, Paris, 15 June 1818, *Sbornik*, CXIX, no. 328, pp. 739–740.

166. Tatishchev to [Zea Bermúdez?], Madrid, June 1818, AHN, *legajo* 6127, *caja* 1 (copy).

167. Pozzo di Borgo to Nesselrode, Paris, 12 July 1818, *Sbornik*, CXIX, no. 337, p. 755.

168. Pozzo di Borgo to Nesselrode, Paris, 6 August 1818, *Sbornik*, CXIX, no. 351, pp. 785–787.

169. Webster, *The Foreign Policy of Castlereagh*, pp. 121–123.

170. K. R. Nesselrode, *Lettres et papiers au chancelier de Nesselrode, 1760–1850*, V, p. 287.

171. See four separate memoranda submitted by the tsarist government to the Spanish crown in June 1818, AHN, *legajo* 6127, *caja* 1.

172. Also present at the Congress of Aix-la-Chapelle were Counts Nesselrode and Capo d'Istria, the Austrian chancellor Prince Metternich, Prussian ministers Count Bernstorff and Prince Hardenberg, and, representing France, the Duke of Richelieu. (William Spence Robertson, *France and Latin-American Independence*, p. 150.)

173. "De la négotiation relative à la question du Rio de la Plata, et, en général, de la pacification des colonies," *Sbornik*, CXIX, no. 223, pp. 474–482.

174. Robertson, "Russia and the Emancipation of Spanish America," p. 207.

175. Alexander I to Ferdinand VII, Vienne, 22 December 1818, AHN, *legajo* 2849, *carpeta* 16.

176. Slëzkin, *Rossiia i voina za nezavisimost'*, pp. 176–177.

177. Ibid.; Bolkhovitinov, *Russko-amerikanskie otnosheniia*, pp. 59–60.

Chapter 7: The Final Years: Russian Responses to Colonial Emancipation

1. Gentz to Nesselrode, Vienne, 27 January 1818, in K. R. Nesselrode, *Lettres et papiers du chancelier de Nesselrode, 1760–1850*, V, 293–294.

2. Ibid., p. 294.

3. See, for example, Pozzo di Borgo to Nesselrode, Paris, 26 September 1814, *Sbornik*, CXII, no. 78, p. 92; Pozzo di Borgo to Capo d'Istria, Paris, 20 May 1817, *Sbornik*, CXIX, no. 97, p. 192; Saldanha to Aguiar, São Petersburgo, 19 April 1817, AHI, Vol. 338/3/4.

4. Zea Bermúdez to Casa Yrujo, San Petersburgo, 21 March (2 April) 1819, AGI, *legajo* 104 (in cipher).

5. Zea Bermúdez to Casa Yrujo, San Petersburgo, 5(17) March 1819, AGI, *legajo* 104 (in cipher).

6. Ibid.

7. Nesselrode to Zea Bermúdez, St. Pétersbourg, n.d. [late March or early April 1819], AGI, *legajo* 104 (copy).

8. Ibid.

9. Saldanha to Villanova Portugal, Funchal, 26 March 1819, ANTT, *caixa* 14, fols. 1–2.

10. Abreu to Villanova Portugal, S. Petersburgo, 2 July 1819, ANTT, *caixa* 14, fol. 1.

11. *Le Conservateur Impartial* (1818): 415.

12. Ibid. (1819): 120.

13. Ibid. (1819): 276.

14. Ibid. (1820): 24.

15. Casa Flores to Casa Yrujo, Río de Janeiro, 5 January 1819, AGI, *legajo* 103. The ship was seized in the port of Talcahuano and subsequently became the flagship of the Chilean navy.

16. *Le Conservateur Impartial* (1820): 14.

17. For a narrative account, see Miguel Artola Gallego, *La España de Fernando VII*, pp. 638–677.

18. *Le Conservateur Impartial* (1820): 1813–1815.

19. August Friedrich Ferdinand von Kotzebue (1761–1819) was the father of Otto von Kotzebue (1787–1846), a Russian mariner who as noted above participated in the Kruzenshtern expedition of 1803–1806 and subsequently himself commanded two voyages to the New World. August von Kotzebue entered Russian service in 1781 as secretary to the governor-general of St. Petersburg, settling two years later in the Estonian city of Revel, where he produced much of his literary work. In 1816 he was attached to the Russian ministry of foreign affairs. The following year he returned to Germany as a tsarist agent, in which capacity he was murdered by a German student of liberal persuasion. Kotzebue's long association with the Russian imperial service contributed greatly to tsarist shock at his assassination.

20. Patricia Kennedy Grimsted, *The Foreign Ministers of Alexander I*, p. 234.

21. Quoted ibid.

22. Zea Bermúdez to Ministère Imperial, St. Pétersbourg, 7(19) April 1820, ANTT, *caixa* 14. Copy forwarded to the Portuguese court by Visconde da Lapa, 9 May 1820.

23. Ministère Imperial to Zea Burmúdez, St. Pétersbourg, 18(30) April 1820, ANTT, *caixa* 14. Copy forwarded to the Portuguese court by Visconde da Lapa, 9 May 1820.

24. San Fernando to Capo d'Istria, Madrid, 14 February 1820, AHN, *legajo* 6129, *caja* 2.

25. Zea Bermúdez to San Fernando, San Petersburgo, 10 January 1820, AGI, *legajo* 104.

26. Adrien Maggiolo, *Corse, France et Russie. Pozzo di Borgo, 1764–1842*, pp. 261–262.

27. Grimsted, *The Foreign Ministers of Alexander I*, pp. 282–283.

28. L. Yu. Slëzkin, *Rossiia i voina za nezavisimost'*, p. 214.

29. Abreu to Palmella, São Petersburgo, 23 August 1823, ANTT, *caixa* 15.

30. Quoted in Artola Gallego, *La España de Fernando VII*, p. 804.

31. Slëzkin, *Rossiia i voina za nezavisimost'*, p. 216.

32. Artola Gallego, *La España de Fernando VII*, p. 804.

33. Fernando VII to Alexander I, Madrid, 26 June 1821, ADPT, fols. 1–2 (copy).

34. Artola Gallego, *La España de Fernando VII*, p. 804.

35. Ibid.

36. Russia severed relations with Spain on 21 January 1823. See Nesselrode to Argaiz, St. Pétersbourg, 21 January 1823, AHN, *legajo* 6133, *caja* 1.

37. Quoted in Slëzkin, *Rossiia i voina za nezavisimost'*, pp. 288–289.

38. Abreu to Palmella, São Petersburgo, 19 November 1823, ANTT, *caixa* 15, fol. 2.

39. "Instrucciones reservadas a los representantes de S. M. en Londres, París, Viena, Petersburgo y Berlín," Madrid, 6 May 1822, AGI, *legajo* 90.

40. Ibid.

41. Slëzkin, *Rossiia i voina za nezavisimost'*, pp. 235–236.

42. Argaiz to Martínez de la Rosa, Petersburgo, 2 June 1822, AGI, *legajo* 90.

43. Nesselrode to Argaiz, St. Pétersbourg, 13(25) June 1822, AHN, *legajo* 6132, *caja* 1. Also copy, ANTT, *caixa* 15.

44. See, for example, William Spence Robertson, *France and Latin-American Independence*, pp. 260–271.

45. In addition to the monograph by N. N. Bolkhovitinov cited in the Introduction, see idem, "Russkaia Amerika i provozglashenie doktriny Monro," *Voprosy istorii*, no. 9 (September 1971): 69–84; and idem, *Russko-amerikanskie otnosheniia, 1815–1832 gg.*, pp. 183–243.

46. Bolkhovitinov, *Russko-amerikanskie otnosheniia*, pp. 191–197.

47. Irby C. Nichols, Jr., "The Russian Ukase and the Monroe Doctrine: A Re-evaluation," *Pacific Historical Review* 36, no. 1 (February 1967): 17.

48. Ibid., p. 18.

49. Bolkhovitinov, *Russko-amerikanskie otnosheniia*, p. 193.

50. Ibid., pp. 196–197.

51. Ibid., p. 197.

52. John Quincy Adams, *Memoirs*, IV, 381.

53. Bolkhovitinov, *Russko-amerikanskie otnosheniia*, pp. 68–77.

54. Capo d'Istria to Poletica, Varsovie, 18 April 1818, Documents, *The American Historical Review* 18, no. 2 (January 1913): 312.

55. Nesselrode to Poletica, Aix-la-Chapelle, 9(21) November 1818, Documents, *The American Historical Review* 18, no. 2 (January 1913): 317.

56. Ibid.; Bolkhovitinov, *Russko-amerikanskie otnosheniia*, pp. 68–70.

57. Nesselrode to Tuyll, St. Pétersbourg, 13 July 1822, Documents, *The American Historical Review* 18, no. 2 (January 1913): 341–342.

58. Quoted in Maggiolo, *Corse, France et Russie*, pp. 275–276.

59. On Langsdorff's life and work, see B. N. Komissarov, *Grigorii Ivanovich Langsdorf*. Also Russell H. Bartley, "The Inception of Russo-Brazilian Relations (1808–1828)," *The Hispanic American Historical Review* 56, no. 2 (May 1976): 217–240; idem, "G. I. Langsdorf i russko-brazil'skie otnosheniia v pervoi treti XIX v.," *Latinskaia Amerika*, no. 3 (May–June 1976): 164–169.

60. James Henderson, *A History of the Brazil*, p. 99.

61. Alexander Caldcleugh, *Travels in South America, During the Years 1819–20–21*, II, 194.

62. John Luccock, *Notas sôbre o Rio-de-Janeiro e partes meridionais do Brasil, tomadas durante uma estada de dez anos nesse país, de 1808 a 1818*, p. 247.

63. J. B. von Spix and K. F. P. von Martius, *Travels in Brazil, in the Years 1817–1820*, I, p. 229.

64. Auguste de Saint-Hilaire, *Voyage dans les provinces de Rio de Janeiro et de Minas Gerais*, I, 129–130.

65. B. N. Komissarov, "Akademik G. I. Langsdorf i ego ekspeditsiia v Braziliiu v 1821–1829 gg.," in D. E. Bertel's et al. (comps.), *Materialy ekspe-*

ditsii akademika Grigoriia Ivanovicha Langsdorfa v Braziliiu v 1821–1829 gg., p. 13.

66. Henderson, *A History of the Brazil*, p. 99.

67. Spix and Martius, *Travels in Brazil*, I, 237.

68. Requerimento de Jorge de Langsdorff, cônsul-general da Rússia, ANTT, *caixa* 2, fol. 3.

69. Ibid., fol. 1.

70. Quoted in Komissarov, "Akademik G. I. Langsdorf i ego ekspeditsiia v Braziliiu," p. 15.

71. Abreu to Pinheiro Ferreira, S. Petersburgo, 6(18) July 1821, ANTT, *caixa* 15, fols. 1–2.

72. Quoted in Komissarov, "Akademik G. I. Langsdorf i ego ekspeditsiia v Braziliiu," p. 15.

73. Abreu to Pinheiro Ferreira, S. Petersburgo, 6(18) July 1821, ANTT, *caixa* 15.

74. Komissarov, "Akademik G. I. Langsdorf i ego ekspeditsiia v Braziliiu," pp. 15–16.

75. Langsdorff to Andrade e Silva, à bord du navire Doris, 5 March 1822, AHI, Vol. 289/1/13.

76. See Russell H. Bartley, "Akademik G. I. Langsdorf i stanovlenie russko-brazil'skikh otnoshenii (1804–1828 gg.)."

77. Langsdorff to Andrade e Silva, Rio de Janeiro, 27 March 1822, AHI, Vol. 289/1/13. See, also, N. Ivashintsov, *Russkie krugosvetnye puteshestviia, s 1803 po 1849 god*, pp. 55–60.

78. See Komissarov, "Akademik G. I. Langsdorf i ego ekspeditsiia v Braziliiu," pp. 15–36; Roderick J. Barman, "The Forgotten Journey: Georg Heinrich Langsdorff and the Russian Imperial Scientific Expedition to Brazil, 1821–1829," *Terrae Incognitae* 3 (1971): 67–96.

79. Akademiia nauk SSSR, *Vsemirnaia istoriia*, VI, 706–707, 737.

80. "Considérations sur le commerce de la Russie avec le Portugal," St. Pétersbourg, 24 January (5 February) 1820, ANTT, *caixa* 15, fol. 3.

81. Ibid.

82. Abreu to Pinheiro Ferreira, S. Petersburgo, 24 November 1821, ANTT, *caixa* 15, fol. 1.

83. Visconde da Lapa to Villanova Portugal, S. Petersburgo, 28 February 1821, ANTT, *caixa* 15.

84. B. F. Sukhomlinov, "Ob ustanovlenii russko-brazil'skikh otnoshenii," *Novaia i noveishaia istoriia*, no. 2 (March–April 1965): 95.

85. See *Le Conservateur Impartial* (1821): 216.

86. Sukhomlinov, "Ob ustanovlenii russko-brazil'skikh otnoshenii," p. 95.

87. Langsdorff to Andrade e Silva, Mandioca, 10 December 1822, AHI, Vol. 289/1/13.

88. Ibid.

89. Abreu to Palmella, S. Petersburgo, 24 August 1824, ANTT, *caixa* 16, fol. 1.

90. Abreu to Palmella, S. Petersburgo, 2 July 1824, ANTT, *caixa* 16, fol. 2.

91. See, for example, Kielchen to Visconde de Inhambupe, Rio de Janeiro, 30 April 1926, AHI, Vol. 289/1/13.

92. On Decembrist views of the struggle for Latin American independence, see Bolkhovitinov, *Russko-amerikanskie otnosheniia*, pp. 492–521; Slëzkin,

Rossiia i voina za nezavisimost', pp. 327–353; L. A. Shur, *Rossiia i Latinskaia Amerika*, pp. 50–65.

93. Páez de la Cadena to Duque del Infantado, San Petersburgo, 8 April 1826, AHN, *legajo* 6134, *caja* 1.

94. Páez de la Cadena to Duque del Infantado, Moscú, 26 September 1826, AHN, *legajo* 6134, *caja* 2.

95. Bolkhovitinov, *Russko-amerikanskie otnosheniia*, p. 300.

96. S. B. Okun, *Rossiisko-amerikanskaia kompaniia*, pp. 158–160.

97. On the surface, Russian adherence to the position of the United States in the matter of recognition was "inconceivable." See, for example, Benjamin Platt Thomas, *Russo-American Relations, 1815–1867*, p. 49.

98. Ibid., pp. 47–48; Bolkhovitinov, *Russko-amerikanskie otnosheniia*, pp. 308–314.

99. Quoted in Bolkhovitinov, *Russko-amerikanskie otnosheniia*, p. 301.

100. Ibid.

101. Ibid., p. 303; Okun, *Rossiisko-amerikanskaia kompaniia*, p. 161.

102. Quoted in Bolkhovitinov, *Russko-amerikanskie otnosheniia*, pp. 301–302.

103. "Eshchë o gaitskoi privilegii," AM, VIII, 112.

104. Ibid.

105. Ibid., pp. 112–113.

106. Ibid., p. 113.

107. Bolkhovitinov, *Russko-amerikanskie otnosheniia*, pp. 302–303.

108. Ibid., p. 302.

109. Ibid., pp. 303–304.

110. Okun, *Rossiisko-amerikanskaia kompaniia*, pp. 128, 132–134.

111. Bolkhovitinov, *Russko-amerikanskie otnosheniia*, p. 299.

112. Ibid., p. 296.

113. Okun, *Rossiisko-amerikanskaia kompaniia*, p. 125.

114. C. Alan Hutchinson, *Frontier Settlement in Mexican California*, pp. 96–105.

115. Kruzenshtern, for example, had suggested that the port of San Francisco might be ceded to Russia as compensation for the Russian warships transferred to Spain in 1817–1818, final payment for which remained outstanding. (See Okun, *Rossiisko-amerikanskaia kompaniia*, p. 125.)

116. Quoted ibid., p. 126.

117. In early 1836, F. P. Vrangel, governor-general of Russian America (1830–1835), traveled to Mexico for informal talks with Mexican authorities about the full range of Russian interests in Alta California. (See his Mexican diary in L. A. Shur, *K beregam Novogo Sveta*, pp. 190–277.) These talks sought only to learn first-hand the Mexican position on an expanded Russian presence in the region and in no way implied a new tsarist diplomatic initiative. Indeed, throughout the 1830s the tsarist government remained loath to sanction Mexican independence even tacitly through direct bilateral discussions of the territorial question. In the meantime, the gradual influx of Anglo-American settlers into California effectively blocked any further expansion of Russian holdings there and, in 1841, finally moved the Russian-American Company to withdraw from California altogether.

118. Cruz Guerreiro to Porto Santo, S. Petersburgo, 9(21) December 1825, ANTT, *caixa* 16; Cruz Guerreiro to Porto Santo, S. Petersburgo, 11(23) Jan-

uary, 23 January (4 February), 6(18) February, and 17 February (1 March) 1826, ANTT, *caixa* 17.

119. Russia, Ministerstvo inostrannykh del, *Ocherk istorii Ministerstva inostrannykh del, 1802–1902*, Prilozheniia, p. 22.

120. P. Miguel Benavente, S. J., "Reflexiones sobre los establecimientos que podían hacer los rusos en las Californias" [1764], BNM, Mss. 3101, fol. 319.

121. Fëdor Smirnov, *Yuzhnaia pri-atlanticheskaia Amerika*, p. 1.

Bibliography

The bibliographic materials listed below represent only the basic sources from which the present study has been drawn. The nature and scope of the topic precluded from the outset an exhaustive investigation of all pertinent sources, especially in the area of unpublished archival materials. The sheer mass of potentially relevant manuscripts, spread over three continents, alone imposed severe strictures of selectivity. Limited access to Soviet archives proved particularly vexatious, as it denied me the opportunity to consult key manuscript collections in Moscow and Leningrad. This serious shortcoming was partially offset by a full examination of related materials in the state archives of Spain, Portugal, and Brazil, as well as by the generous assistance of Soviet colleagues who contributed much from their own researches. Many of these materials, in turn, are here cited for the first time and thus broaden significantly the documentary bases for the continued study of Russian New World interests in the eighteenth and nineteenth centuries.

Unpublished Documents

Archivo General de Indias (Seville).
> *Sección Novena (Papeles de Estado), legajos* 86–92 and 98–105, *América en General.*

Archivo Histórico Nacional (Madrid).
> *Sección de Estado.*
>> *Alejandro I, legajo* 2,849, *carpeta* 16, *cuatro cartas a Fernando VII.*
>> *Inglaterra, Embajada de España, legajos* 5,469–5,470 (1817–1819), *correspondencia; legajo* 5,591 (1815–1818), *expedientes.*
>> *Rusia, Embajada de España, legajos* 6,123–6,134 (1806–1826), *correspondencia y expedientes.*

Arquivo Histórico do Itamaratí, Ministério das Relações Exteriores do Brasil (Rio de Janeiro).
> *Documentos Autógrafos de D. João VI, lata* 169, *pasta* 3, *maço* 3.
> *Legação em S. Petersburgo, volumes* 338/3/2–4, *ostensivos* (1808–1820).
> *Legação Imperial na Rússia, volume* 230/2/1, *ofícios* (1825–1831).
> *Representações Diplomáticas Estrangeiras no Brasil, Rússia, volumes* 289/1/13–14 (1821–1899), *Consulado da Rússia, notas recebidas; volume* 289/1/21 (1818–1892), *Consulado da Rússia, notas expedidas; volume* 289/2/1 (1811–1876), *Consulado da Rússia, notas expedidas.*

Arquivo Nacional Tôrre do Tombo (Lisbon).
> *Ministério dos Negócios Estrangeiros.*

Correspondência de diversos para Rodrigo Navarro de Andrade, Encarregado de Negócios em S. Petersburgo (1804–1817), caixa 11, maços 1–3.

Embaixada extraordinária ao Imperador da Rússia (1814), originaes encadernados de despachos e documentos da embaixada do Marquez de Marialva, maço 62.

Legação da Rússia em Portugal, caixas 1–2 (1780–1828).

Legação de Portugal na Rússia, caixas 12–17 (1806–1828).

Bancroft Library (Berkeley, California).

Rossiisko-Amerikanskaia Kompaniia. Korrespondentsiia, Sitka (1802–1867), microfilm.

  Letters received by the Governors-General (1802–1866), reels 1–5 (18 April 1802 to 13 December 1827).

  Letters sent by the Governors-General, 1818–1867, reels 26–30 (11 January 1818 to 29 December 1827).

Miscellaneous Mss.

Biblioteca del Museo Naval (Madrid).

Colección de documentos relativos al segundo ministerio del Exmo. Sr. D. José Vázquez Figueroa, Mss. 432–445.

Biblioteca Nacional (Madrid).

Sección de Manuscritos.

  P. Miguel Benavente, S. J., "Reflexiones sobre los establecimientos que podían hacer los rusos en las Californias," [1764], Ms. 3101 (bound *legajo*, eighteenth century), fols. 314–336.

Lenin State Library (Moscow).

Otdel rukopisei.

Arkhiv Vladimira Mikhailovicha Miroshevskogo, fond 469.

Saltykov-Shchedrin State Public Library (Leningrad).

Otdel rukopisei.

Arkhiv Dmitriia Pavlovicha Tatishcheva, fond 762.

Published Documents

Andreev, A. I., ed. *Russkie otkrytiia v Tikhom okeane i Severnoi Amerike v XVIII–XIX vekakh. Sbornik materialov.* Moscow-Leningrad: Izd-vo AN SSSR, 1944.

Archivo del General Miranda. 15 vols. Caracas: Editorial Sur-Americana and Tipografía Americana, 1929–1938.

Arkhiv grafov Mordvinovykh. 10 vols. St. Petersburg: Tipografiia I. N. Skorokhodova, 1901–1903.

Bolkhovitinov, N. N., comp. "Otnoshenie Rossii k nachalu voiny Latinskoi Ameriki za nezavisimost'," *Istoricheskii arkhiv*, no. 3 (1962): 120–131.

Brazil. Ministério das Relações Exteriores. *Archivo diplomático da Independência.* 6 vols. Rio de Janeiro: Litho-Typo. Fluminense, 1922–1925.

———. Statutes. *Codigo Brasiliense, ou Collecção das Leis, Alvarás, Decretos, Cartas Regias, &c. promulgados no Brasil desde a feliz chegada do Principe Regente N.S. a estes estados.* 3 vols. Rio de Janeiro: Impressão Regia, 1811–1820.

———. ———. *Collecção das Leis do Brasil, 1808–1819, 1821–1826.* 18 vols.

Rio de Janeiro: Typographia Nacional and Imprensa Nacional, 1880–1891.

Calvo, Carlos. *Colección completa de los tratados, convenios, capitulaciones, armisticios y otros actos diplomáticos de todos los estados de la América Latina.* . . . 6 vols. Madrid: Carlos Bailly-Bailliere, 1864.

Cardoso de Oliveira, José Manoel. *Actos diplomáticos do Brasil. Tratados do periodo colonial e varios documentos desde 1493.* 2 vols. Rio de Janeiro: Typo. do Jornal do Commercio, 1912.

Documents. "Correspondence of the Russian Ministers in Washington, 1818–1825," *The American Historical Review* 18, no. 2 (January 1913): 309–345; no. 3 (April 1913): 537–562.

Du Four, Clarence John. Documentary appendix to "The Russian Withdrawal from California," *Quarterly of the California Historical Society* 12, no. 3 (September 1933): 249–276.

Humphreys, R. A., ed. *British Consular Reports on the Trade and Politics of Latin America, 1824–1826.* London: Royal Historical Society, 1940.

Manning, William Ray, comp. *Diplomatic Correspondence of the United States Concerning the Independence of the Latin-American Nations.* 3 vols. New York: Oxford University Press, 1925.

Mukhanov, P., and M. Semevskii, eds. "Zapiska o finansakh, politike i torgovle Rossiiskogo gosudarstva v 1810 g.," *Chteniia v Imperatorskom obshchestve istorii i drevnostei rossiiskikh pri Moskovskom universitete* 4 (1868): 129–151.

Nesselrode, K. R. *Lettres et papiers au chancelier de Nesselrode, 1760–1850.* 11 vols. Paris: A. Lahure, [1904–1912].

Nikolai Mikhailovich, velikii kniaz', comp. *Diplomaticheskie snosheniia Rossii i Frantsii, po doneseniiam poslov Imperatorov Aleksandra i Napoleona, 1808–1812.* 7 vols. St. Petersburg: Ekspeditsiia zagotovleniia gosudarstvennykh bumag, 1905–1914.

——, ed. Appendices to *Imperator Aleksandr I. Opyt istoricheskogo issledovaniia.* 2 vols. St. Petersburg: Ekspeditsiia zagotovleniia gosudarstvennykh bumag, 1912.

Palmella (Duque de). *Despachos e correspondência.* 4 vols. Lisbon: Imp. Nacional, 1851–1869.

Pavlov, P. N. et al., eds. *K istorii Rossiisko-Amerikanskoi Kompanii. Sbornik dokumental'nykh materialov.* Krasnoiarsk: Krasnoiarskii Kraevoi Gosudarstvennyi Arkhiv and Krasnoiarskii Gosudarstvennyi Pedagogicheskii Institut, 1957.

Pokrovskii, A., ed. *Ekspeditsiia Beringa. Sbornik dokumentov.* Moscow: Glavnoe arkhivnoe upravlenie NKVD SSSR, 1941.

"Proekt zavoevaniia Ameriki, podannyi Petru Velikomu," *Moskvitianin* 1 (1851): 121–124.

Raventós y Noguer, M., and I. de Oyarzábal Velarde. *Colección de textos internacionales.* Vol. 1. Barcelona: Bosch-Casa Editorial, 1936.

Russia. Gosudarstvennyi sovet. *Arkhiv Gosudarstvennogo soveta.* 5 vols. in 16. St. Petersburg: Tipografiia Vtorogo otdeleniia Sobstvennoi E. I. V. Kantseliarii, 1869–1904.

——. Imperatorskoe Russkoe Istoricheskoe Obshchestvo. *Sbornik.* 148 vols. St. Petersburg: Gosudarstvennaia Tipografiia, 1867–1916.

————. Komitet ob ustroistve russkikh amerikanskikh kolonii. *Doklad.* St. Petersburg: Tipografiia Departamenta vneshnei torgovli, 1863.

————. Laws. *Polnoe sobranie zakonov Rossiiskoi imperii.* 1st ser., 1649 to 12 December 1825. 49 vols. St. Petersburg: Tipografiia Vtorogo otdeleniia Sobstvennoi E. I. V. Kantseliarii, 1830.

————. Ministerstvo inostrannykh del. *Dokumenty dlia istorii diplomaticheskikh snoshenii Rossii s zapadnymi dezhavami, ot zakliucheniia vseobschego mira v 1814 do kongressa v Verone v 1822 godu.* 2 vols. St. Petersburg: Voennaia tipografiia Glavnogo shtaba, 1823–1825.

————. ————. *Vneshniaia politika Rossii XIX i nachala XX veka. Dokumenty rossiiskogo ministerstva inostrannykh del.* 1st ser. (1801–1815). 8 vols. Moscow: Gosudarstvennoe izd-vo politicheskoi literatury, 1960–1972.

————. Morskoe ministerstvo. *Materialy dlia istorii russkikh zaselenii po beregam vostochnogo okeana.* Supplement to *Morskoi sbornik,* no. 1 (1861). St. Petersburg: Tipografiia Morskogo ministerstva, 1861.

"Russkie diplomaty o voine za nezavisimost' v Latinskoi Amerike," *Novaia i noveishaia istoriia,* no. 1 (January-February 1966): 112–121.

Schnaiderman, Boris. "Documentos russos sôbre o Brasil," *Revista de História* 33, no. 67 (July-September 1966): 215–228.

Sirotkin, V. G., comp. "Dokumenty o politike Rossii na Dal'nom Vostoke v nachale XIX v." *Istoricheskii arkhiv,* no. 6 (1962): 85–99.

Webster, C. K., ed. *Britain and the Independence of Latin America, 1812–1830. Select Documents from the Foreign Office Archives.* 2 vols. London, New York, and Toronto: Published for the Ibero-American Institute of Great Britain by the Oxford University Press, 1938.

Memoirs, Diaries, and Contemporary Accounts

Adams, John Quincy. *Memoirs.* 12 vols. Edited by Charles Francis Adams. Philadelphia: J. P. Lippincott & Co., 1874–1877.

"Braziliia v opisaniiakh uchastnikov russkoi ekspeditsii 1821–1829 godov," *Novaia i noveishaia istoriia,* no. 3 (May–June 1966): 115–127.

Caldcleugh, Alexander. *Travels in South America, During the Years 1819–20–21.* 2 vols. London: John Murray, 1825.

Chateaubriand, [François Auguste René, viscomte ` de]. *Congrès de Vérone. Guerre d'Espagne. Négociations. Colonies espagnoles.* 2 vols. Paris: Delloye, Acquéreur et Éditeur, 1838.

García de León y Pizarro, José. *Memorias.* 2 vols. Madrid: Revista de Occidente, 1953.

Golovnin, V. M. *Puteshestvie Rossiiskogo Imperatorskogo shliupa Diana, iz Kronshtadta v Kamchatku, sovershennoe . . . v 1807, 1808 i 1809 godakh.* 2 vols. St. Petersburg: Morskaia Tipografiia, 1819.

————. *Puteshestvie vokrug sveta, po poveleniiu Gosudaria imperatora, sovershennoe no voennom shliupe Kamchatke, v 1817, 1818 i 1819 godakh.* 2 vols. St. Petersburg: Morskaia Tipografiia, 1822.

————. *V. M. Golovnin Detained in Simon's Bay. The Story of the Detention of the Imperial Russian Sloop Diana, April 1808–May 1809.* Translated from the Russian by Mrs. Lisa Millner. Edited with additional notes and index by O. H. Spohr. Cape Town: Friends of the South African Library, 1964.

————. *Voyage de M. Golownin, capitaine de vaisseau de la marine impériale de Russie . . . pendant les années 1811, 1812 et 1813. . . .* 2 vols. Paris: Imprim. de Smith,·1818.

Henderson, James. *A History of Brazil.* London: Longman, Hurst, Rees, Orme, and Brown, 1821.

Humboldt, Alexander von. *Political Essay on the Kingdom of New Spain.* Translated from the original French by John Black. 2 vols. London: Longman, Hurst, Rees, Orme, and Brown, 1811.

Khlebnikov, E. T. "Memoirs of California." Translated from the Russian with a biographical sketch of the author by Anatole G. Mazour, *Pacific Historical Review*, 9, no. 3 (September 1940): 307–336.

Kotzebue, O. E. *Puteshestvie v Yuzhnyi okean i Beringov proliv dlia otyskaniia severo-vostochnogo morskogo prokhoda, predpriniatoe v 1815–1818 gg. na korable "Riurik."* St. Petersburg: Morskaia Tipografiia, 1823.

————. *Puteshestvie vokrug sveta, sovershennoe po poveleniiu Gosudaria Imperatora Aleksandra Pervogo na voennom shliupe Predpriiatii, v 1823, 24, 25, i 26 godakh.* St. Petersburg: Morskaia Tipografiia, 1828.

Kotzebue, Otto von. *A New Voyage Round the World, in the Years 1823, 24, 25, and 26.* 2 vols. London: Henry Colburn and Richard Bentley, 1830.

————. *A Voyage of Discovery, into the South Sea and Beering's Straits, for the Purpose of Exploring a North-East Passage, undertaken in the Years 1815–1818, at the Expense of His Highness the Chancellor of the Empire, Count Romanzoff, in the Ship Rurick.* 3 vols. London: Longman, Hurst, Rees, Orme, and Brown, 1821.

Krusenstern, Captain A. J. *Voyage Round the World, in the Years 1803, 1804, 1805, & 1806, by Order of His Imperial Majesty Alexander the First, on board the Ships Nadeshda and Neva.* 2 vols. London: Printed by C. Roworth; for John Murray, Bookseller to the Admiralty and the Board of Longitude, 1813.

Kruzenshtern, I. F. *Puteshestvie vokrug sveta v 1803, 1804, 1805 i 1806 godakh, po poveleniiu Ego Imperatorskogo Velichestva Aleksandra Pervogo na korabliakh Nadezhde i Neve.* 3 vols. St. Petersburg: Morskaia Tipografiia, 1809–1812.

Langsdorff, G. de. *Mémoire sur le Brésil pour servir de guide a ceux qui désirent s'y établir.* Paris: Imprimerie de Denugon, 1820.

Langsdorff, G. H. von. *Langsdorff's Narrative of the Rezanov Voyage to Nueva California in 1806.* Revised English translation by Thomas C. Russell. San Francisco: The Private Press of T. C. Russell, 1927.

————. *Voyages and Travels in Various Parts of the World, During the Years 1803, 1804, 1805, 1806, and 1807.* 2 vols. London: Printed for Henry Colburn, 1813–1814.

Lazarev, Andrei. *Plavanie vokrug sveta na shliupe Ladoge v 1822, 1823 i 1824 godakh.* St. Petersburg: Morskaia Tipografiia, 1832.

Lisiansky, Urey. *A Voyage Round the World, in the Years 1803, 4, 5, & 6; Performed by Order of His Imperial Majesty Alexander the First, Emperor of Russia, in the Ship Neva.* London: Printed for John Booth and Longman, Hurst, Rees, Orme, & Brown by S. Hamilton, 1813.

Luccock, John. *Notas sôbre o Rio-de-Janeiro e partes meridionais do Brasil, tomadas durante uma estada de dez anos nesse pais, de 1808 a 1818.* 2nd ed. São Paulo: Libraria Martins, 1951.

"O Brasil meridional visto por um oficial de marinha russo no início do século XIX." Translated with notes by Conde Emanuel de Bennigsen, *Revista de História* 2, no. 6 (April-June 1951): 391–410.

Pradt, Dominique Georges Frédéric de. *Des colonies et de la révolution actuelle de l'Amérique.* Paris: F. Béchet, 1817.

Russia. Glavnoe arkhivnoe upravlenie MVD SSSR. Tsentral'nyi gosudarstvennyi arkhiv Voenno-morskogo flota. *M. P. Lazarev. Dokumenty.* Vol. I of a projected multivolume collection. Moscow: Voenno-morskoe izd-vo Voenno-morskogo ministerstva Soiuza SSR, 1952.

Saint-Hilaire, Auguste de. *Voyage dans les provinces de Rio de Janeiro et de Minas Gerais.* 2 vols. Paris: Grimbert et Dorez, 1830.

Shur, L. A. "Braziliia nachala XIX v. v neopublikovannom 'zhurnale krugosvetnogo plavaniia' M. I. Ratmanova," *Latinskaia Amerika*, no. 3 (May-June 1969): 176–184.

———. *K beregam Novogo Sveta. Iz neopublikovannykh zapisok russkikh puteshestvennikov nachala XIX veka.* Moscow: Nauka, 1971.

Spix, J. B. von, and K. P. F. von Martius. *Travels in Brazil, in the Years 1817–1820.* 2 vols. London: Longman, Hurst, Rees, Orme, Brown, and Greene, 1824.

Tarakanoff, Vasili Petrovich. *Statement of My Captivity Among the Californians.* Written down by Ivan Shiskin and translated from the Russian by Ivan Petroff, with notes by Arthur Woodward. Los Angeles: Early California Travel Series, Glen Dawson, 1953.

Tchitchinoff, Zakahar. *Adventures in California of Zakahar Tchitchinoff, 1818–1828.* Introduction by Arthur Woodward. Los Angeles: Early California Travel Series, Glen Dawson, 1956.

Torrubia, F. Giuseppe. *I Moscoviti nella California o sia dimostrazione della verità del passo all'America Settentrionale nuovamente scoperto dai Russi, e di quelle anticamente praticato dalli Popolatori, che vi transmigrarono dall'Asia. Dissertazione storico-geografica.* Rome: Generoso Salomoni, 1759.

Yanovskii, Semën Ivanovich. "Zapiski," *Izvestiia Kaluzhskoi Uchënoi Arkhivnoi Komissii*, supplements to *vypuski* 5–6, 7–8, 9–10, 11–12 (1898).

Zavalishin, D. "Delo o kolonii Ross," *Russkii vestnik* 62 (1866): 36–65.

———. "Kaliforniia v 1824 godu," *Russkii vestnik* 60 (1865): 322–368.

———. "Krugosvetnoe plavanie fregata 'Kreiser.' V 1822–1825 gg. pod komandoiu Mikhaila Petrovicha Lazareva," *Drevniaia i novaia Rossiia* 2 (May-August 1877): 54–67, 115–125, 199–214; 3 (September-December 1877): 39–52, 143–158, 210–223.

Periodicals

Colección de antiguos periódicos chilenos. Vols. 1–15. Santiago de Chile: Biblioteca Nacional, 1951–1965.

Le Conservateur Impartial. St. Petersburg, 1813–1824.

Correio Braziliense ou armazem literario. London, 1808–1822.

Dukh zhurnalov. St. Petersburg, 1817–1820.

Gaceta de Buenos Ayres. Buenos Aires, 1810–1821.

Gazeta de Madrid. Madrid, 1808–1818.

Istoricheskii, statisticheskii i geograficheskii zhurnal. Moscow, 1808–1818.

Journal de St.-Pétersbourg, Politique et Littéraire. St. Petersburg, 1825–1830.
National Intelligencer. Washington, 1810.
Russkii invalid. St. Petersburg, 1820–1826.
Sankt-Peterburgskie vedomosti. St. Petersburg, 1809–1812.
Sanktpeterburgskie kommercheskie vedomosti. St. Petersburg, 1807–1810.
Syn otechestva. St. Petersburg, 1812–1826.
Vestnik Evropy. Moscow, 1808–1812.

Reference and Statistical Publications
Azbuchnyi ukazatel' imën russkikh deiatelei dlia russkogo biograficheskogo slovaria. 2 vols. St. Petersburg: Gosudarstvennaia Tipografiia, 1887–1888.
Bol'shaia entsiklopediia. Slovar' obshchedostupnykh svedenii po vsem otrasliam znaniia. 22 vols. St. Petersburg: Knigoizdatel'skoe Tovarishchestvo "Prosveshchenie," 1900–1909.
Bol'shaia sovetskaia entsiklopediia. 2nd ed., 50 vols. Moscow: Gosudarstvennoe nauchnoe izd-vo "Bol'shaia Sovetskaia Entsiklopediia," 1949–1957.
Brazil. Secretaria de Estado das Relações Exteriores. *Relações diplomáticas do Brasil. Contendo os nomes dos representantes diplomáticos do Brasil no estrangeiro e os dos representantes diplomáticos dos diversos paizes no Rio de Janeiro de 1808 a 1912.* Rio de Janeiro: Typo. do Jornal do Commercio, 1913.
Entsiklopedicheskii slovar'. 82 vols. St. Petersburg: F. A. Brokgauz (Leipzig) and I. A. Efron (St. Petersburg), 1890–1904.
Kabuzan, V. M. *Narodonaselenie Rossii v XVIII-pervoi polovine XIX v. (po materialam revizii).* Moscow: Izd-vo AN SSSR, 1963.
Nebol'sin, Grigorii. *Statisticheskoe obozrenie vneshnei torgovli Rossii.* 2 vols. St. Petersburg: Tipografiia Departamenta vneshnei torgovli, 1850.
Pokrovskii, V. I., ed. *Sbornik svedenii po istorii i statistike vneshnei torgovli Rossii.* Vol. I. St. Petersburg: Izdanie Departamenta tamozhennykh sborov, 1902.
Rashin, A. G. *Formirovanie promyshlennogo proletariata v Rossii. Statistiko-ekonomicheskie ocherki.* Moscow: Gosudarstvennoe sotsial'no-ekonomicheskoe izd-vo, 1940.
———. *Naselenie Rossii za 100 let (1811–1913). Statisticheskie ocherki.* Moscow: Gosudarstvennoe sotsial'no-ekonomicheskoe izd-vo, 1956.
[Rumiantsev, N. P.] *Gosudarstvennaia torgovlia v raznykh eë vidakh.* 6 vols. St. Petersburg: Gosudarstvennaia Kommerts-Kollegiia, 1803–1808.
Russkii biograficheskii slovar'. 25 vols. St. Petersburg: Imperatorskoe Russkoe Istoricheskoe Obshchestvo, 1896–1918.
Spain. Ministerio de la Marina. *Estado general de la Armada para el año 1849.* Madrid: Imprenta y Librería de Don Román Matute, 1848.
Ziablovskii, Evdokim. *Statisticheskoe opisanie Rossiiskoi Imperii v nyneshnem eë sostoianii, s predvaritel'nymi poniatiiami o statistike i o Evrope voobshche v statisticheskom vide.* 5 vols. in 2. St. Petersburg: Tipografiia Imperatorskogo Teatra and Imperatorskaia Akademiia Nauk, 1808.

Articles and Papers
Alekseev, A. I., and B. N. Komissarov. "N. G. Rubtsov i ego rol' v issledovanii

Brazilii," *Izvestiia Vsesoiuznogo Geograficheskogo Obshchestva* 98, Vyp. 6 (1966): 500–506.

Alekseev, M. P. "Ispanistika v svete istorii ispano-russkikh kul'turnykh sviazei," *Voprosy ispanskoi filologii*, seriia "Dreviaia i novaia Romaniia," Vyp. 1 (1974): 10–24.

Al'perovich, M. S. "Ispanskaia Amerika i voina za nezavisimost' SShA," *Novaia i noveishaia istoriia*, no. 2 (March-April 1975): 73–87.

————. "Izuchenie istorii Latinskoi Ameriki v Sovetskom Soiuze (Kratkii obzor)," in V. V. Vol'skii et al., eds., *Latinskaia Amerika v proshlom i nastoiashchem* (Moscow: Izd-vo sotsial'no-ekonomicheskoi literatury, 1960): 450–463.

————. "Izuchenie istorii stran Latinskoi Ameriki," in *Sovetskaia istoricheskaia nauka ot XX k XXII s"ezdu KPSS. Istoriia Zapadnoi Evropy i Ameriki* (Moscow: Izd-vo AN SSSR, 1963): 151–170.

————. "Miranda i 'Velikaia Kolumbiia,'" *Novaia i noveishaia istoriia*, no. 4 (July-August 1966): 56–66.

————. "Soviet Historiography of the Latin American Countries," *Latin American Research Review* 5, no. 1 (Spring 1970): 63–70.

Andrews, Clarence L. "Russian Plans for American Dominion," *The Washington Historical Quarterly* 18, no. 2 (April 1927): 83–92.

Augel, Moema Parente. "Um diário inédito de Ludwig Riedel, 1820–1823 (São Petersburgo–Bahia–Rio de Janeiro)." Paper read at XLI International Congress of Americanists, Mexico City, 2–7 September 1974.

Barman, Roderick J. "The Forgotten Journey: Georg Heinrich Langsdorff and the Russian Imperial Scientific Expedition to Brazil, 1821–1829," *Terrae Incognitae* 3 (1971): 67–96.

Bartley, Russell H. "Akademik G. I. Langsdorf i stanovlenie russko-brazil-skikh otnoshenii (1804–1828 gg.)." Paper read at international conference on Americanist studies sponsored by the USSR Academy of Sciences and the All-Union Geographic Society of the USSR, Leningrad, 22–24 October 1974.

————. "A Decade of Soviet Scholarship in Brazilian History: 1958–1968," *The Hispanic American Historical Review* 50, no. 3 (August 1970): 445–466.

————. "G. I. Langsdorf i russko-brazil'skie otnosheniia v pervoi treti XIX v.," *Latinskaia Amerika*, no. 3 (May-June 1976): 164–169.

————. "The Inception of Russo-Brazilian Relations (1808–1828)," *The Hispanic American Historical Review* 56, no. 2 (May 1976): 217–240.

————. "On Scholarly Dialogue: The Case of U. S. and Soviet Latin Americanists," *Latin American Research Review* 5, no. 1 (Spring 1970): 59–62.

Baykov, Alexander. "The Economic Development of Russia," *The Economic History Review*, 2nd ser., 7, no. 2 (1954): 137–149.

Baylen, Joseph O., and Dorothy Woodward. "Francisco de Miranda in Russia," *The Americas* 6, no. 4 (April 1950): 431–446.

Bennigsen, Conde Emanuel de. "Nota acêrca de alguns projetos de colonização russa na América do Sul durante o século XVIII," *Revista de História* 4, no. 15 (July-September 1953): 169–177.

Béthencourt, A. "Proyecto de un establecimiento ruso en Brasil (1732–1733)," *Revista de Indias* 10, nos. 37–38 (July-December 1949): 651–668.

Bolkhovitinov, N. N. "Avantiura doktora Sheffera na Gavaiiakh v 1815–1819 gg.," *Novaia i noveishaia istoriia*, no. 1 (January-February 1972): 121–137.

———. "K voprosu ob ugroze interventsii Sviashchennogo soiuza v Latinskuiu Ameriku (iz predystorii doktriny Monro)," *Novaia i noveishaia istoriia*, no. 3 (May-June 1957): 46–66.

———. "Novye raboty o russko-amerikanskoi torgovle v XVIII-nachale XIX veka," *Novaia i noveishaia istoriia*, no. 4 (July-August 1967): 122–126.

———. "Russkaia Amerika i provozglashenie doktriny Monro," *Voprosy istorii*, no. 9 (September 1971): 69–84.

———. "Voina Latinskoi Ameriki za nezavisimost' i pozitsiia Rossii," *Voprosy istorii*, no. 11 (November 1965): 153–159.

Brooks, Philip Coolidge. "The Pacific Coast's First International Boundary Delineation, 1816–1819," *Pacific Historical Review* 3, no. 1 (August 1934): 62–79.

Casal, Esther Suzzi. "Las discusiones en Europa acerca de la invasión lusitana a la Banda Oriental," *Cuarto Congreso Internacional de Historia de América* (Buenos Aires, 1966), VII, 35–63.

"Chto bylo v kreposti Ross v 1817 godu," *Novaia zaria* (San Francisco, 5 August 1972): 4.

Dabagian, E. S. "Izuchenie Brazilii v SSSR," in A. V. Efimov et al., eds., *Braziliia. Ekonomika, politika, kul'tura* (Moscow: Izd-vo AN SSSR, 1963): 458–472.

———. "50 let sovetskoi latinoamerikanistiki (bibliograficheskii ocherk)," in V. V. Vol'skii, ed., *SSSR i Latinskaia Amerika, 1917–1967* (Moscow: Mezhdunarodnye otnosheniia, 1967): 176–209.

De Bertier de Sauvigny, Guillaume. "Sainte-Alliance et Alliance dans les conceptions de Metternich," *Revue Historique* 223 (April-June 1960): 249–274.

Delgado, Jaime. "La 'pacificación de América' en 1818," *Revista de Indias* 10, no. 39 (January-March 1950): 7–67.

Divin, V. A. "Russkie moreplavaniia k beregam Ameriki posle Beringa i Chirikova," in I. R. Grigulevich et al. (eds.), *Ot Aliaski do Ognennoi Zemli* (Moscow: Nauka, 1967): 85–94.

Du Four, Clarence John. "The Russian Withdrawal from California," *Quarterly of the California Historical Society* 12, no. 3 (1933): 240–249.

Efimov, A. V. "Otkrytiia Ameriki so storony Azii." Paper delivered at VII International Congress of Anthropological and Ethnographic Sciences, Moscow, August 1964.

Ermolaev, V. I. "Nekotorye voprosy osvoboditel'noi bor'by amerikanskikh kolonii Ispanii i Portugalii (K 150-letiiu nachala voiny za nezavisimost' 1810–1826 gg.)," *Novaia i noveishaia istoriia*, no. 3 (May-June 1960): 23–37.

Essig, O. E. "The Russian Settlement at Ross," *Quarterly of the California Historical Society* 12, no. 3 (September 1933): 191–209.

Farrelly, Theodore S. "The Russians and Pre-Bering Alaska," *Pacific Historical Review* 3, no. 4 (November 1934): 444–448.

Ford, Worthington C. "John Quincy Adams and the Monroe Doctrine," *The American Historical Review* 7 (July 1902): 676–696; 8 (October 1902): 28–52.

Gil Novales, Alberto. "L'indipendenza americana nella coscienza spagnola (1820–1823)," *Revista Storica Italiana*, 85, *fascicolo* 4 (December 1973): 1117–1139.

Goebel, Dorothy Burne. "British Trade to the Spanish Colonies, 1796–1823," *The American Historical Review* 43 (January 1938): 288–320.

Guber, A. A. "Problemy natsional'no-osvoboditel'noi bor'by v Latinskoi Amerike (1810–1826 gg.) v. trudakh sovetskikh istorikov," *Novaia i noveishaia istoriia*, no. 1 (January-February 1970): 32–38.

————, and N. M. Lavrov. "K 150-letiiu voiny za nezavisimost' Latinskoi Ameriki," *Novaia i noveishaia istoriia*, no. 4 (July–August 1960): 11–18.

Hart, Albert B. "The Monroe Doctrine and the Doctrine of Permanent Interest," *The American Historical Review* 7 (October 1901): 77–91.

Holborn, Hajo. "Russia and the European Political System," in Ivo J. Lederer, ed., *Russian Foreign Policy. Essays in Historical Perspective* (New Haven and London: Yale University Press, 1962), pp. 377–415.

Humphreys, R. A. "Richard Oswald's Plan for an English and Russian Attack on Spanish America, 1781–1782," *The Hispanic American Historical Review* 18, no. 1 (February 1938): 95–101.

Kahan, Arcadius. "The Costs of 'Westernization' in Russia: The Gentry and the Economy in the Eighteenth Century," *Slavic Review* 25, no. 1 (March 1966): 40–66.

Kashevaroff, Rev. A. P. "Fort Ross. An Account of the Russian Settlement in San Francisco Bay," *Alaska Magazine* 1, no. 5 (May 1927): 235–242.

Komissarov, B. N. "Akademik G. I. Langsdorf i ego ekspeditsiia v Braziliiu v 1821–1829 gg.," in D. E. Bertel's, B. N. Komissarov, and T. I. Lysenko, comps., L. A. Shur, ed., *Materialy ekspeditsii akademika Grigoriia Ivanovicha Langsdorfa v Braziliiu v 1821–1829 gg. Nauchnoe opisanie* (Leningrad: Nauka, Leningrad branch, 1973), pp. 7–43.

————. "Arkhiv ekspeditsii G. I. Langsdorfa v Braziliiu (1821–1829)," in I. R. Grigulevich et al., eds., *Ot Aliaski do Ognennoi Zemli* (Moscow: Nauka, 1967), pp. 275–285.

————. "Materialy ekspeditsii G. I. Langsdorfa 1821–1829 godov kak istochnik po istorii Brazilii," *Novaia i noveishaia istoriia*, no. 1 (January-February 1968): 139–150.

————. "Ob otnoshenii Rossii k voine Ispanskoi Ameriki za nezavisimost' (po materialam arkhiva V. M. Miroshevskogo)," *Vestnik Leningradskogo Universiteta*, no. 8 (seriia istorii, iazyka i literatury), Vyp. 2 (1964): 60–71.

————. "Peru nakanune nezavisimosti (3 zapiski russkikh moreplavatelei o Peru 1817–1818 gg.," in I. S. Kon, ed., *Sbornik studencheskikh nauchnykh rabot (ekonomicheskogo, istoricheskogo, filosofskogo, iuridicheskogo, filologicheskogo i vostochnogo fakul'tetov)* (Leningrad: Izd-vo Leningradskogo universiteta, 1963): 147–157.

————. "Spor o russko-ispanskoi konventsii," *Voprosy istorii*, no. 6 (June 1966): 195–197.

————, and S. L. Tret'iakov. "Materialy po statistike naseleniia Brazilii pervoi chetverti XIX v. v arkhive ekspeditsii G. I. Langsdorfa," in V. K. Furaev, B. N. Komissarov, and K. B. Vinogradov, eds., *Issledovaniia po novoi i noveishei istorii. Sbornik statei, posviashchennyi 60-letiiu so dnia rozhdeniia doktora istoricheskikh nauk professora V. G. Revunenkova* (Leningrad: Izd-vo Leningradskogo universiteta, 1972): 17–30.

Krylova, T. K. "Otnosheniia Rossii i Ispanii v pervoi chetverti XVIII veka," in A. M. Deborin et al., eds., *Kul'tura Ispanii*. *Sbornik* (Moscow: Izd-vo Akademii nauk SSSR, 1940): 327–352.

Lanning, John Tate. "Great Britain and Spanish Recognition of the Hispanic American States," *The Hispanic American Historical Review* 10, no. 4 (November 1930): 429–456.

Lingelbach, W. E. "Historical Investigation and the Commercial History of the Napoleonic Era," *The American Historical Review* 19 (January 1914): 257–281.

Lozinski, G. "Le Général Miranda en Russie (1786–1787)," *Le Monde Slave*, nouvelle série, 2, no. 4 (April 1933): 72–90; 2, no. 5 (May 1933): 186–218.

Manchester, Alan K. "The Recognition of Brazilian Independence," *The Hispanic American Historical Review* 31, no. 1 (February 1951): 80–96.

Masterson, James R., and Helen Brower. "Bering's Successors, 1745–1780. Contributions of Peter Simon Pallas to the History of Russian Exploration toward Alaska," *Pacific Northwest Quarterly* 38, no. 1 (January 1947): 35–83; 38, no. 2 (April 1947): 109–155.

Mazour, Anatole G. "Dimitry Zavalishin: Dreamer of a Russian-American Empire," *Pacific Historical Review* 5, no. 1 (February 1936): 26–37.

———. "Doctor Yegor Scheffer: Dreamer of a Russian Empire in the Pacific," *Pacific Historical Review* 6, no. 1 (February 1937): 15–20.

———. "The Russian-American and Anglo-Russian Conventions, 1824–1825: An Interpretation," *Pacific Historical Review* 14, no. 3 (September 1945): 303–310.

———. "The Russian-American Company: Private or Government Enterprise?" *Pacific Historical Review* 13, no. 2 (June 1944): 168–173.

Metford, J. C. J. "The Recognition by Great Britain of the United Provinces of the Río de la Plata," *Bulletin of Hispanic Studies* 29, no. 113 (January–March 1952): 201–224.

Mikhailov, S. S. "Izuchenie Latinskoi Ameriki v Sovetskom Soiuze," *Voprosy istorii*, no. 4 (April 1962): 98–106.

———. "Izuchenie problem Latinskoi Ameriki," *Vestnik AN SSSR* 32, no. 5 (1962): 54–59.

———. "Nekotorye voprosy izucheniia Latinskoi Ameriki," *Novaia i noveishaia istoriia*, no. 2 (March-April 1964): 29–36.

Miroshevskii, V. M. "Ekaterina II i Fransisko Miranda (K voprosu o mezhdunarodnykh sviaziakh ispanoamerikanskikh separatistov v XVIII veke)," *Istorik-Marksist*, no. 2 (1940): 125–132.

Moriakov, V. I. "Russkii perevod 'Istorii obeikh Indii' Reinalia," *Vestnik Moskovskogo Universiteta*, seriia IX (istoriia), no. 1 (1972): 55–68.

Morison, S. E. "The Origin of the Monroe Doctrine, 1775–1823," *Economica* 4, no. 10 (October 1924): 27–51.

Mullett, Charles F. "British Schemes against Spanish America in 1806," *The Hispanic American Historical Review* 27, no. 2 (May 1947): 269–278.

Neumann, William L. "United States Aid to the Chilean Wars of Independence," *The Hispanic American Historical Review* 27, no. 2 (May 1947): 204–219.

Nichols, Irby C., Jr. "The Russian Ukase and the Monroe Doctrine: A Reevaluation," *Pacific Historical Review* 36, no. 1 (February 1967): 13–26.

Norris, John M. "The Policy of the British Cabinet in the Nootka Crisis," *The English Historical Review* 70, no. 277 (October 1955): 562–580.

"O sud'be Forta Ross," *Novaia zaria* (San Francisco, 5 August 1972): 4.

Ogden, Adele. "Russian Sea-Otter and Seal Hunting on the California Coast, 1803–1841," *Quarterly of the California Historical Society* 12, no. 3 (September 1933): 217–239.

Perkins, Dexter. "Europe, Spanish America, and the Monroe Doctrine," *The American Historical Review* 27 (January 1922): 207–218.

———. "Russia and the Spanish Colonies, 1817–1818," *The American Historical Review* 28, no. 4 (July 1923): 656–672.

Portal, Roger. "Manufactures et classes sociales en Russie au XVIIIᵉ siècle," *Revue historique* 201 (April-June 1949): 161–185; 202 (July-September 1949): 1–23.

Potekhin, V. "Selenie Ross," *Zhurnal manufaktur i torgovli* 8 (1859), "Otdel torgovli" (V): 1–42.

Pratt, E. J. "Anglo-American Commercial and Political Rivalry on the Plata, 1820–1830," *The Hispanic American Historical Review* 11, no. 3 (August 1931): 302–335.

Preobrazhenskii, A. A. "O sostave aktsionerov Rossiisko-Amerikanskoi Kompanii v nachale XIX v.," *Istoricheskie zapiski* 67 (1960): 286–298.

Resnick, Enoch. "Spain's Reaction to Portugal's Invasion of the Banda Oriental in 1816," *Revista de Historia de América*, no. 73–74 (January-December 1972): 131–144.

Robertson, William Spence. "An Early Threat of Intervention by Force in South America," *The Hispanic American Historical Review* 23, no. 4 (November 1943): 611–631.

———. "Metternich's Attitude toward Revolutions in Latin America," *The Hispanic American Historical Review* 21, no. 4 (November 1941): 538–558.

———. "The Monroe Doctrine Abroad in 1823–24," *American Political Science Review* 6, no. 4 (November 1912): 546–563.

———. "The Policy of Spain toward Its Revolted Colonies, 1820–1823," *The Hispanic American Historical Review* 6, nos. 1–3 (February-August 1926): 21–46.

———. "The Recognition of the Hispanic American Nations by the United States," *The Hispanic American Historical Review* 1, no. 3 (August 1918): 239–269.

———. "Russia and the Emancipation of Spanish America, 1816–1826," *The Hispanic American Historical Review* 21, no. 2 (May 1941): 196–221.

———. "The United States and Spain in 1822," *The American Historical Review* 20 (July 1915): 781–800.

Rose, J. Holland. "Canning and the Spanish Patriots in 1808," *The American Historical Review* 12 (October 1906): 39–52.

Rydjord, John. "British Mediation between Spain and Her Colonies: 1811–1813," *The Hispanic American Historical Review* 21, no. 1 (February 1941): 29–50.

Seco Serrano, Carlos. "Doña Carlota Joaquina de Borbón y la cuestión uruguaya. Notas en torno a unas cartas," *Revista de Indias* 8, nos. 28–29 (April-September 1947): 405–464.

Shashkov, S. S. "Rossiisko-Amerikanskaia Kompaniia," in *Sobranie sochinenii*, 2 vols. St. Petersburg: Izdanie O. N. Polovoi, 1898), II, 632–652.

Shirokii, V. F. "Iz istorii khoziaistvennoi deiatel'nosti Rossiisko-Amerikanskoi Kompanii," *Istoricheskie zapiski* 13 (1942): 207–221.

Shtrakhov, A. I. "Osvoboditel'naia bor'ba naroda La-Platy v 1810–1816 godakh," *Novaia i noveishaia istoriia*, no. 4 (July-August 1960): 19–35.

Shur, L. A. "Braziliia i Peru epokhi voiny za nezavisimost' v neopublikovannom dnevnike F. F. Matiushkina," *Latinskaia Amerika*, no. 1 (January-February 1971): 137–144.

————. "Ispanskaia Amerika nachala XIX v. v dnevnike F. P. Litke," *Novaia i noveishaia istoriia*, no. 3 (May-June 1971): 150–153.

————. "Ispanskaia i Portugal'skaia Amerika v russkoi pechati XVIII-pervoi chetverti XIX v.," in V. V. Vol'skii et al., eds., *Latinskaia Amerika v proshlom i natoiashchem* (Moscow: Izd-vo sotsial'no-ekonomicheskoi literatury, 1960): 340–369.

————. "Kul'turnye i literaturnye sviazi Rossii i Brazilii v XVIII–XIX vv.," in A. V. Efimov et al., eds., *Braziliia. Ekonomika, politika, kul'tura* (Moscow: Izd-vo AN SSSR, 1963): 473–512.

————. "Materialy russkikh puteshestvennikov XVIII–XIX vv. kak istochnik po geografii, istorii i etnografii stran Latinskoi Ameriki," *Izvestiia Vsesoiuznogo Geograficheskogo Obshchestva* 100, no. 3 (1968): 230–236.

————. "Putevye zapiski i dnevniki russkikh puteshestvennikov kak istochnik po istorii Kalifornii (pervaia polovina XIX v.)," in *Amerikanskaia ezhegodnik. 1971* (Moscow: Nauka, 1971): 295–319.

Slëzkin, L. Yu. "O solidarnosti peredovoi russkoi obshchestvennosti s patriotami Latinskoi Ameriki," *Novaia i noveishaia istorii*, no. 4 (July-August 1960): 71–80.

————. "Politika evropeiskikh derzhav i SShA v voprose o priznanii nezavisimosti stran Latinskoi Ameriki (1822 g.)," in N. M. Lavrov et al., eds., *Voina za nezavisimost' v Latinskoi Amerike (1810–1826 gg.)* (Moscow: Nauka, 1964): 240–269.

————. "Voina Ispanskoi Ameriki za nezavisimost' v otsenke russkikh diplomatov (1810–1816 gg.)," in V. V. Vol'skii et al., eds., *Latkinskaia Amerika v proshlom i nastoiashchem* (Moscow: Izd-vo sotsial'no-ekonomicheskoi literatury, 1960): 370–394.

Slusser, Robert M. "The Role of the Foreign Ministry," in Ivo J. Lederer, ed., *Russian Foreign Policy. Essays in Historical Perspective* (New Haven and London: Yale University Press, 1962), pp. 197–239.

Sokol, A. E. "Russian Expansion and Exploration in the Pacific," *The American Slavic and East European Review* 11, no. 2 (April 1952): 85–105.

Stoliarov, V. I. "Provozglashenie nezavisimosti Venesuely," *Novaia i noveishaia istoriia*, no. 4 (July-August 1971): 61–72.

Street, J. "Lord Strangford and Río de la Plata, 1808–1815," *The Hispanic American Historical Review* 33, no. 4 (November 1953): 477–510.

Sukhomlinov, B. F. "Ob ustanovlenii russko-brazil'skikh otnoshenii," *Novaia i noveishaia istoriia*, no. 2 (March-April 1965): 89–96.

Svet, Ya. M., and L. A. Shur. "Russko-latinoamerikanskie otnosheniia XVI–XIX vv. v osveshchenii zarubezhnykh issledovatelei," *Latinskaia Amerika*, no. 6 (November-December 1970): 138–159.

Swärd, Sven Ola. "As relações sueco-brasileiras no início do XIX século," *Revista de História* 29, no. 59 (July-September 1964): 133–146.

Tambs, Lewis A. "Anglo-Russian Enterprises Against Hispanic South America, 1732–1737," *The Slavonic and East European Review* 48, no. 112 (July 1970): 357–372.

Taylor, George P. "Spanish-Russian Rivalry in the Pacific, 1769–1820," *The Americas* 15, no. 2 (October 1958): 109–127.

Temperley, H. W. V. "Canning and the Conferences of the Four Allied Governments at Paris, 1823–1826," *The Hispanic American Historical Review* 30 (October 1924): 16–43.

———. "French Designs on Spanish America in 1820-5," *The English Historical Review* 40, no. 157 (January 1925): 34–53.

———. "The Later American Policy of George Canning," *The American Historical Review* 11 (July 1906): 779–797.

Tompkins, Stuart R., and Max L. Moorhead. "Russia's Approach to America: From Russian Sources, 1741–1761," *The British Columbia Historical Quarterly* 13 (1949): 55–66.

———. "Russia's Approach to America: From Spanish Sources, 1761–1775," *The British Columbia Historical Quarterly* 13 (1949): 231–255.

Vishniakov, N. "Rossiia, Kaliforniia i Sandvichevy ostrova," *Russkaia starina* 36 (1905): 249–289.

Vital-Hawell, V. "El aspecto internacional de las usurpaciones americanas en las provincias españolas limítrofes con los Estados Unidos de 1810 a 1814," *Revista de Indias* 25, nos. 99–100 (January-June 1965): 115–153.

———. "La cuestión de las colonias españolas y Europa en vísperas del Congreso de Aquisgrán (1811–1818)," *Revista de Indias* 21, nos. 85–86 (July-December 1961): 459–484.

Vol'skii, Victor V. "The Study of Latin America in the U. S. S. R.," *Latin American Research Review* 3, no. 1 (Fall 1967): 77–87.

Webb, Edith. "Agriculture in the Days of the Early California Padres," *The Americas* 4, no. 3 (January 1948): 325–344.

Webster, C. K. "Castlereagh and the Spanish Colonies, 1815–1818," *The English Historical Review* 27, no. 105 (January 1912): 78–95.

———. "Castlereagh and the Spanish Colonies, 1818–1822," *The English Historical Review* 30, no. 120 (October 1915): 631–645.

Woodward, Margaret L. "The Spanish Army and the Loss of America, 1810–1824," *The Hispanic American Historical Review* 48, no. 4 (November 1968): 586–607.

Zak, L. A. "Iz istorii diplomaticheskoi bor'by na venskom kongresse," *Voprosy istorii*, no. 3 (March 1966): 70–82.

Zimmerman, A. F. "Spain and Its Colonies, 1808–1820," *The Hispanic American Historical Review* 11, no. 4 (November 1931): 439–463.

Zvavich, I. "Ispaniia v diplomaticheskikh otnosheniiakh Rossii v 1812 godu," *Istoricheskii zhurnal*, nos. 3–4 (1943): 45–49.

Monographs, Special Studies, and Related Works

Akademiia nauk SSSR. *Vsemirnaia istoriia*. 10 vols. Moscow: Nauka, 1956–1965.

Alekseev, M. P. *Ocherki istorii ispano-russkikh literaturnykh otnoshenii XVI–XIX vv.* Leningrad: Izd-vo Leningradskogo universiteta, 1964.

Al'perovich, M. S. *Sovetskaia istoriografiia stran Latinskoi Ameriki.* Moscow: Nauka, 1968.

———. *Voina za nezavisimost' Meksiki (1810–1824).* Moscow: Nauka, 1964.

Armitage, John. *The History of Brazil, from the period of the arrival of the Braganza Family in 1808, to the abdication of Don Pedro the First in 1831.* 2 vols. London: Smith, Elder and Co., 1836.

Artola Gallego, Miguel. *La España de Fernando VII.* Vol. 26 of *Historia de España,* edited by Ramón Menéndez Pidal. Madrid: Espasa-Calpe, 1968.

Auchmuty, James Johnston. *The United States Government and Latin American Independence, 1810–1830.* London: P. S. King & Son, Ltd., 1937.

Bancroft, Hubert Howe. *History of Alaska. 1730–1885.* San Francisco: The History Company, Publishers, 1886.

———. *History of California.* Vol. 2 (1801–1824). San Francisco: The History Company, Publishers, 1886.

———. *History of the Northwest Coast.* Vol. 2 (1800–1846). San Francisco: The History Company, Publishers, 1886.

Bartley, Russell H., ed. *Soviet Historians on Latin America. Recent Scholarly Contributions.* Madison, Milwaukee, and London: Published for the Conference on Latin American History by the University of Wisconsin Press, forthcoming.

Bécker, Jerónimo. *Historia de las relaciones exteriores de España durante el siglo XIX. (Apuntes para una historia diplomática).* Vol. 1 (1800–1839). Madrid: Establecimiento Tipográfico de Jaime Ratés, 1924.

———. *La independencia de América (su reconocimiento por España).* Madrid: Establecimiento Tipográfico de Jaime Ratés, 1922.

Berg, L. S. *Istoriia russkikh geograficheskikh otkrytii.* Moscow: Izd-vo AN SSSR, 1962.

———. *Otkrytie Kamchatki i ekspeditsii Beringa, 1725–1742.* 3rd ed. Moscow-Leningrad: Izd-vo AN SSSR, 1946.

Bertel's, D. E., B. N. Komissarov, and T. I. Lysenko, comps., L. A. Shur, ed. *Materialy ekspeditsii akademika Grigoriia Ivanovicha Langsdorfa v Braziliiu v 1821–1829 gg. Nauchnoe opisanie.* Leningrad: Nauka, Leningrad branch, 1973.

Blackwell, William L., ed. *Russian Economic Development from Peter the Great to Stalin.* New York: New Viewpoints, 1974.

Blum, Jerome. *Lord and Peasant in Russia from the Ninth to the Nineteenth Century.* New York: Atheneum, 1965.

Bolkhovitinov, N. N. *Doktrina Monro (proizkhozhdenie i kharakter).* Moscow: Izd-vo Instituta mezhdunarodnykh otnoshenii, 1959.

———. *Russko-amerikanskie otnosheniia, 1815–1832 gg.* Moscow: Nauka, 1975.

———. *Stanovlenie russko-amerikanskikh otnoshenii, 1775–1815.* Moscow: Nauka, 1966.

Bonnel, Ulane. *La France, les États-Unis et la guerre de course (1797–1815).* Paris: Nouvelles Éditions Latines, 1961.

Bruun, Geoffrey. *Europe and the French Imperium, 1799–1814.* New York and London: Harper & Brothers, Publishers, 1938.

Calmon, Pedro. *O Rei do Brasil. Vida de D. João VI.* Rio de Janeiro: Livraria José Olympio, 1935.

Calógeras, João Pandiá. *A política exterior do Imperio.* 2 vols. Rio de Janeiro: Impresa Nacional, 1927–1928.

Chevigny, Hector. *Lord of Alaska. Baranov and the Russian Adventure.* New York: The Viking Press, 1942.

———. *Russian America. The Great Alaskan Venture, 1741–1867.* New York: The Viking Press, 1965.

Cook, Warren L. *Flood Tide of Empire. Spain and the Pacific Northwest, 1543–1819.* New Haven and London: Yale University Press, 1973.

Crouzet, François. *L'économie britannique et le blocus continental (1806–1813).* 2 vols. Paris: Presses Universitaires, 1958.

Delgado de Carvalho, Carlos. *História diplomática do Brasil.* São Paulo: Companhia Editôra Nacional, 1959.

Dozer, Donald Marquand, ed. *The Monroe Doctrine. Its Modern Significance.* New York: Alfred A. Knopf, 1965.

Driesch, Wilhelm von den. *Die ausländischen Kaufleute während des 18. Jahrhunderts in Spanien und ihre Beteiligung am Kolonialhandel.* Cologne and Vienna: Böhlau, 1972.

Efimov, A. V. *Iz istorii velikikh russkikh geograficheskikh otkrytii.* Rev. ed. Moscow: Nauka, 1971.

Eggers, Eduardo R., and Enrique Feune de Colombí. *Francisco de Zea Bermúdez y su época, 1779–1850.* Madrid: Consejo de Investigaciones Científicas, Escuela de Historia Moderna, 1958.

Falkus, M. E. *The Industrialization of Russia, 1700–1914.* London and Basingstoke: Macmillan, 1972.

Fedorova, S. G. *Russkoe naselenie Aliaski i Kalifornii. Konets XVIII veka–1867 g.* Moscow: Nauka, 1971.

Fernández Duro, Cesáreo. *Armada española desde la unión de los reinos de Castilla y de Aragón.* 9 vols. Madrid: Est. Tipográfico "Sucesores de Rivadeneyra," 1895–1903.

Gil, Federico G. *Latin American–United States Relations.* New York: Harcourt, Brace, Jovanovich, Inc., 1971.

Gille, Bertrand. *Histoire économique et sociale de la Russie du moyen-âge au vingtième siècle.* Paris: Payot, 1949.

Golder, F. A. *Russian Expansion on the Pacific, 1641–1850. An Account of the Earliest and Later Expeditions Made by the Russians along the Pacific Coast of Asia and North America; Including Some Related Expeditions to the Arctic Regions.* Cleveland: The Arthur H. Clark Company, 1914.

Griffin, Charles Carroll. *The United States and the Disruption of the Spanish Empire, 1810–1822. A Study of the Relations of the United States with the Rebel Spanish Colonies.* New York: Columbia University Press, 1937.

Grimsted, Patricia Kennedy. *The Foreign Ministers of Alexander I. Political Attitudes and the Conduct of Russian Diplomacy, 1801–1825.* Berkeley and Los Angeles: University of California Press, 1969.

Gulishambarov, St. O. *Vsemirnaia torgovlia v XIX v. i uchastie v nei Rossii.* St. Petersburg: Tipografiia V. Kirshbauma, 1898.

Hatch, Flora Faith. *The Russian Advance into California.* San Francisco: R and E Research Associates, 1971.

Haumant, Émile. *La culture française en Russie (1700–1900).* 2nd rev. ed. Paris: Librairie Hachette et Cie, 1913.

Heckscher, Eli F. *The Continental System. An Economic Interpretation.* Oxford: Clarendon Press, 1922.

Hernández Sánchez-Barba, Mario. *La última expansión española en América.* Madrid: Instituto de Estudios Políticos, 1957.

Hobsbawm, E. J. *The Age of Revolution, 1789–1848.* Cleveland and New York: The World Publishing Company, 1962.

Hölzle, Erwin. *Russland und Amerika. Aufbruch und Begegnung zweier Weltmächte.* Munich: Verlag R. Oldenbourg, 1953.

Hutchinson, C. Alan. *Frontier Settlement in Mexican California. The Hijar-Padrés Colony and Its Origins, 1769–1835.* New Haven and London: Yale University Press, 1969.

Ivashintsov, N. *Russkie krugosvetnye puteshestviia, s 1803 po 1849 god.* St. Petersburg: Tipografiia Morskogo ministerstva, 1872.

Jelavich, Barbara. *A Century of Russian Foreign Policy, 1814–1914.* Philadelphia and New York: J. B. Lippincott Company, 1964.

Jong, Theo P. M. de. *Nederland en Latijns-Amerika (1816–1826).* Groningen: 1963.

Kabuzan, V. M. *Izmeneniia v razmeshchenii naseleniia Rossii v XVIII-pervoi polovine XIX v. Po materialam revizii.* Moscow: Nauka, 1971.

Kaufmann, William W. *British Policy and the Independence of Latin America, 1804–1828.* New Haven: Yale University Press, 1951.

Kerner, Robert J. *The Urge to the Sea. The Course of Russian History. The Role of Rivers, Portages, Ostrogs, Monasteries, and Furs.* Berkeley and Los Angeles: University of California Press, 1946.

[Khlebnikov, Kiril]. *Zhizneopisanie Aleksandra Andreevicha Baranova, glavnogo pravitelia rossiiskikh kolonii v Amerike.* St. Petersburg: Morskaia Tipografiia, 1835.

Khromov, P. A. *Ekonomicheskoe razvitie Rossii v XIX–XX vekakh, 1800–1917.* Moscow: Gosudarstvennoe izd-vo politicheskoi literatury, 1950.

Kliuchevskii, V. O. *Sochineniia.* 8 vols. Moscow: Gosudarstvennoe izd-vo politicheskoi literatury and Izd-vo sotsial'no-ekonomicheskoi literatury, 1956–1959.

Komissarov, B. N. *Grigorii Ivanovich Langsdorf.* Leningrad: Nauka, Leningrad branch, 1975.

Kossok, Manfred. *Im Schatten der Heiligen Allianz. Deutschland und Lateinamerika, 1815–1830. Zur Politik der deutschen Staaten gegenüber der Unabhängigkeitsbewegung Mittel- und Südamerikas.* Berlin: Akademie-Verlag, 1964.

————. *La Santa Alianza y la política de los estados alemanes ante la emancipación latinoamericana (1815–1830).* Montevideo: Universidad de la República Oriental del Uruguay, Facultad de Humanidades y Ciencias, 1965.

Kuleshov, V. I. *Literaturnye sviazi Rossii i Zapadnoi Evropy v XIX veke (pervaia polovina).* Moscow: Izd-vo Moskovskogo universiteta, 1965.

Lavretskii, I. R. *Miranda.* Moscow: Molodaia Gvardiia, 1965.

Lavrov, N. M., A. I. Shtrakhov, and B. I. Koval, eds. *Voina za nezavisimost' v Latinskoi Amerike (1810–1826).* Moscow: Nauka, 1964.

Lebedev, D. M., and V. A. Esakov. *Russkie geograficheskie otkrytiia i issledovaniia s drevneishikh vremën do 1917 goda.* Moscow: Mysl', 1971.

Lederer, Ivo J., ed. *Russian Foreign Policy. Essays in Historical Perspective.* New Haven and London: Yale University Press, 1962.

Leroy-Beaulieu, Anatole. *L'empire des tsars et les russes.* 3rd rev. ed., 3 vols. Paris: Librairie Hachette, 1889–1893.

Leslie, R. F. *The Age of Transformation, 1789–1871.* New York: Harper & Row, 1967.

Liashchenko, P. I. *Istoriia narodnogo khoziaistva SSSR.* Vol. 1: *Dokapitalisticheskie formatsii.* 4th ed. Moscow: Gosudarstvennoe izd-vo politicheskoi literatury, 1956.

Lobanov-Rostovsky, Andrei A. *Russia and Europe, 1789–1825.* Durham, N. C.: Duke University Press, 1947.

Lynch, John. *The Spanish-American Revolutions, 1808–1826.* New York: Norton, 1973.

Macedo, Jorge de. *O bloqueio continental. Economia e guerra peninsular.* Lisbon: Editôra Gráfica Portuguesa, Lda., 1962.

Maggiolo, Adrien. *Corse, France et Russie. Pozzo di Borgo, 1764–1842.* Paris: Calmann Lévy, 1890.

Magidovich, I. P. *Istoriia otkrytiia i issledovaniia Tsentral'noi i Yuzhnoi Ameriki.* Moscow: Mysl', 1965.

Maiskii, I. M. *Ispaniia, 1808–1917. Istoricheskii ocherk.* Moscow: Izd-vo AN SSSR, 1957.

Manchester, Alan K. *British Preëminence in Brazil, Its Rise and Decline. A Study in European Expansion.* New York: Octagon Books, Inc., 1964.

Manizer, G. G. *Ekspeditsiia akademika G. I. Langsdorfa v Braziliiu (1821–1828).* Edited with introduction and notes by N. G. Shprintsin. Moscow: Gosudarstvennoe izd-vo geograficheskoi literatury, 1948.

Manning, William Ray. *The Nootka Sound Controversy.* In American Historical Association, Annual Report for the Year 1904 (Washington, D. C., 1905): 279–478.

Mavor, James. *An Economic History of Russia.* 2nd ed., 2 vols. New York: Russell & Russell, Inc., 1965.

Melvin, Frank Edgar. *Napoleon's Navigation System. A Study of Trade Control during the Continental Blockade.* New York: D. Appleton and Company, 1919.

Miliukov, P. *Ocherki po istorii russkoi kul'tury.* 3rd rev. ed., 3 vols. St. Petersburg: Izdanie redaktsii zhurnala "Mir Bozhi," 1898–1901.

Miroshevskii, V. M. *Osvoboditel'nye dvizheniia v amerikanskikh koloniiakh Ispanii ot ikh zavoevaniia do voiny za nezavisimost' (1492–1810 gg.).* Moscow: Nauka, 1946.

Mitchell, Mairin. *The Maritime History of Russia. 848–1948.* London: Sidgwick and Jackson, Ltd., 1949.

Nevskii, V. V. *Pervoe puteshestvie rossiian vokrug sveta.* [Moscow]: Gosudarstvennoe izd-vo geograficheskoi literatury, 1951.

Nicolson, Harold. *The Congress of Vienna. A Study in Allied Unity: 1812–1822.* New York: Harcourt, Brace and Company, 1946.

Nikolai Mikhailovich, velikii kniaz'. *Imperator Aleksandr I. Opyt istoricheskogo issledovaniia.* St. Petersburg: Ekspeditsiia zagotovleniia gosudarstvennykh bumag, 1912.

Nikul'chenkov, K. L. *Admiral Lazarev.* Moscow: Voennoe izd-vo Ministerstva oborony Soiuza SSR, 1956.

Norton, Luiz, *A Côrte de Portugal no Brasil.* São Paulo: Companhia Editôra Nacional, 1938.

Okun, S. B. *Ocherki istorii SSSR. Konets XVIII–pervaia chetvert' XIX veka.* Leningrad: Gosudarstvennoe uchebno-pedagogicheskoe izd-vo Ministerstva prosveshcheniia RSFSR, Leningradskoe otdelenie, 1956.

————. *Rossiisko-amerikanskaia kompaniia.* Moscow-Leningrad: Gosudarstvennoe sotsial'no-ekonomicheskoe izd-vo, 1939.

Oliveira Lima, Manoel de. *Dom João VI no Brazil. 1808–1821.* 2 vols. Rio de Janeiro: Typ. do Jornal do Commercio, 1908.

————. *História diplomática do Brazil. O reconhecimento do Império.* Paris and Rio de Janeiro: H. Garnier, Livreiro-Editor, [1901].

Perkins, Dexter. *A History of the Monroe Doctrine.* 3rd ed. Boston and Toronto: Little, Brown and Company, 1963.

————. *The Monroe Doctrine, 1823–1826.* Cambridge, Mass.: Harvard University Press, 1932.

Phillips, Walter Alison. *The Confederation of Europe. A Study of the European Alliance, 1813–1823, as an Experiment in the International Organization of Peace.* 2nd ed. New York: Howard Fertig, 1966.

Piccirilli, Ricardo. *Argentinos en Río de Janeiro, 1815–1820. Diplomacia. Monarquía. Independencia.* Buenos Aires: Editorial Pleamar, 1969.

Pilder, Hans. *Die Russisch-Amerikanische Handels-Kompanie bis 1825.* Berlin and Leipzig: G. J. Göschen'sche Verlagshandlung G. m.b.H., 1914.

Pirenne, Jacques-Henri. *La Sainte-Alliance. Organisation européenne de la paix mondiale.* 2 vols. Neuchatel: Éditions de la Baconnière, 1946.

Pokrovskii, M. N. *Diplomatiia i voiny tsarskoi Rossii v XIX stoletii. Sbornik statei.* Moscow: Krasnaia nov', 1923.

Pokrovskii, S. A. *Vneshniaia torgovlia i vneshniaia torgovaia politika Rossii.* Moscow: Mezhdunarodnaia kniga, 1947.

Poniatowski, Michel. *Histoire de la Russie d'Amérique et de Alaska.* Paris: Horizons de France, 1958.

Prado Júnior, Caio. *História econômica do Brasil.* 8th rev. ed. São Paulo: Editôra Brasiliense, 1963.

Pypin, A. N. *Obshchestvennoe dvizhenie v Rossii pri Aleksandre I.* 5th ed. Petrograd: Ogni, 1918.

Rippy, J. Fred. *Latin America in World Politics. An Outline Survey.* New York: Alfred A. Knopf, 1928.

————. *Rivalry of the United States and Great Britain Over Latin America (1808–1830).* Baltimore: The Johns Hopkins Press, 1929.

Robertson, William Spence. *France and Latin-American Independence.* New York: Octagon Books, Inc., 1967.

————. *The Life of Miranda.* 2 vols. Chapel Hill, N. C.: University of North Carolina Press, 1929.

Rozhkova, M. K., ed. *Ocherki ekonomicheskoi istorii Rossii pervoi poloviny XIX veka. Sbornik statei.* Moscow: Izd-vo sotsial'no-ekonomicheskoi literatury, 1959.

Russia. Ministerstvo inostrannykh del. *Ocherk istorii Ministerstva inostrannykh del, 1802–1902.* St. Petersburg: Tovarishchestvo R. Golike i A. Vil'borg, 1902.

————. Morskoe ministerstvo. *Istoricheskii obzor razvitiia i deiatel'nosti Morskogo Ministerstva, za sto let ego sushchestvovaniia (1802–1902 gg.).* St. Petersburg: Tipografiia Morskogo ministerstva, 1902.

Ryndziunskii, P. G. *Gorodskoe grazhdanstvo doreformennoi Rossii.* Moscow: Izd-vo AN SSSR, 1958.

Saralegui y Medina, Manuel de. *Un negocio escandaloso en tiempos de Fernando VII. Narración histórica.* Madrid: Imprenta de Jaime Ratés Martín, 1904.

Saul, Norman E. *Russia and the Mediterranean, 1797–1807.* Chicago and London: University of Chicago Press, 1970.

Schop Soler, Ana María. *Die spanisch-russischen Beziehungen im 18. Jahrhundert.* Wiesbaden: O. Harrassowitz, 1970.

Schurz, William Lytle. *The Manila Galleon.* New York: E. P. Dutton & Co., 1959.

Sebastiani, Pedro. "Russko-ispanskaia konventsiia 1817 goda." Diplomnaia rabota, Leningrad State University, 1973.

Semënov, A. *Izuchenie istoricheskikh svedenii o Rossiiskoi vneshnei torgovle, i promyshlennosti s poloviny XVII-go stoletiia po 1858 god.* 3 vols. St. Petersburg: Tipografiia I. I. Glazunova i K°., 1859.

Semyonov, Yuri. *Siberia. Its Conquest and Development.* Baltimore: Helicon Press, 1963.

Severin, N. A. *Otechestvennye puteshestvenniki i issledovateli.* Moscow: Gosudarstvennoe uchebno-pedagogicheskoe izd-vo Ministerstva prosveshcheniia RSFSR, 1956.

Sherwood, Morgan B., ed. *Alaska and Its History.* Seattle and London: University of Washington Press, 1967.

Shur, L. A. *Rossiia i Latinskaia Amerika. Ocherki politicheskikh, ekonomicheskikh i kul'turnykh otnoshenii.* Moscow: Mysl', 1964.

Simonsen, Roberto C. *História econômica do Brasil (1500–1820).* 4th ed. São Paulo: Companhia Editôra Nacional, 1962.

Sirotkin, N. N. *Duel' dvukh diplomatii. Rossiia i Frantsiia v 1801–1812 gg.* Moscow: Nauka, 1966.

Slëzkin, L. Yu. *Rossiia i voina za nezavisimost' v Ispanskoi Amerike.* Moscow: Nauka, 1964.

Smirnov, Fëdor. *Yuzhnaia pri-atlanticheskaia Amerika. Politiko-ekonomicheskie ocherki s zametkami o russkoi torgovle v Brazilii.* St. Petersburg: Obshchestvennaia pol'za, 1872.

Sodré, Nelson Werneck. *As razões da independencia.* Rio de Janeiro: Editôra Civilização Brasileira, 1965.

Sumner, B. H. *Peter the Great and the Emergence of Russia.* New York: Collier Books, 1965.

Tarle, E. V. *Kontinental'naia blokada. Issledovaniia po istorii promyshlennosti i vneshnei torgovli Frantsii v epokhu Napoleona.* Moscow: Zadruga, 1913.

―――. *Ocherki istorii kolonial'noi politiki zapadnoevropeiskikh gosudarstv (konets XV-nachalo XIX v.).* Moscow-Leningrad: Nauka, 1965.

Tatum, Edward Howland, Jr. *The United States and Europe, 1815–1823. A Study in the Background of the Monroe Doctrine.* Berkeley: University of California Press, 1936.

Teixeira Soares, Alvaro. *Diplomacia do Império no Rio da Prata (até 1865).* Rio de Janeiro: Editôra Brand Ltda., 1955.

Temperley, Harold. *The Foreign Policy of Canning, 1822–1827. England, the*

Neo-Holy Alliance, and the New World. 2nd ed. Hamden, Conn.: Archon Books, 1966.

Thomas, Benjamin Platt. *Russo-American Relations, 1815–1867.* Baltimore: The Johns Hopkins Press, 1930.

Thompson, R. A. *The Russian Settlement in California Known as Fort Ross, Founded 1812 . . . Abandoned 1841. Why the Russians Came and Why they Left.* Santa Rosa: Sonoma Democrat Publishing Company, 1896.

Thorning, Joseph F. *Miranda. World Citizen.* Gainesville: University of Florida Press, 1962.

Tikhmenev, P. *Istoricheskoe obozrenie obrazovaniia Rossiisko-amerikanskoi kompanii i deistvii eë do nastoiashchego vremeni.* 2 vols. St. Petersburg: Tipografiia Eduarda Veimara, 1861–1863.

Tompkins, Stuart Ramsay. *Alaska. Promyshlennik and Sourdough.* 2nd printing. Norman: University of Oklahoma Press, 1952.

Trachevskii, A. *Ispaniia deviatnadtsatogo veka.* Vol. 1. Moscow: Izd-vo K. T. Soldatenkova, 1872.

Vianna, Hélio. *História diplomática do Brasil.* Rio de Janeiro: Biblioteca do Exército-Editôra, 1958.

Vila Vilar, Enriqueta. *Los rusos en América.* Seville: Escuela de Estudios Hispano-Americanos, 1966.

Völkl, Ekkehard. *Russland und Lateinamerika, 1741–1841.* Wiesbaden: Otto Harrassowitz, 1968.

Vogarskii, Ya. E. *Naselenie Rossii za 400 let (XVI-nachalo XX vv.).* Moscow: Prosveshchenie, 1973.

Webster, Sir Charles. *The Congress of Vienna, 1814–1815.* 6th ed. London and Southhampton: The Camelot Press, Ltd., 1963.

———. *The Foreign Policy of Castlereagh, 1815–1822. Britain and the European Alliance.* London: G. Bell and Sons, Ltd., 1947.

Whitaker, Arthur Preston. *The United States and the Independence of Latin America, 1800–1830.* 2nd ed. New York: W. W. Norton & Company, 1964.

Woodhouse, C. M. *Capodistria. The Founder of Greek Independence.* London and New York: Oxford University Press, 1973.

Woodward, E. L. *The Age of Reform, 1815–1870.* 7th ed. London: Oxford University Press, [1958].

Yarmolinsky, Avrahm. *Russian Americana. Sixteenth to Eighteenth Centuries. A Bibliographical and Historical Study.* New York: The New York Public Library, 1943.

Zlotnikov, M. F. *Kontinental'naia blokada i Rossiia.* Moscow-Leningrad: Nauka, 1966.

Zubov. N. N. *Otechestvennye moreplavateli-issledovateli morei i okeanov.* Moscow: Gosudarstvennoe izd-vo geograficheskoi literatury, 1954.

Index